Good Intentions
Are Not Enough

Transformative Leadership for Communities of Difference

Carolyn M. Shields

A SCARECROWEDUCATION BOOK

The Scarecrow Press, Inc.
Lanham, Maryland, and Oxford
2003

A SCARECROWEDUCATION BOOK

Published in the United States of America
by Scarecrow Press, Inc.
A Member of the Rowman & Littlefield Publishing Group
4720 Boston Way, Lanham, Maryland 20706
www.scarecrowpress.com

PO Box 317
Oxford
OX2 9RU, UK

British Library Cataloguing in Publication Information Available

Library of Congress Cataloging-in-Publication Data

Shields, Carolyn M.
  Good intentions are not enough : transformative leadership for
communities of difference / Carolyn M. Shields.
      p. cm.
Includes bibliographical references (p.) and index.
    ISBN 0-8108-4513-X (hardback : alk. paper)—ISBN 0-8108-4514-8 (pbk.
: alk. paper)
1. Educational leadership. 2. Multicultural education. I. Title.
LB2806.S355 2003
371.2—dc21

                                                              2002009746

To those
who
create spaces where others can
ask questions:
who are we walling in? who are we walling out?
to whom are we giving offense?

To students and scholars
colleagues and educators
who passionately want to create schools
that are
socially just and academically excellent.

To my friends and family
who are always willing to go beyond my "sayings"
and to challenge and inspire me.

With love and thanks.

Contents

Illustrations

TABLES

FIGURES

Acronyms

CHILD	Children Happily Inquiring, Learning, Developing
EMO	Educational management organization
ESL	English as a second language
NAFTA	North American Free Trade Agreement
PAC	Parent advisory council
SEOP	Student educational and occupational plan
SES	Socioeconomic status
YRS	Year-round school
MT-YRS	Multitrack year-round school
ST-YRS	Single-track year-round school

Introduction

Over thirty years ago, I was walking home from a corner store in a Newfoundland town, when an elderly gentleman stopped me and said, "You don't belong here do you?" Startled, I began to stammer that my husband (a United Church minister) and I had just moved into the parsonage down the street, and we did "belong." I quickly realized he meant something quite different. He then asked my name (Cooke) and proceeded to attempt to place me. "Cook. Are you the Cook from Hant's Harbor? No, you can't be; they are all Catholic . . . What about the Cookes from . . . ?" At that point I realized I would never belong, at least in his terms, because I had not been born there.

The memory of that encounter remains vivid, even though it has been thirty years since I lived in Newfoundland. I sometimes recall the incident when I talk to people whose origins (unlike my own) are not white, Anglo-Saxon Canadian. A friend tells of the sting of schoolyard taunts like, "Go home you f— — Punjab, back where you belong!" A teacher colleague recalls having eggs broken on her head when she was in elementary school because she was from a visible minority group. Another tells of being pelted with snowballs with stones inside them. A Navajo student I interviewed spoke about a teacher who told her that "all Navajo are stupid." A Muslim friend was told by a Caucasian Christian lady that there was not enough room on a bus for both of them.

For me, as an adult, being told I did not belong was a curious anomaly. It was an isolated, momentary, and individual occurrence. Because I thought I understood the standpoint of the questioner, it caused me neither angst nor sleepless nights. It definitely did not cause me to question who I was or whether I had a right to live in that community. For many people from ethnic, socioeconomic, and class affiliations perceived to be outside the mainstream, growing up with repeated and consistent messages of being misfits or intruders in society has caused a deep-seated sense of inferiority and anguish. Their experiences are both qualitatively and quantitatively different from mine. Mine represent individualistic and isolated incidents. Theirs reflect systemic marginalization and discrimination that were pervasive and communal, that reached to the core of who they were. Sadly, systemic messages of exclusion are still conveyed to children in our schools; such messages are profoundly inexcusable.

On one level, my Newfoundland encounter was a simple reflection of what locals might have called a way of making connections, determining place of origin. At the time, neither they nor I would have interpreted the man's comments as an example of discrimination. (We were both white and English-speaking, so how could it have been?) Since then, I have come to understand that discussions of birthplace and origins are closely tied to issues of race and color, to the presence (or lack thereof) of power and privilege. Such concerns play a very large role in determining whether one is an outsider or an insider, whether one has, or has not, the right to belong.

This book is intended to help educators create schools in which belonging is not equated with circumstances of birth. It focuses on ways to create what I call communities of difference—school communities in which we value and respect one another as we learn how to live and work together. These schools are communities in which all students, regardless of home situations or backgrounds, are expected to learn and are helped to achieve to high standards. They are communities in which difference is neither feared nor excluded but included, understood, and respected.

It must be said at the outset that diversity is not new. Schools and other social institutions have always been populated by people from diverse backgrounds who have different perspectives, beliefs, and values. What may be new today is that, with shifting demographic patterns, our daily exposure to diversity seems heightened, more intense, more extensive. To meet the changing social and academic needs of all students, educational leaders need to create school communities in which students are compelled by respect and high expectations, communities in which they learn to live and study together in peace and justice as they prepare for a diverse and global community beyond school.

To help us think seriously about diversity, I present many stories from schools and the people who work in them. I hope they will help educators understand the need to overcome unreasonable fear of difference, include alternative perspectives, and recognize the limitations of good intentions. To create schools in which all students and their teachers can feel they belong, we need to develop new approaches and new models for implementing socially just educational practices for the coming decades. We need to listen to the narratives of educational leaders, teachers, and students, and carefully explore both relevant theoretical perspectives and exemplars of practice.

This book is intended for theorists and practitioners, school administrators and students of educational leadership, and anyone who cares deeply about improving the quality of education that our students receive. It is written in the hope that we may tear down the walls that divide us and, together, create more inclusive school communities.

GOOD INTENTIONS ARE NOT ENOUGH (FROST SAID SO TOO)

When I hear tales of rejection and exclusion, privilege and power, I am deeply concerned, not only about their effect on the recipients but about how we have come to believe that to live together as neighbors, we need to either resemble those beside us or build walls to keep us apart. I am reminded of an often quoted but rarely understood poem by Robert Frost. In his poem "Mending Wall" (1915) a misguided farmer stubbornly holds to his position that "Good fences make good neighbors." We hear the phrase often but fail to understand that Frost is really challenging the concept. This poem exemplifies the notion of misguided, good intentions so well that I have chosen to use it as a leitmotiv running through the book. Here is the poem in its entirety:

Mending Wall
Something there is that doesn't love a wall,
That sends the frozen-ground-swell under it
And spills the upper boulders in the sun,
And makes gaps even two can pass abreast.

The work of hunters is another thing:
I have come after them and made repair
Where they have left not one stone on a stone,
But they would have the rabbit out of hiding,
To please the yelping dogs. The gaps I mean,
No one has seen them made or heard them made,
But at spring mending-time we find them there.
I let my neighbor know beyond the hill;
And on a day we meet to walk the line
And set the wall between us once again.
We keep the wall between us as we go.
To each the boulders that have fallen to each.
And some are loaves and some so nearly balls
We have to use a spell to make them balance:
"Stay where you are until our backs are turned!"
We wear our fingers rough with handling them.
Oh, just another kind of outdoor game,
One on a side. It comes to little more:
There where it is we do not need the wall:
He is all pine and I am apple orchard.
My apple trees will never get across
And eat the cones under his pines, I tell him.
He only says, "Good fences make good neighbors."
Spring is the mischief in me, and I wonder
If I could put a notion in his head:
"Why do they make good neighbors? Isn't it
Where there are cows? But here there are no cows.
Before I built a wall I'd ask to know
What I was walling in or walling out,
And to whom I was like to give offense.
Something there is that doesn't love a wall,
That wants it down." I could say "Elves" to him,
But it's not elves exactly, and I'd rather
He said it for himself. I see him there,
Bringing a stone grasped firmly by the top
In each hand, like an old-stone savage armed.
He moves in darkness as it seems to me,
Not of woods only and the shade of trees.
He will not go behind his father's saying,
And he likes having thought of it so well
He says again, "Good fences make good neighbors."

The neighbors meet annually to walk the wall together. They remain on opposite sides of the wall. They talk superficially, never really sharing what they think. It seems too dangerous and difficult to disagree, to let conflict into the open. Yet the wall that divides is fragile; it takes some luck and a magic "spell" to balance the stones, to rebuild the wall so it will stay in place another year, or at least until they turn their backs again. They are different (or at least their trees are); one has pine, the other apples. They do not stop to understand or appreciate as they simply build and rebuild the wall.

Only the narrator recognizes the activity for what it is—a game, for where they build, he says, there is no need for a wall. There are no cows, no threats to the safety or security of either field, and so he asks tentatively whether there is really any need for a wall. But the neighbor responds, as he has always done, and as his father has done before him, "Good fences make good neighbors."

The poet muses, "Before I built a wall I'd ask to know / What I was walling in or walling out, / And to whom I was like to give offense." But he does not raise the questions aloud; there is no exploration, no dialogue. He longs for a way to move his neighbor out of "the darkness" in which he seems to move, yet takes no action to that end. They both work hard, their fingers rough with handling the stones. Their intentions are good. But one is bound by tradition, his father's saying; the other is fearful of breaking the tenuous peace and wants his neighbor to say "it for himself."

BUILDING WALLS IN SCHOOL

Schools today are built of pine and apple trees, elm, oak, kauri, japonica—more kinds than most of us can name or identify. But we seem to fear the variety, believing that difference is dangerous. Diversity upsets the status quo; it challenges existing norms and beliefs. As in Frost's adjacent orchards, there are no cows here and no enemies within our walls—no intrinsic threats to the welfare of the students from those who are in some way different. On occasion, friendships develop, a glimmer of understanding occurs—a gap is created silently, as in the poem: "no one has seen or heard." But we quickly close in the wall. In most developed English-speaking countries, even with rapidly changing demographics, an apparently shrinking world, and increasingly diverse school populations, large numbers of children are being given the message, both overtly and covertly, that they belong behind a wall.

Sometimes, in a well-intentioned attempt to provide a sense of belonging, we permit our schools and society to become fragmented, creating separate institutions for various social and ethnic groups, encouraging, for example, charter schools, magnet schools, independent schools for different ethnic and religious groups. In today's climate of tight fiscal resources, increasing emphasis on accountability, and growing demands for choice, there is definitely a place for new and innovative forms of schooling. My concern is that, as new models are developed, choice does not become synonymous with hegemony and exclusion on social, economic, or racial grounds. We must voice our niggling doubts and engage in meaningful dialogue to explore issues like equity and social justice in schooling. We cannot afford to follow the example of Frost's farmers, failing to ask whom we are walling in, whom we are keeping out, failing to consider to whom we are giving offense. This book will help us reflect critically on these and similar issues.

OVERVIEW OF THE BOOK

The book is divided into three parts. In the first, I develop three key concepts: educational leaders as *transformative cross-cultural leaders,* schools as *communities of difference,* and the need for *critical criteria* that may help us examine our schools and educational programs with greater clarity. The concepts are developed with reference to academic and other literature, as well as to data drawn from my studies of schools. In the first section, many of the illustrations I give are examples of attitudes and activities I have found in schools that represent good intentions of hard-working educators but do not adequately or justly serve the needs of children, their families, or society. The focus changes dramatically in the subsequent chapters.

In part 2, I demonstrate unequivocally that there are alternative conceptions of schooling. I draw heavily on my ten years of empirical work in the United States and Canada as well as shorter periods of time spent in schools elsewhere, including New Zealand and Fiji. These glimpses of real life are combined with powerful theoretical perspectives to stimulate our thinking and provide support for efforts to implement models of schooling that more effectively and equitably address the needs of diverse student bodies. Throughout, I introduce the narratives and experiences of others to emphasize or elaborate specific ideas. You will meet some creative, innovative, hard-working, and caring educators and you will visit their schools. Some will be introduced early and will reappear throughout the book; others will be introduced later as their experiences or perspectives are relevant to illuminate a specific point. Overall, you will be enriched by these glimpses of real people challenging inequities in the status quo and making a difference where they live.

In part 3, I combine theoretical perspectives and empirical data into a framework for those wishing to create or recreate schools that respect and incorporate diversity. This framework emphasizes the need to rethink notions of school leadership if we are to change how we organize educational experiences for students. It unifies the ideas that have been developed through the book and focuses on ways in which educational leaders may improve the educational experiences of children in their schools. The book concludes with a chapter in which I present a case study based, once again, on events and individuals I have seen in schools; the case is then analyzed through a dialogue between the author and a school-based educator in which we discuss some of the possibilities and challenges of trying to implement the ideas contained in this book. I hope that in this dialogue you will find some of your own questions and responses and that you will engage thoughtfully and critically with us as we wrestle with how best to implement these ideas in environments that often seem reluctant to consider educational change.

Audience

There are many similarities in educational systems around the world and there are also differences due to the political, social, and fiscal environments in which school systems have developed. My premise is that regardless of similarities or differences, we can learn from one another. Ideas from less-developed countries that may seem foreign or unusual to a reader in a developed country may help educational leaders to reflect on why practices are so different elsewhere. Likewise, practices common in developed countries may help educators in less developed countries to find alternative approaches to education. In each case, hearing about different methods and perspectives may challenge us to think differently about how we organize schools for instruction or for social interaction or how we involve the wider community.

The book is not primarily designed as a textbook, although it may be used for that purpose. It is intended to provoke dialogue and reflection and to further that goal, in appendix A, "For Further Reflection," I pose a few questions that may guide the reader through some of the key ideas in each chapter.

This book is written primarily for educators in schools in English-speaking developed countries. Despite contextual differences, educational leaders in such geographically distinct countries as Australia, Britain, Canada, New Zealand, and the United States experience many similar challenges—challenges related to increasing heterogeneity, fiscal constraint, school governance and parental involvement, political and cultural expectations, accountability and high-stakes testing, and other legislative policies.

Literature and Theoretical Perspectives

The literature I use in this book comes from a wide range of sources and theoretical perspectives. I draw, for example, on ideas from cultural studies, organizational theory, leadership studies, and identity studies, as well as various perspectives including postmodernism, critical multiculturalism, and feminism. My intention is not to provide a comprehensive discussion of theoretical positions but to use relevant aspects of theories in accessible ways to help us reflect on and better understand how to make schools more just, caring, and optimistic places for the children and adults who spend their days in them.

I use pseudonyms for most of the individuals, schools, and districts that have generously permitted me to spend time visiting, observing, questioning, probing, interviewing, and taking pictures. The pseudonyms are intended to protect the confidentiality of my respondents and to prevent any errors, which are entirely mine, from reflecting on them. Pseudonyms also acknowledge that schools are fluid institutions and that my descriptions are but snapshots, moments in time, that may or may not be accurate when this book goes to press or in succeeding years. In schooling, changes in context, governance, or leadership are often accompanied by philosophical as well as practical changes. Nevertheless, the stories contained in this book illustrate some of the possibilities inherent in the concepts of transformative cross-cultural leadership and communities of difference that I will be developing. I do not use pseudonyms for country names that help contextualize the data, for real names used as part of a historical record or reports published elsewhere, or for personal friends who have generously permitted me to incorporate some of their writing into my text. I acknowledge their contributions to my thinking. To all who have helped me and whose stories appear in these pages, I owe a tremendous debt of thanks.

One final comment about pseudonyms. The stories I share in the following pages are powerful. If I presented real names, it might suggest that these educators are exceptional and that the stories are intended to praise and glorify them. In some ways, of course, they are unusual; but in other ways, they represent many other thoughtful, caring, excellent leaders I have met. Hence, there is a sense in which using pseudonyms avoids privileging some stories, experiences, and knowledge at the expense of others.

Several phrases are repeated throughout the book as a sort of mantra. Phrases such as "good intentions are not enough" or schools need to be "just, democratic, empathetic, and optimistic" or "leaders operate on the souls of their followers" provide the basis for leadership which helps to create schools that are both socially just and academically excellent. The terms *transformative cross-cultural leadership* and *communities of difference* are developed as key framing concepts for new ways of thinking about schools. I intend them to become guiding principles for those who read this book.

STARTING POINTS

Approximately a quarter century ago, Schwartz and Ogilvy (1979) examined ways in which disciplinary thinking had changed. They found that in every area they studied (for example, philosophy, physics, religion and spirituality, mathematics, linguistics, the arts, brain theory, and psychology), there had been a basic shift in thinking in ordering, knowing, and causing. These ideas are important for educators seeking ways to effect positive change in schools.

New Ways of Ordering

It is no longer possible, Schwartz and Ogilvy found, to think about the world as *ordered* like a clock—a giant mechanism, effectively put together and set in motion that will carry on forever, fulfilling its function of time keeping.[1] It is more accurate to understand the structures that order the universe as holographic and interconnected instead of hierarchical. Implied in a new way of thinking about order is the realization that a change in any one part of an organization is likely to bring about a series of changes as other areas adapt to the new condition.

Educational organizations, like other human institutions, are ordered in somewhat unpredictable and complex ways. Wheatley (1993) suggests it is akin to aspects of chaos theory. Just as we cannot predict with absolute accuracy how an individual will respond to certain stimuli or a given situation, so we can neither predict nor control organizational behavior. For that reason, trying to control or manage discrete relationships is unproductive; examining patterns, and finding meaning in them, may be more useful.

New Ways of Knowing

We no longer think about *knowing* in fixed and finite ways. While not denying that some information is factual, it is important to recognize that knowledge is also constructed and depends in large part on individual and cultural interpretations. If I were to tell you that Versailles is close to Paris and is home to the magnificent castle built by Louis XIV, you might say, "of course." However, a student of architecture would be sure to tell me that it had been built over time by numerous workers; indeed, Louis XIV set up his home and installed his government in the chateau, but it was neither *built* nor designed by him. Louis Le Vau was commissioned to renovate and extend an old hunting lodge, Le Notre created the gardens from swampland, and Mansart masterminded the hydraulic display of the fountains.[2] Moreover, should you be a resident of Versailles, Missouri, you would likely start by telling me that I had mispronounced the name of your city and that it was not located in France and did not house the famous chateau. Instead, you might tell me it is located close to Lake of the Ozarks and that the main tourist attraction is nearby caves. Schwartz and Ogilvy point out that new ways of knowing lead to "a process of knowledge that is more interpretive, inevitably ambiguous, and partial. The process has rules, but they are rules for engagement rather than for objectifying" (Schwartz and Ogilvy 1979, 51). If we had dismissed either perspective on Versailles as ridiculous, we might never have realized the partial truth of each, apparently irreconcilable, position.

New Ways of Causing

Causing is the third element identified by Schwartz and Ogilvy. They state that in the past, cause and effect were considered to be simple one-to-one processes, but that

> the movement in the new view is from the simple to the more complex, from single agents to multiple sources, from unidirectional to mutual, from determinate or probabilistic outcomes to innovation, and from control to influence. (1979, 51)

It used to be thought that if a teacher told a student to sit down or "get to work," the very statement would cause the desired behavior. However, the reality, as teachers all know, is quite different. One student might comply, another might sit down but start to cry, a third might talk back, still another might storm out of the classroom. Multiple factors help determine what the response may be. In other words, we cannot make things happen by waving a wand, by creating a policy, or by telling someone to do something. Instead, we must work together to build toward some shared goals and visions. If we try to implement a new social studies curriculum, some teachers may attempt to implement it faithfully, others will introduce components of it, and still others will continue to teach as before. The result of the new policy is likely to be more variance in instruction, rather than greater conformity as was likely intended. Increased dialogue, exploration, and interaction are necessary as we work together to build shared goals and visions that may lead to desirable changes. Nevertheless, changes rarely simplify our work.

Heterarchic Leadership

In terms of leadership, Schwartz and Ogilvy talk about the need for a change from hierarchic to heterarchic leadership. Heterarchic leadership, they suggest, resembles the familiar children's game "scissors, stone, paper." The combination of hand positions proffered at the same time determines which element is dominant (scissors beat paper, paper beats stone, stone beats scissors). Sometimes scissors are dominant; at other times the "leader" is paper or stone. In like fashion, Schwartz and Ogilvy suggest, leaders need to recognize that in some situations, their knowledge will take a backseat to the knowledge of colleagues— or even outsiders. In some circumstances one person will need to take the lead; at other times, another person's skill or expertise will be required.

So it is with changing a school to meet the needs of students, teachers, and its broader community in an age of rapid demographic, social, fiscal, cultural, and political change. New ways of ordering, knowing, causing, and leading are necessary. If we are to succeed, we must not only value everyone's skill, background, expertise, and knowledge, but recognize that each person is essential. In the following chapters, I discuss leadership for a school community that is just, democratic, empathetic, and optimistic based on the assumption that no one person is the leader—but that numerous people are bound together in a moral commitment, a sort of covenant, to effect educational change.

Underlying Assumptions

This book is based on seven assumptions. My first assumption is that, as presently organized and managed, most schools do not take into account a changed and changing society. I am convinced that despite the hard work and good intentions of many individual school administrators and teachers, schools too often fail to meet the needs of all members of the student body. Although there are some outstanding examples of inclusive and excellent practices in various schools and classrooms in the English-speaking world and beyond, schools and school systems in general have failed to respond to the rapid changes in the rest of society and hence are often unsuccessful in facilitating either academic or social success for many students.

My second assumption is that the need for change is systemic. The norms of schooling must change if schools are to be excellent, inclusive, respectful, and caring institutions where students may attain high levels of academic success. I develop the concept of schools as communities of difference as one way in which educators may better achieve these goals.

Third, I recognize that if schools are to undergo fundamental change, then school leaders must play key roles. Directors, superintendents, principals, and teacher-leaders will all have to be actively engaged in the quest to transform educational practice. Learning to engage in what I call transformative cross-cultural leadership is key to successful educational leadership for changing times.

Fourth, I am convinced that we need to develop a clear picture of what we are trying to accomplish and identify criteria to help us assess our progress. We need to have more clarity about what it means to talk about schools that are equitable and excellent, in which students both feel they belong and achieve to high levels, in which there is no trade-off of either the social or the academic components or goals of schooling.

This point warrants elaboration as a separate assumption. My fifth assumption is that one of the primary reasons for the existence of schools is the education of children. Although this book focuses on leadership for the creation of inclusive school communities, preparing children to take their rightful place in society does not simply require social skills (religious or civil organizations, churches, or YMCAs can do that well). Indeed schools need to be primarily educative—both in terms of providing all children with appropriate, high-quality academic education (broadly conceived) and helping them develop competencies in other related areas, such as social, emotional, cultural, and political realms.

The last two assumptions work together. The sixth assumption is that theory needs to be brought to bear on educational practice; the seventh is that excellent and exemplary educational practice must inform the development of educational theory. In other words, theory and practice are not independent concepts, one located in the university and the other in schools. Rather, I believe that all educators need to work together and learn from one another for the good of students and the ultimate benefit of society. Our specific responsibilities may be different, but the general mission is the same: the creation of a more just and more excellent education system.

Before We Move On

I am an educator. As a classroom teacher, I have had eighteen years of experience teaching children from kindergarten to senior high school, from a remote community in Labrador, accessible at the time only by cable car or by boat, to an inner-city high school, from pullout remedial to "regular" to integrated gifted classes, in homogeneous and diverse schools. I have been guilty of good intentions and little knowledge. I have been complicit in accepting the status quo without engaging in critique or reflection. I have been culpable of perpetrating inequity. Perhaps that is why I am now so passionately concerned about the issues I raise in these pages. I firmly believe that as educators, we—myself included—can and must do better. And I am earnestly attempting to do so in my own practice.

ACKNOWLEDGMENTS

I could not have written this book without the help of many caring, concerned, and dedicated educators. Some of them you will meet in the following pages; others have been just as influential, but their names and faces do not appear. Many other thank-yous are also in order—for the funding I received from the Hampton Fund of the University of British Columbia and from the Social Sciences and Humanities Research Council (SSHRC) of the Canadian government, and for other kinds of support I received from colleagues around the world who welcomed and assisted me. I am reminded again about the importance of community, collaboration, and support, for none of us, John Donne once said, can possibly stand alone as an educational island.

It is my hope that this book will prompt reflection about how academics prepare school leaders, about how practitioners engage in educational leadership, and how together we conceptualize and realize high-quality, just, and caring schools. Educators who wish to be both responsible and accountable in the complex and dynamic environment of the next few decades will take steps to challenge inequities in the status quo and develop schools that are both equitable and excellent, inclusive and caring. If these chapters prompt dialogue and debate, challenge educators to become more critically reflective practitioners, and stimulate the search for new ways of living and working together in schools, I will have accomplished my goal.

NOTES

1. I have a colleague whose research interest is time. He likes to use the example of the Uccello clock (a clock that actually moves backward) to remind us that even time is a relative and constructed concept. It is, I think, a nice way of rethinking the relationship of a created instrument to the concept it embodies. For more information about this clock, see S. Pintus, "That strange clock by Paolo Uccello," at www.catpress.com/fanmega/art/tiduomq .htm.

2. For an overview, see *Paris Tourisme* at www.paris-tourisme.com/places/ Versailles/index.html.

PART 1

Laying the Groundwork:
Leading a Community That Is
Socially Just and Academically Excellent

I see him there,
Bringing a stone grasped firmly by the top
In each hand, like an old-stone savage armed.
He moves in darkness as it seems to me,
Not of woods only and the shade of trees.
He will not go beyond his father's saying,
And he likes having thought of it so well,
He says again, "Good fences make good neighbors."

The image of an educational leader standing, armed with the tools, strategies, and ideas of the past is, unfortunately, still too familiar to many people concerned with education. Yet it is readily apparent to one who walks through the doors of many schools today that the face of education has changed. How, then, should our thinking about educational leadership, school communities, and educational practices reflect the visible changes in school populations and cultures?

When I went to school, there were few students from other countries, few from visible minority groups, and the differences that were acknowledged tended to be those of preference—my friend preferred strawberry ice cream; she was a better basketball player, but perhaps I learned more easily. Multiculturalism, racism, sexuality were ideas about which my early experiences of schooling remained silent. And yet I recall, with a niggling sense of shame, the tall, silent boy sitting at the back of my third-grade class, quiet, neglected, not causing any trouble but not participating either. He never laughed; he did not join in any of our activities. He wore a sports jacket, he spoke little English, he had a strong accent. He was "different" and we ignored him—teachers and students alike. I still wonder what we lost by not getting to know him. And I fear that nothing in Gerhard's future could have compensated him for what he lost by being marginalized in our school setting.

In the three chapters that make up part 1, I lay the theoretical and conceptual groundwork for three key concepts that permeate the rest of the book. Chapter 1 introduces the concept of *transformative cross-cultural leadership*. Here I draw on traditional concepts from centuries of thinking and writing about leadership as well as more recent research; I also incorporate ideas missing from most discussions of leadership: the need to attend to issues of power, multiculturalism, and transformation, not only in our society but also in our schools. Educational leaders cannot afford to rely on tradition, depend on good intentions, or fall back on what has always worked in the past. Society has changed; schools have changed; and so too must our thinking about educational leadership change. Here I argue that many different styles and approaches to leadership may be effective—if leaders are deeply grounded in moral principles, have a clear sense of vision, and act authentically, in accordance with their values and vision.

The second chapter in this section, "Schools as Communities of Difference," starts with the notion that diversity is a reality in our world, that our communities and schools are composed of people from many different backgrounds with various religious, ethnic, and cultural traditions; differing talents, abilities, disabilities, sexual orientations; and a wide range of class and socioeconomic backgrounds. I examine how an educational leader might create a sense of in-school community and begin to develop positive, collaborative, and mutually supportive relationships with parents and other members of the wider community. In this chapter I introduce the idea of a *community of difference* to suggest that community must build on, not eliminate, difference. We must value the intrinsic worth of all members of the community, come together with respect, engage in dialogue, form new understandings, discover shared values, and create a more inclusive, more socially just community in which all children may also succeed academically.

I am often asked what I mean by the term *social justice*. Answering this question is the task I take up in chapter 3, "Criteria for Excellence and Social Justice." I suggest four criteria, which I believe must be taken together, to help us understand how education must focus simultaneously on social justice and academic excellence and promote a society that reflects these same values. I argue (as do Kincheloe and Steinberg 1995) that education must be just, democratic, empathetic, and optimistic. *Justice* requires educational leaders to ensure that all students have access to high-quality, challenging programs; that all children are held to high standards and expected to learn. Too often children whose home language is not English or who come from poverty or abuse are written off: less is expected of them, their home situation is blamed, and we assume they will not succeed as well as their more advantaged peers. This is not socially just. The belief that some groups of children are intrinsically more able than other groups because of the color of their skin or their life circumstances is simply wrong, and the practices that stem from this assumption are often misguided. *Democratic* schools are inclusive. They acknowledge the worth of every individual—student, parent, teacher, and community member—and the right of those affected by educational decisions to participate in the decision-making processes. *Empathetic* schools and educators recognize that education is fundamentally relational. We learn and grow through interaction with others. Hence, learning occurs best in a caring, supportive environment in which each learner feels safe, respected, and valued. *Optimism* is a criterion not often associated with schools, yet it is the glue that holds the rest in balance. An education that is optimistic enhances the life choices and chances of all children, not only those who come to our schools with the most apparent social and cultural advantages. It opens windows of understanding and doors of opportunity for all children.

The clear message from this section is that educational leaders cannot and must not rely on past attitudes and practices, even though they may have "worked" when school communities seemed more homogeneous than they appear at present. Instead, educational leaders must become transformative—changing their organizations from communities that rely on traditional assumptions about shared norms, beliefs, and values to ones that may be described as *communities of difference*. Leaders must be *cross-cultural,* open to learning from others whose traditions and perspectives are different from their own, and *transformative,* leading from moral principles and ethical practice. Finally, educational leaders in heterogeneous school communities must base decisions on explicit criteria related to social justice and academic excellence. They will ask questions about who is being advantaged, included, and privileged by decisions about instruction, resource allocation, and social activities; they will attempt to identify those who may be marginalized, excluded, or disadvantaged by a specific action or decision and they will act in ways that emphasize justice, democracy, empathy, and optimism.

In 1993 McDaniel wrote:

> Typically school districts do an excellent job of conducting feasibility studies, gathering research and evaluative information, organizing implementation committees, solving logistical problems, and developing community action plans. Where we fall down is on the political side of the equation. As educators, we often assume that all we have to do is develop a good idea and tell the community about it. We neglect to recognize or act on the understanding that educational change is a political struggle, a discussion, or a debate, at its worst it is a destructive battle over what is important to people or perceived to be important to people. (1993, 4)

The ideas in this section must be considered and implemented with these comments in mind. Educational change is difficult. It often challenges our values, beliefs, and practices; it may threaten things that seem important to us. At its worst, as McDaniel points out, educational change can be divisive and destructive. At its best, educational change permits us to redress past wrongs, challenge inequities in the status quo, and provide more children with a just and caring education and optimistic opportunities in the present and for the future.

To accomplish this, we must be prepared to relinquish the stones of the past and stand not in darkness but in the light, to move out of the shade and go beyond the sayings of our predecessors. To do this, we must challenge old norms, past practices, even good intentions. We must begin to tear down the walls that divide us from others in our school communities, walls that prevent us from achieving education that is socially just and academically excellent for all students. We must become agents of change and transformation whether we find ourselves in classrooms, offices, or the boardrooms of our education systems.

CHAPTER 1

Transformative Cross-Cultural Leadership

Alicia[1] is the principal of Canyon Collegiate, located on the Navajo reservation. The school is characterized by its remote location, high poverty, and ESL challenges. Alicia has consistently seen her students and community as a place of rich cultural resources and great educational opportunity. Her positive attitude and approach are turning her school into a state of the art technological site. . . . To list Alicia's accomplishments on a single sheet of paper is impossible, but she is the heart of Canyon Collegiate.

The above excerpt is taken from Alicia's nomination, made by her district director of secondary schools, for a prestigious Milken[2] Award. It attests to the importance of school leadership. Alicia is described as the heart of the school. The nomination continues, "Alicia has the ability to channel all school programs into a force to accomplish meaningful reform." How does Alicia, or any other educational leader for that matter, achieve such accomplishments?

The title of this chapter, "Transformative Cross-Cultural Leadership," introduces several concepts that are essential in approaching the task of educational leadership for meaningful reform. I develop the ideas in reverse order in this chapter. First I focus on the importance of leadership, a concept that has been studied from the beginning of organized society but is still poorly understood. I then introduce the term *cross-cultural* to emphasize the need to explore what one means by culture and how one might lead "across" it. Finally I explain the use of the term *transformative*, rather than the more common word, transformational, and suggest that it better captures the type of changes required in education today.

LEADERSHIP: A UBIQUITOUS FUZZY CONCEPT

Over the centuries, there have been numerous attempts to define excellence in leadership. Early attempts focused on individuals in positions of formal authority and the qualities and approaches deemed necessary for success.

Sun Tsu, a Chinese general from the sixth century B.C., developed some aphorisms for good military leadership that have become popular in thinking about modern institutional leadership, including leadership in education, business, and political organizations.[3] While some people may be uncomfortable with using a military metaphor to inform educational leadership, and some may reject outright the possibility of learning anything from Sun Tsu, many of his ideas seem applicable to good educational leadership. His bedrock principle, even in war, was honor. In a time when warfare was becoming more vicious, he advised his leaders to reflect carefully on what they were doing and how they were proceeding. He counseled, for example, that "he who excels in resolving difficulties does so before they arise" (Sun Tsu 1997, 38), "the supreme excellence in war is to attack the enemy's plans" (p. 39), and "he whose ranks are united in purpose will be victorious" (p. 42). There is obvious wisdom in these words. But no matter how many precepts a leader may attempt to implement, there is no guarantee that he or she will become a good or successful leader.

Plato chose a different approach and began with the assumption that not everyone was fit to lead. He argued that society needed a philosopher-king—someone not from the masses, but one selected to be properly schooled for the role who would ponder ethical questions related to topics like what constitutes the "good life." The emphasis on moral vision is essential today; reflections about what constitutes the good life, a good education, or a well-educated citizen still prompt much educational debate. Nevertheless, finding "the correct answer" to such questions does not guarantee excellence in leadership.

Discussions of leadership in Western civilizations for many centuries centered on discussions of military leaders and strategy, political rulers (mostly royalty and lords), and religious leaders and clerics. In contrast to Sun Tsu or Plato, Machiavelli is often considered the epitome of the cruel or unjust leader. In *The Prince,* Machiavelli addressed the topic of whether it is better for a leader to be loved or feared. Although few people have read *The Prince,* many have heard that the author came down on the side of being feared. Despite the fact that he was not advocating that a leader inspire fear in his followers, the term *Machiavellian* perpetuates the distortion and his reputation for cruelty. On closer examination, what Machiavelli was struggling with was the dilemma that sometimes a good leader may have to act in ways that seem heartless. In language that may be extreme, Machiavelli says that although a leader may wish to be both loved and feared, if one has to choose, being feared is safer because it does not rely on the fickle goodwill of followers. Leaders cannot expect to be liked by everyone and must be careful not to misuse clemency in an attempt to be loved. Being feared and hated, however, are two different things.

Later, Napoleon wrestled with many of the same issues.[4] Indeed, history continues to debate whether he was a tyrant or a revolutionary. He was elected in a landslide victory to a four-year term of office. Wanting to retain power, he conducted a coup d'état (1799), assumed dictatorial powers, and changed the law to permit a ten-year term. During that time, although he is renowned for his code of law and many civic improvements in France, he also crushed and oppressed many adversaries.

The difficulties of identifying and engaging in good, effective, and moral leadership have been documented for centuries. Nevertheless, there is a continuing sense that good leadership is essential to effective organizational life. Perhaps that is why innumerable approaches to studying or practicing leadership continue to emerge. Grint, for example, reports that in the 1990s in the English language alone, ten articles were published about leadership every minute (1997, 2). A search on the word *leader* at the Internet site of an online book retailer once provided 1,077 titles, many of which suggested a simple recipe for becoming a successful leader. A few representative titles were: *Alchemy of a Leader; The Art of the Leader; The Articulate Executive: Learn to Look, Act, and Sound Like a Leader; Be the Leader You Were Meant to Be; Common Sense Leadership: A Handbook for Success as a Leader; The Confident Leader: A Powerful and Practical Tool Kit for Managers and Supervisors; Developing the Leader within You; Discover Your Leaderself; Training the Leader inside You; Phantom Leader; Seven*

Traits of a Successful Leader; Shadow Leader; and *Smart Moves for People in Charge: 130 Checklists to Help You Be a Better Leader.*

Choosing the right book to inspire and direct one's leadership practice is not an easy matter. Some are simplistic, taking no account of organizational differences or contexts. Others purport to provide a recipe for leadership in a few easy lessons. One simple, if cynical, guide through the maze is to consider that the word *the* constitutes a red flag. Anything that purports to be *the* answer, *the* right tool, or *the* best practice should be approached with caution and a great number of questions such as, Best for whom? Under what circumstances? How do we know?

In the first part of the twentieth century, there were numerous scientific attempts to identify such things as the best leadership traits or the quintessential leadership qualities of great men of history. Bass and Stogdill describe studies conducted in the first half of the twentieth century which examined such things as height, weight, talkativeness, physique, energy, responsibility, self-confidence—the list is endless (see Bass 1990, chap. 4).

DRAWING ON MORE RECENT LEADERSHIP THEORIES

Clearly, interest in leadership continues unabated. In the last half of the twentieth century, however, many new, more nuanced, and perhaps more promising theories of leadership have emerged. Some people (Ogawa and Bossert 1995) recognize the importance of both formal and informal networks of communication and insist that leadership is not solely an individual but also an organizational quality. Others (Gemmil and Oakley 1997; Kets de Vries 1997) suggest that leaders may not only have a positive impact, but if they are not careful may create a kind of unhealthy dependency or learned helplessness among the followers. Some go further and seem to despair about leaders altogether, suggesting that the power that accompanies formal leadership positions frequently develops from a pathological desire for power and sense of self-importance (Kets de Vries 1997).

Sibicky analyzes the persistent tendency of followers to comply with the instructions they received during the famous Milgram experiments (in which subjects thought they were administering successively greater electric shocks to victims). He concludes that we cannot "assume that one's personality, character, or moral upbringing will inoculate one from destructive behavior" (Sibicky 1996, 123). His observations make an important contribution to our understanding of both the dark side and the moral nature of leadership. They also raise questions about how one learns to be an effective (and just) educational leader despite outside pressure from what appear to be legitimate situations, moral peer groups, or powerful authority figures.

In this section, I examine more recent approaches to educational leadership in order to develop a more comprehensive, theory-based approach. Among them are transactional, transformational, feminist, multicultural, democratic, critical, and emancipatory leadership concepts. I draw from multiple theories and integrate their disparate concepts in order to build a scaffold for what I call *transformative cross-cultural leadership*. My description of the leadership theories is of necessity incomplete, in that it is intended to simply highlight aspects of several approaches that may inform a just and caring conception of educational leadership.

Some writers have insisted that there is a crucial distinction between leading and managing, summed up in the aphorism "Managers are people who do things right and leaders are people who do the right things" (Bennis and Nannus 1985, 21). However appealing the distinction in the abstract, its validity becomes less convincing in practice. Consider one principal who was so busy "doing the right things," for example, listening to each student's story about who stole some bottles of pop concentrate from a cupboard in the gym area, that she did not have time to approve textbook orders or authorize repairs to the photocopier. Her staff might have wanted her to do "things right." What about the leader who was so busy ensuring that everything was done right, spending countless hours checking up on the arrival and departure time of teachers, making sure that every student rule infraction received appropriate disciplinary action, and helping the secretary allocate appropriate supplies to each unit, that he seldom attended any student activities, performances, or sports events. His staff may well have recognized that doing things right is not enough; indeed, he also needed to do the right things. These extreme examples are rarely found because most people recognize that good leaders need to do both well.

Gardner (1990) rejects the frequent dichotomization of the work of leaders (doing the right things) and of managers (doing things right) and, in my opinion, more correctly identified the need for leader/managers. He says that managers do not necessarily demonstrate leadership behaviors, nor do leaders automatically attend to the day-to-day needs of an organization; but leader/managers balance both types of behavior. Leader/managers distinguish themselves, Gardner suggests, in that they think differently from either managers or leaders (p. 4). They are more concerned about the longer term, they think in terms of renewal, and they place heavy emphasis on intangibles such as vision, values, and motivation. They recognize the nonrational aspects of organizations and leadership, attend to the political realities of having multiple constituencies, grasp the relationships between their unit and larger realities, and attend to constituents beyond their organization's boundaries.

Despite the importance of an educational leader being able to attend to (or delegate) essential managerial tasks, in the next few pages, I focus on the types of orientations most closely associated with the leader/manager, with particular emphasis on the school principal.

Transactional Leadership

negotiate find ways to help each person/group achieve

During the last half of the twentieth century, many theorists (Gardner 1990; Hodgkinson 1983; Senge 1990, 2000) noted the serious shortcomings of early approaches to leadership (described variously as rational, technical, prescriptive, or functionalist) that were characterized by understandings of leadership as hierarchical, emphasizing control, command, and order within an organization. In 1978 Burns first distinguished between the common transactional leadership style and transformational leadership, a distinction that has attracted a number of subsequent writers as well. Starratt states that transactional leadership focuses on organizational transactions—people entering into agreements through a process of "bargaining between the individual interests of persons or groups in return for their cooperation in the leader's agenda" (1995, 109). Transactional leadership is often rejected as being too technical, too focused on bargaining and making individual deals for mutual benefit. While such bargaining should not be the primary focus of educational leaders, the notion of finding a balance be-

Burns

tween individual and collective interests should not be dismissed out of hand. Leaders wanting to be effective in today's complex organizations will pay attention to competing interests and find ways to help each person and group achieve some benefit.

Transformational Leadership

Transformational leadership is generally described as leadership that focuses more on the collective interests of a group or community. Firestone and Louis (1999) have described the model of transformational leadership developed by Leithwood and his colleagues as "one of the most complete models of transformational leadership in education" (p. 315). The model identifies several dimensions of what a transformational leader does: creating a school vision, setting high performance expectations, creating consensus around group goals, developing an intellectually stimulating climate, creating a productive school culture, developing structures to foster participation in school decisions, offering individualized support, and modeling best practices and organizational values. It includes overt and covert behaviors, individual and collective strategies for leadership, and may be applied in either diverse or homogeneous settings. Yet, as will be seen a little later, the transformation described here is organizational, and it may occur without attention to issues of equity or social justice. Thus the most common concept of transformational leadership in educational circles in North America is an institutional theory that remains silent about the moral components of leadership. In this book, to remind the reader that leadership requires more than an institutional focus, I have chosen to use the term *transformative* rather than transformational.

Feminist Approaches to Leadership

Feminist approaches to leadership highlight the need for attention to be paid to the place of sex and gender in understanding leadership and organizational life. Shakeschaft's (1987) position is that most theories of educational administration and organizational development have been "based on a white male behavior and worldview" (p. 96) that do not "hold up when applied to women and people of color" (p. 96). She argues that education will benefit by paying considerably more attention to the "experiences of girls and women" (p. 107). Others (Blackmore 1989; Ferguson 1994) suggest that a feminist reconstruction of leadership forces a reexamination of power relationships. They urge leaders to move beyond thinking of power *over* another and to focus on empowerment and power used *with* another person, and power to accomplish a specific purpose. Feminism includes a view of power that is multidimensional and multidirectional and an understanding that leadership is practiced differently in different contexts.

Although some claim that women tend "to be more nurturing, interested in others, and more socially sensitive" than men (Bass and Avolio 1997, 207), other scholars (Hoff-Somers 1994; Young 1994) caution against the tendency to use feminist theories to polarize the field by essentializing women or making sweeping claims about the superiority of women as educational leaders. Indeed such claims have much in common with the positions of previous centuries that claimed superiority for whites over other ethnic and racial groups[5] or that denied women's ability to hold political positions and to vote[6] knowledgeably. Generalizations about a group are often more harmful than helpful because they tend to polarize perspectives and promote division.

The body of work on gender and leadership challenges institutional norms and traditional power bases and validates new ways of thinking and working. It raises important questions about the values of institutional life by emphasizing interest in others, relationships, and a sense of social responsibility. But it is limited in that it privileges a focus on gender over other forms of difference and may be used to perpetuate division and prejudice rather than overcome them.

Multicultural Approaches to Leadership

Multicultural approaches to leadership are, in many ways, similar to feminist approaches, in that they also challenge the existing norms, values, and power relationships of organizational life, but by focusing on race and ethnicity. Multiculturalists often stress the need to diversify the pool of teachers or administrators in order to create schools that are inclusive, caring, and respectful. Some writers (for example, Ah Nee-Benham and Cooper 1998; Baber 1995; Dillard 1995; Murtadha-Watts 1999b; Nieto 1992) emphasize that leaders of color play an important role in today's schools, despite their under-representation. As numbers of visible minority educators increase, they convince others of their competence and hence contribute to the creation of a society that recognizes and respects the expertise of its diverse people. Increasing the diversity of the educational workforce brings new sensitivities, new perspectives, needed balanced, and new role models to our schools.

As important as it is to diversify the cadre of educators, it is not always possible to attain proportional representation of diverse groups. Moreover, focusing on one characteristic is never enough because ethnicity is only one component of diversity. Regardless of the gender, class, or ethnic group from which a school leader comes, there will be staff members, students, and families who come from other groups.

New ways of understanding are essential if we are to attend to the various learning needs of all children and adequately prepare them for adult life in a diverse and multicultural society. Too often, educators in schools with superficially homogeneous populations report that they have no need to incorporate diverse perspectives into their instruction (Schmuck 1993; Shields 2002a). Yet visible minority status is just one way to think about and identify diversity. By rejecting or neglecting difference, these educators fail to prepare their students for adult life in a diverse, multicultural, and global community.

Many schools have as part of their mission statement a form of the aphorism that all children can learn. However, as Skrla and Scheurich argue, "actual practices and programs in these same schools are suffused with deficit views of the educability of children of color and children from low-income homes" (2001, 3). They report that there are also glimmers of hope and cite one superintendent who stated that his thinking had changed from paying lip service to the concept of high expectations for all to really believing it:

> I have made this transformation that all kids can learn, from one that thought we were going to have an extremely difficult time with these kids because of their low socioeconomic condition. . . . It isn't something I've had all my life. (Skrla and Scheurich 2001, 8)

Realizing that all children actually means *all* children is a starting point. But stating that all children can learn (unless there are severe neurological impairments) is simply a truism. This is exemplified by the daily demonstrations provided by all children as they dress themselves, talk, arrive at school, and so on. A more significant educational question is, What can all children learn? Perhaps more importantly, we need to begin to ask, What do we want and expect children to learn?

Democratic Leadership

Sometimes the term *democratic leadership* is used to advocate a desirable form of organizational leadership and recognize the need to prepare all students for future participation in a democratic society. In some quarters, the clarion call for democratic leadership suggests it would be a panacea. Here, too, although democratic leadership may be attractive, both caution and increased clarity are in order.

It is essential to distinguish between direct democracy (one person, one vote) and other forms of representative or participatory democracy in which checks and balances have been instituted as safeguards. In the former, the majority may easily overrule a legitimate minority position and perpetuate inequities existing in the status quo. In Athens, a displeased populous could, for example, vote the immediate death of an offending ruler. More recently, in Emmen, Switzerland, a vote of all of the town's eligible electorate resulted in only the members of four Italian families out of fifty-six candidates being accepted as full citizens (Bachmann 2000). One highly controversial aspect of the process was the rejection of all others—including people from the former Yugoslavia, Turkey, Hungary, and Poland, some of whom had even been born in Switzerland. The mayor was both uncritical and unapologetic, stating that the process was highly democratic and that the people had spoken. In the name of democracy, one powerful group was able to prevent people whom they perceived to be undesirable and different from gaining access to claims to what many would argue are rightful claims to citizenship.

In Canada, the Liberal government in British Columbia, elected with a landslide victory in May 2001, promised to hold a public referendum on an agreement by the previous government to settle aboriginal[7] (*Nisga'a*) land claims. Many critiqued this type of referendum, in which the majority is asked to vote on the rights of a minority, as an example of the misuse of democratic leadership. Rarely will the majority vote for the rights of the minority and against its own perceived self-interest.

Yet, where appropriate checks and balances are introduced, democracy can be effective. In 1994 Proposition 187 was passed in California, denying educational access to children of illegal immigrants. A federal judge subsequently froze the decision. The 104th Congress took up the matter as an amendment to the omnibus immigration reform bill (H.R. 2202). The provision was passed by the full House of Representatives, but the conference committee later eliminated it, partly because no vote had been taken in the Senate on the issue. Due in part to a series of checks and balances, the provisions of the bill were never enacted.

Thus it is important to distinguish between the concept of democratic leadership and fuzzy conceptions of democracy. Inequitable practices may be perpetuated under some forms of democracy in which majorities determine policies that perpetuate inequities in their self-interest. These are often justified in the name of democracy, while issues of equity and social justice may remain unaddressed. A concept of democratic leadership that takes the rights of all citizens into account, ensures checks and balances, and includes all members of the society, regardless of their social or political position, needs to be clearly articulated.

Green wrote that "in recent years, an odd international alliance of conservative and liberal political theorists has advocated a purely 'formal,' institutional conception of democracy" (1999, vi). She maintains that this is quite different from "a deeper conception of democracy that expresses the experience-based possibility of more equal, respectful, and mutually beneficial ways of community life" (p. vi). Democratic leadership includes different voices in the processes of decision making and social inquiry. It is based on negotiation, dialogue, and collaborative reconstruction, as well as a concept of multiculturalism that goes beyond the common one-person-one-vote notion of democracy. Viewed in this way, educational leadership must be democratic.

Critical Approaches to Leadership

The form of what Green calls "deeply democratic leadership" resembles other leadership theories that may broadly be categorized as

critical perspectives. I use the term *critical* in a pragmatic way, applying it to any approach based on a fundamental desire to critique and
change, rather than to understand and describe, the status quo. Although this broad use of *critical* does not attend to the many nuances
and differences among various theories, it is consistent with the use of
others and encompasses the categories Burrell and Morgan (1979) call
radical perspectives. Many writers (Capper 1992; Reyes, Velez, and
Peña 1993; Riehl 2000) use *critical* in this way, prodding us to "raise
legitimate questions about social structure: the questions of class,
power, and culture" (Foster 1986, 637).

Leadership that is both democratic and critical may be *deeply disruptive* and *deeply beneficial*. It requires those who hold positions of
privilege and power within organizations or society to respect, engage
in dialogue with, and cooperate with "those whose values are different
than but not unalterably antagonistic to one's own" (Green 1999, 60).
It is, however, not a relativistic, anything-goes type of leadership, but
one firmly grounded in moral and ethical principles.

On one occasion, the angry older brother of a female student in the
ninth grade confronted a principal. He insisted that his culture required
him, in the absence of his father, to take action to punish another student whose attention he believed was disrespectful to his younger sister. He demanded that the principal call the young man to her office so
he could defend his sister's honor in a fight. In this case, the principal
needed to have a clear sense of guiding principles. She had to acknowledge the brother's right to hold both an emotional and a cultural
sense of outrage; but she also had to hold firmly to the knowledge that
the right to beat someone up was antagonistic to the laws and culture
of the school. She could not simply abrogate her responsibilities to provide a safe learning environment for all students in order to permit the
exercise of a cultural norm of physical punishment.

A number of writers explicate other aspects of critical leadership.
Foster identifies understanding, critique, and education as three components of a critical approach to leadership (1986, 624). The leader's
task includes "developing understandings of the various people and positions involved in running a school" and creating "a critical appraisal
of the extant reality of schooling." It also entails preparing individuals
for both democratic participation and occupational involvement (p.

637). The leader would try to understand why the brother was upset and to work with him to find mutually acceptable ways to deal with the situation. Perhaps she would also work with the sister to develop shared understandings about acceptable behavior and relationships both at school and in the community.

Anderson claims that to develop a critical constructivist approach to leadership, the school leader needs to attend to questions of invisibility, legitimation, and nonevents and to understand "the invisible and unobtrusive forms of control that are exercised in schools and school districts" (1990, 39). An example of an invisible (and invisibly legitimated) educational issue identified by one principal was his realization that no students enrolled in English as a second language programs appeared on school honor roll lists. On investigating, he found that these students were enrolled in a self-contained classroom program and did not receive discrete grades for different subjects. Hence, when honor role calculations were made, the students were disqualified because they did not have a grade point average based on six eligible subjects. The school policy had created an invisible barrier for some students. Only when the situation was made visible could the principal begin to take steps to rectify it.

Starratt also advocates critical leadership and, in order to create a model of ethical schooling, combines it with two additional concepts. He proposes that educational administrators combine three ethics—critique, justice, and caring. An ethic of critique will lead the administrator to ask such questions as: Who benefits by these arrangements? Which group dominates this social arrangement? Who defines the way things are structured here? (Starratt 1991, 189). An ethic of justice will lead an administrator to ensure that "learning activities are structured within curricular and extra-curricular programs to encourage discussion of individual choices as well as discussions of school community choices" (p. 193). In other words, educators will find ways to balance individual and community needs. An ethic of caring "focuses on the demands of relationships . . . reaches beyond concerns with efficiency" (p. 195), and leads us to act out of a sense of compassion. Starratt's model requires a holistic approach: consideration of individual and group, of structure and culture, of justice and caring.

In one urban school, two competing parent groups, one English-speaking and the other Mandarin-speaking, had developed over time.

In this case, the principal needed to explore the status of the two groups. Who could make decisions? Which group was considered official? Why did parents feel that they needed two groups? Who felt unwelcome and silenced? He needed to find ways to bring all interested parents together rather than permit the continued legitimation of two groups—one dominant, the other marginalized, due to differences in language and ethnicity. Instituting two parent groups may allow a principal to hear from both groups. It may give more individuals an opportunity to express themselves, but it does nothing to bring the groups together, to understand each other better, or to create a sense of common purpose.

When educational leaders adopt a critical approach, they must not only take account of a school's faculty and student body; they must also consider the needs of the groups and communities the students represent. They must ensure that they do not suppress difficult and uncomfortable ideas; therefore, they must be prepared to deal with conflicts, help people explore the basis for differences in opinion, and find ways to work together.

In one school in which 10 percent of the student body was African American, 60 percent of students suspended were African American. The explanation was simplistic and one-dimensional. An administrator explained, "Those who were fighting get expelled. It's not my fault that the African Americans fight more than the other students."

Yet critical leadership would not stop there. A principal who recognized the discrepancy in the number of students being severely disciplined related to their proportion of the student body might begin to ask probing questions. She might begin by reflecting that since there is definitely no evidence of a genetic predisposition to violence among African Americans, but a disproportionate number of African American students were being suspended, she needed to try to find other reasons to explain the high incidence of violence among a certain sector of a school population. She might ask such questions as: Are these students appropriately placed in educational programs? Are they included in the power and decision-making structures of the school? Are there factors in their home or community situations that create a likelihood of tension or violence? Once some hypotheses had been developed, the leader would proceed to collect data to determine whether there were

institutional and social barriers in the school itself that led to disproportionate incidents of rule infringements.

Some educators advocate what are, in my opinion, more repressive
approaches to student discipline. Vergon, for example, supports increasing the direct control mechanisms for students engaged in unacceptable behaviors. On finding that African American students were
engaged in a greater number of disciplinary incidents than other students, he proposed that "clearer and stricter discipline measures" would
reduce the "disparate exclusion of students of color" (2000, 6). A critical leader would reject this approach and find ways to explore why one
group seems to feel disenfranchised in the present system, perhaps
seeking ways to defuse tensions by examining their often difficult and
painful histories in the community.

Involving the African American students, their parents, and other
members of their community in the identification of the problem and
its solutions is consistent with Maxcy's (1991) belief that a leader's
task is to help release the power of those he or she is leading in order
for them to practice self-, as well as social, emancipation. Words like
freedom, liberation, emancipation, equality, and *justice,* while not often associated with the daily operation of public schools, are central to
the concept of school leadership I am developing.

Transformative Leadership

Although some people use the terms *transformational* and *transformative* as synonyms, there is a subtle but important difference. Transformational leadership, as already noted, focuses on the collective interests of a group or an organization. Using Leithwood and Jantzi's
(1990) model, we could determine that transformational leadership is
present in situations where the leader is directly involved in developing
an identifiable shared vision, fostering consensus, setting high performance standards, developing an intellectually stimulating climate,
building a productive school culture, and developing structures to foster participation in school decisions. Each of these elements may be
identified in the following illustration.

In a controversial decision, a western Canadian school district chose to
implement a user-pay half-day kindergarten to supplement the existing

publicly funded kindergarten. The rationale was that too many of the relatively wealthy, high-status parents in the district were opting to send their children to private schools, hence depriving the board of provincial funding. Ignoring cries of elitism and concerns about increasing the achievement gap between more and less socially and economically advantaged children, the district implemented the full-day kindergarten wherever there were enough participants to make it fiscally feasible. The name of the activity was changed from kindergarten to CHILD[8] to circumvent legal concerns raised by the province.

Starratt states that transformational leadership "changes people's operative attitudes, values, and beliefs from self-centered to higher, altruistic beliefs, attitudes, and values" (1995, 110). Using his definition, one might argue that the foregoing illustration fulfills the conditions for transformational leadership. Advocates of the user-pay kindergarten within the school district might claim that their personal goals were transformed into altruistic ones that bettered both the school system and the parents and children who participated in the CHILD program.

On the other hand, one might argue that the transformation proceeded to the benefit of those with the money and power to profit, and to the detriment of children already marginalized through class, socioeconomic status (SES), or other home factors, who could not afford the user-pay program. There is no provision here for the inclusion of groups whose situations do not permit them to benefit from the program.

In the same jurisdiction (and others), the government sponsors a full-day kindergarten for aboriginal students. Taxpayers support these extended educational services for children from a group whose members tend to have less ability to pay and whose children are among the least successful in the education system. This full-day kindergarten is an attempt to provide some equity in the preschool experiences the children have encountered and to equip them to be more successful in their subsequent schooling. This program seems more altruistic, although many children who might benefit from additional educational experiences are still excluded. Choosing to offer supplementary services to those who most need them is an example of transformative leadership.

I use the term *transformative* to imply moral leadership, leadership that would consider the financial situation of students and their parents and that would be more likely to advocate using the resources of the most wealthy to help those in need than to support a program like

CHILD. Goeglein and Hall define *transformative leadership* as a "reciprocal process whereby one or more individuals engage with others in such a way that leaders and followers raise one another to higher levels of motivation and morality" (2001, 1). Transformative leadership, they assert, is "based in values." Astin and Astin emphasize that transformative leadership is essentially value-based leadership in a given social context that "can open up new possibilities for transformation and change" (2000, 2). They summarize their hope that transformative leadership may help to change society in these words:

> We believe that the value ends of leadership should be to enhance equity, social justice, and the quality of life; to expand access and opportunity; to encourage respect for difference and diversity; to strengthen democracy, civic life, and civic responsibility; and to promote cultural enrichment, creative expression, intellectual honesty, the advancement of knowledge, and personal freedom coupled with responsibility. (p. 6)

Transformative (rather than transformational) leadership focuses on social justice.

The framework as created to this point is complex and demanding for educational leaders. We must attend to both individual and organizational needs, we must engage in transactional, transformational, and above all, transformative processes. To do this, we must understand the composition of our organizations, address issues of power, gender, ethnicity, and culture, and use processes that are deeply democratic and appropriately critical.

These concepts of leadership all emphasize the need for transformation, but they do not directly address the rapidly changing nature of school populations and the concomitant demands on school leaders. I use the term *cross-cultural* to highlight the demographic changes that have occurred in much of the English-speaking world and to suggest the need for educational leaders to take account of these changes.

CROSS-CULTURAL LEADERSHIP:
LEADING MULTIPLE CULTURES

In 1984 Craft noted that approximately 6 percent of British society and 20 percent of Australian society did not speak English as a home language

(1984, 18). In Canada, according to the 1996 census, approximately 4 million people (13.7 percent of the population) had immigrated during the previous forty years. A *USA Today* "snapshot," "26.4 Foreign-Born Live in USA," (2000) reported that in 1999, 26.4 million people (approximately 9.7 percent of the American population) had been born outside the United States.

As world demographics change, so too do school populations. Because the white population of California, Florida, and Texas has dropped below 50 percent, many schools call themselves majority-minority schools to describe the situation in which the previously dominant, middle-class, white, English-speaking majority now represents less than 50 percent of the total population. Schools have also changed with respect to dominant language, religion, class, values, beliefs, and practices. Yet the most common educational response is to ignore or decry the changes. We too often fail to consider how we conceptualize school organization, culture, curriculum, community, and even school leadership in majority terms, ignoring the increasingly diverse student body. Indeed, we sometimes ignore diversity in the hope that it will disappear.

When we want to learn about others, we often turn to research literature for direction and insights. For that reason, in the next section, I examine the literature related to cross-cultural leadership in order to show what it does, but also what it does not, contribute to thinking about school leadership.

Examining the Literature on Cross-Cultural Leadership

It is perhaps surprising, given the widespread changes in social demographics and their impact on schools, that there is no coherent body of literature related to cross-cultural leadership in education. The term *cross-cultural leadership* has, however, received considerable attention in other social science literature, particularly from business and health care. In general, the term *cross-cultural* is used to describe a search for a leadership model that holds across cultures, for example, a model that would enhance the success of an American executive taking a position in Hong Kong. In this research, the focus is on comparing current practices and assessing their transferability across cultures and in other contexts (Hofstede 1991; Kakabadse et al. 1997; Trompenaars 1993). Hofstede, whose work is frequently mentioned in discussions of cross-cultural research, maintains that unless one understands that dimensions such as individualism, power distance, uncertainty avoidance, and gender orientation may be approached quite differently from culture to culture, the outcomes of interaction may often be unintended conflict (Hofstede 1991, 208). He also recognized that unanticipated consequences may occur when a leader from one society moves to another, accompanied by inappropriate and even "irrelevant materials" and assumptions (p. 217).

Although many of these studies suggest that a common approach in business management may not be possible, some educators (see Hallinger 1995; Hallinger and Leithwood 1996; Heck 1998) have embarked on a similar quest: to determine whether there is a general model of school-principal leadership that holds across settings. Chapman, Sackney, and Aspin (1999), in a recent overview of *internationalization* in education, further describe the quest for generalizable approaches in education. Citing Professor Ebuchi of Japan, they write that internationalization is "a process by which the education provision . . . becomes more sophisticated, enriched and broadly applicable to students from all backgrounds and countries" (Chapman, Sackney, and Aspin 1999, 74).

In the business context, the success of a cross-national team may depend on minimizing difference and achieving a common management style. Trying to achieve a common style and to minimize difference may help enhance productivity or economic profit. However, in education, it is inherently problematic, even hegemonic, to strive for uniformity because uniformity will always privilege the experience of some children and minimize or negate that of others. A one-size-fits-all approach to leadership, especially to cross-cultural leadership, does not really fit very well at all.

Educational Cross-Cultural Leadership

When I use the term *cross-cultural leadership,* it is not in search of one model that is applicable across cultures and in many contexts. Rather, I use the term to acknowledge that educational leaders come from cultures that are different from the cultures of many of their students—whether

Look at points of view different from your own.

the differences are in terms of class, ethnicity, education, socioeconomic status, sexual orientation, gender, heritage language, or cultural
traditions. Regardless of how successful we are as educators in attract-
ing teachers and leaders from various minority groups, they too will be
cross-cultural leaders, working with students and teachers who are in
some ways alike and in others different from themselves.

Cross-cultural leadership is critical for schools of the twenty-first
century because all school leaders have to work across cultures. It is
rare indeed for a school principal to work in a school that is so homogeneous there are no identifiable differences of race, ethnicity, or social
class. It is even more unlikely that she will work in an environment in
which there are no significant differences of religion, gender, sexual
orientation, ability, or disability. Yet we still tend to talk and think about
schools in North America as if they were relatively homogeneous, and
as if there were no cultural issues that need to be examined. As one of
my graduate students suggested, if any administrator thinks the student
body in his or her school is homogeneous, it is probably a sign that the
administrator spends too much time in the office.

When I conducted interviews among high school students in one
American school district in which students came predominantly from
three distinct groups (Anglo, Hispanic, and Navajo), white students appeared confused when I asked about what aspects of their culture they
hoped to pass on to their children. Several said they did not understand
the question; others stated that it did not apply to them. Many parents
and teachers made statements on written surveys and questionnaires
like "culture belongs in the home" or "schools should not teach culture" or "culture should only be taught if there is time."

Each of these (and many other) comments suggests a profound mis-
understanding of the nature of culture. Schools are not, and cannot be,
culture-free. There can be, however, so little explicit conversation about
the norms and values of participants that the traditional societal norms
are assumed to apply to everyone. The culture of the majority then becomes *the* culture of the school. Whether it is acknowledged or not,
schools do teach culture. Thus one important task of the cross-cultural
leader is to make the presence of culture(s) explicit and clarify its roles.
He will help people within the immediate population of the school, as
well as its wider community, determine what culture or cultures domi-

nate and which are marginalized and subordinated within the existing orientation of the school.

Sometimes culture is defined as "the way we do things around here." Others have defined it as "keeping the herd moving in a roughly westward direction," or more elegantly as "an ethos created and sustained by social processes, images, symbols, and ritual" (Morgan 1997, 132). If the way we do things around a school is so ingrained that it is not recognized as culture, then the implicit norms of schooling most certainly reflect the beliefs, traditions, and practices of the dominant or majority culture, frequently to the exclusion of minority groups and cultures.

Cross-cultural leaders must seek to understand, explain, and overcome the covert ways in which people are excluded from their school communities. They must help people explore their assumptions and understand how the culture of the school has emerged and how it may be changed to be more inclusive and representative of all children in the school.

PUTTING IT TOGETHER:
TRANSFORMATIVE CROSS-CULTURAL LEADERSHIP

A *transformative cross-cultural leader* would not be manipulative or controlling. She would not misuse or abuse her power as Napoleon did; nor would she ignore issues of purpose, justice, or morality, as so many people seem to do. In contrast, she would focus on identifying inequities, implementing inclusive and just practices, and making moral decisions.

What then of leadership style? Does it make no difference whether one is collaborative? Authoritarian? Caring? I am tempted to respond with a qualified no. There are examples of good—perhaps even excellent—leaders who demonstrate polar-opposite styles and approaches to leadership.

Joe Clark, the legendary secondary-school principal whose story is depicted in the movie *Lean on Me,* is well-known as an energetic, dedicated, bat-wielding school principal. Alternatively called "an obsessed disciplinarian" and a "leader, role model, and friend," he is a familiar example of an energetic and authoritarian educational leader.

Despite the objections of many of his teachers, the skepticism of his board, and drastic measures to control student discipline at the school, Joe succeeded in cleaning up New Jersey's troubled Eastside High School and turned it into a model school. In the process, we are told, he earned the respect and support of his staff and students. Despite his achievements, one would certainly be hard-pressed to consider him democratic.

Martin Luther King was a successful leader who united people from disparate backgrounds and sets of beliefs and convinced them that they should be prepared to sacrifice, even die, for the cause of freedom in the United States. Mahatma Gandhi exemplifies the servant-leader who earned the respect and support of his followers over time through personal sacrifice and fasting.

Attempts to find the character or personality traits that unite these leaders leave us with no clear answers. But they all held strong (and quite different) core values. They were deeply committed to a sense of purpose and they were willing to make personal sacrifices, even break the law if necessary, to achieve their goals. What King, Gandhi, and Clark had in common may have been *authenticity,* a quality that I believe provides the key to effective leadership.

Authenticity as the Key

Terry, introducing the notion of *authentic leadership,* states that the word *authentic* is derived from "Greek sources meaning one who accomplishes. To be authentic is to act, to embody, to engage, and to participate in life" (1993, 107). But it is more. Authentic leadership is not just action but ethical action—being "true to ourselves and true to the world, real in ourselves and real in the world" (p. 139). This could certainly be said of Clark, King, and Gandhi.

Joe Clark was true to his beliefs that drug users should be banned, that the school should be a safe place for students and teachers. Although he illegally chained the doors of his school (in contravention of fire regulations), he succeeded in achieving his goal. King was willing to demonstrate, to preach openly, to risk jail in order to attain equal rights for his people. Gandhi believed in pacifism. Despite the deaths of many followers who joined in passive resistance, his goal of a free India was attained. Although the goals and ends differed, each leader exhibited consistency among stated beliefs, espoused goals, and observable actions. It is this consistency that is basic to authentic leadership.

These three people went further than most educational leaders will be expected to go in taking a stand for their beliefs. All demonstrated a willingness to stand firm and resist political pressure or unjust practices, even when their own personal safety or security were jeopardized. Clark was transferred; King and Gandhi were imprisoned and ultimately killed for their positions. Yet King's position on civil disobedience was evidenced by each of them: if you break the law, even for a just cause, you must be willing to suffer the consequences.

Ethics as the Foundation

In 1978 Burns suggested that ethics is essential to leadership and set off a huge theoretical debate by saying that, for him, this meant there could be no such thing as unethical leadership. His position was extremely controversial, but his point was that it is an inherent contradiction to use the word *leadership* unless whatever is being described has a moral and ethical foundation.

Many recent conceptions of leadership tend to remain silent on the topic of ethics. Evans (1996), for example, builds his concept of authentic leadership on integrity—a fundamental consistency among espoused beliefs and values, stated goals, and observable action—but ignores the moral and ethical underpinnings. Like Evans, Terry (1993) is silent about the need for "participation in life" to be grounded in moral practice. It is possible to suggest that a leader does not need to subscribe to any particular belief system, demonstrate any particular character traits, or adopt any specific leadership strategy—he or she simply should be consistent. Intuitively we know that this is not what we need or want in a leader. One might be evil, amoral, or even immoral—and still be consistent. (Hitler and Stalin are consummate examples.) Even good intentions may not be sufficient unless we carefully define what we mean by terms such as *good, success, effectiveness, excellence,* and *justice*.

Authentic leadership as a concept is incomplete unless it is also leadership with a clear focus on ethics and morality. Temes, writing about

Martin Luther King, states that "the best leaders operate on the souls of their followers" (1996, 80). (Unfortunately so do the worst.) Sergio-vanni talks about the "head, heart, and hand of leadership" (1992, 6) and emphasizes the need for moral leadership:

> By giving more credence to sense experience and intuition, and by ac-cepting sacred authority and emotion as fully legitimate ways of know-ing, equal in value to secular authority, science, and deductive logic, the value systems undergirding management theory and leadership practice will grow large enough to account for a new kind of leadership—one based on moral authority. (p. 16)

One of the difficulties of the successive waves of educational re-form that have occurred during the past few decades has been that too many changes have been proposed and implemented in a moral vacuum. School boards and legislative bodies have attempted to de-centralize decision making or centralize accountability. Teacher and student tests and new forms of school accreditation have been de-veloped, school and class sizes changed, schedules modified, and changes instituted in almost every program or curricular area—with very little lasting impact on students' educational experiences or out-comes.

We often engage in reform without having clarified the underlying purposes or intents. We fail to determine what we mean by a "good" ed-ucation system, an "excellent" program, or a "successful" student. What do we mean when we talk about "educated citizens"? What would it mean if we were to help our students understand how to live "the good life" or to create a "better" society? Each of these is a pro-foundly moral question. To begin to address them, we require leaders who are firmly grounded in moral principles.

CONCLUSION

Leaders who are authentic—consistent in words and actions, com-mitted to a moral cause, and willing to take a stand—may differ widely in their goals, personality traits, or leadership styles, yet they can all be successful leaders. They are transformative, working for change wherever they find inequity. They are cross-cultural, working with people from many different cultural groups in order to enhance equity for all. And they are leaders, exercising both management and leadership skills, both doing the right thing and figuring out how to do things right.

The concept of transformative cross-cultural leadership is summarized in figure 1.1.

A transformative leader rejects the inclination of Frost's farmer to build walls where none are needed. Instead, he or she asks serious questions about to whom our current educational practices are likely to "give

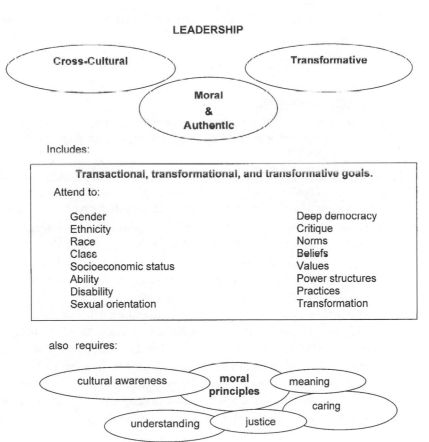

LEADERSHIP

Cross-Cultural

Transformative

Moral
&
Authentic

Includes:

Transactional, transformational, and transformative goals.
Attend to:

Gender	Deep democracy
Ethnicity	Critique
Race	Norms
Class	Beliefs
Socioeconomic status	Values
Ability	Power structures
Disability	Practices
Sexual orientation	Transformation

also requires:

cultural awareness   moral principles   meaning

caring

understanding   justice

Figure 1.1. Transformative Cross-Cultural Leadership

offense" and whom they are intended to benefit. Transformative cross-cultural leaders understand the diverse cultures of their schools and organizations; they develop images of inclusive, caring, high-performing schools that take into account changing school populations and also prepare students for life in a global knowledge economy. They identify and challenge inequities in existing systems, and they act morally, consistently, and persistently, in transformative ways, to create the type of schools described in the next chapter as communities of difference.

NOTES

1. The reader is reminded that these names are pseudonyms. They protect the confidentiality of my respondents, and they also remind us that the purpose of the book is not to glorify individuals, however successful they may be, but to provide ideas on which others may build.

2. The prestigious national award, which includes a $25,000 prize, was awarded to Alicia in June 2000.

3. See, for example, books by Schnarr and Moore (2000), Wing and Sunzi (1988), and Clavell (1998) that apply his concepts to everything from marketing to spiritual peace.

4. For a quick review of these issues, see Owen Connelly, "Napoleon I," at www.encarta.msn.com/encet/refpages/refarticle.aspx?refid=761566988.

5. See the work of George Morton (described in Gould 1996) who examined one thousand skulls in an attempt to prove the superiority of Caucasians (although in doing so, he "needed" to exclude Hindus).

6. Women won the right to vote in the United States in 1920. In Canada, women were able to vote in Manitoba in 1916; other provinces gradually granted suffrage, with Quebec being the last in 1940.

7. I use the term *aboriginal* as a general word to include people who are variously called by other words such as First Nations, Indian, American Indian, Native American, Maori, Aborigine, and so on. The dictionary defines the term as "pertaining to the earliest known inhabitants of a country or region."

8. CHILD is an acronym for Children Happily Inquiring, Learning, Developing. The half-day program is offered at a cost to parents of $280 a month for a three-day option or $350 a month for a five-day option.

CHAPTER 2

Schools as Communities of Difference

During my sabbatical leave, I had the opportunity to spend some time in New Zealand visiting a number of schools and learning how educators worked with diverse student populations. On one occasion, a man from the regional office of the Ministry of Education called me to schedule a visit to what he called a "language nest," a concept that was new to me.

As we walked into the building, I was amazed by the sight of about forty children of various ages from different ethnic groups. In the back was a row of toddlers in high chairs. Three and four year olds were sitting on the floor in front. Adults sitting with the children on the floor held infants on their laps. A few older children were on chairs. All of them were singing.

I recognized the tune, "Jesus Wants Me for a Sunbeam," but the words were unfamiliar. The song ended and another—a totally new one—began. A woman spoke a few words to the children (again in an unfamiliar language), and they began to greet us: *Kia Ora . . . Kia Orana,* Good Morning!

The woman rose, gave my host a hug, and greeted me with a wide smile. This was my introduction to *Kaura Kaupapa Maori*: New Zealand language nests. These preschool classes were established in 1982 as a way to provide support for Maori language and culture. The language nests now flourish in support of New Zealand Maori; some also encourage Cook Island Maori, Samoan, and other cultures. They provide preschool education for those who want their young children to preserve and develop pride in their home culture or to gain rich multicultural experiences and understanding of others. Parents pay a small fee, but the majority of the cost is borne by the government.

I returned several times to that and other language nests. Now, back in North America, I mentally revisit them. I recall the sounds of children playing and speaking in several languages; I delight once again in their enthusiasm. I summon up the faces of the adults and realize that, aside from the woman who greeted us and who was described to me as being "in charge," I really had no idea which adults were parents and which paid workers. Parents were encouraged and welcome to participate. And I frequently ponder the constraints of many of our North American rules and conventions.

Language nests serve children from infancy to age five. Rather than wait for the beginning of a new school year, as is the custom in North America, New Zealand children enter school on the day of their fifth birthday. "Is it disruptive," I repeatedly asked teachers, "having children start at many different points during the school year?" "Not at all," they responded. "It gives each child time to be welcomed and introduced to school on his or her own special day." Children eagerly anticipate their fifth birthday, generally marked by new school clothes, a school bag, and the opportunity to attend school for the first time. Starting at different times, children then progress individually at their own pace, while becoming part of a socially constructed "whole." During the primary grades, children are not promoted in lockstep fashion but are moved to the next class as they are ready, generally at the beginning of a new term.[1]

Some North American teachers have suggested that New Zealand teachers accept this practice, which they see as confusing, because it is all they know. Maybe, but maybe not. I wonder what could happen if we, as educational leaders, more often had the opportunity to experience other ways of doing things. Would it help us break out of our mold?

This chapter explores what our schools could be like if we began to envision a new sense of community, one that is to some extent embodied in the concept of New Zealand language nests. In this chapter, I call this concept a community of difference.

THINKING ABOUT COMMUNITY

Community, like leadership, has been the subject of much discussion and writing in the past few years.[2] Most commonly, *community* describes a group of people who share a specific location, such as those who live in a retirement community, read a community newspaper, or live in a specific school neighborhood. *Community* is also used to refer to a group of people who share a mutual interest, such as an Internet community, a gaming community, or an ancient history community. It is also used to identify a group of people who share common traits, beliefs, or behaviors, such as the Jewish community, the gay community, or the Latino community. Another use of *community* focuses on groups with collective purposes, such as the educational community, the health care community, or the farming community.

The term *global community* is widely used to describe the breakdown of old economic, cultural, and communicative barriers throughout the world and the establishment of new norms. It embodies the common fear of losing what is familiar and of not knowing what may come. At the global level, large institutions such as the World Bank and new economic alliances such as NAFTA and the European Economic Union have garnered international attention. With globalization comes an increasing awareness of paradox: as the world becomes more united by trade and communications networks, it is also becoming more complex and fragmented.

It is difficult to talk about community—about the ways in which people come together to live and learn in relationships—without seeming to imply that community can be, perhaps even should be, homogeneous. It is important to understand that there will always be differences. People are so diverse that they group and regroup, agreeing and disagreeing, supporting and rejecting each other's viewpoints. Even in communities that are apparently homogeneous, there exist what someone has called "cross-cutting cleavages." Thus, although the farm community may come together to lobby the government about better crop insurance, the same members of the community may disagree heartily about the use of pesticides or the importance of organic farming. Not even the best of friends agree on *everything*.

It should also be noted that people live in multiple, intersecting, and overlapping communities. To continue the illustration, although some people may spend most of their work week in a farming community, once or twice a week, they may travel to the city to participate in sporting events or a service club where they interact with people from other communities. Then they may disperse to various churches and temples where they meet with yet another group of friends and acquaintances in order to worship as they choose.

Although community, as it is discussed in this book, may sometimes seem to be a unitary concept, this is unduly simplistic. No community is entirely homogeneous.

COMMUNITY: A FOCUS OF SCHOOL REFORM

The concept of schools as communities has attracted a great deal of attention during the recent plethora of educational reform initiatives. It has been the subject of many books, articles, and special issues of journals. Authors write about professional communities (Louis 1996), learning communities (Dufour 2001; Mitchell 1999), online communities (Powers and Barnes 2001), value communities (Vendler 2001), communities of hope (Neugebauer 2000), and communities of memory (Bellah et al. 1985), to name a few. Educators debate what are sometimes posited as conflicts between professionalism and community (*Peabody Journal of Education* 1998, vol. 73).

In a 1993 address, subsequently published in a 1994 edition of a prestigious journal, Sergiovanni claimed that changing the metaphor from *organization* to *community* would fundamentally change the nature of schools. He urged the creation of school communities in which a sense of collective "we" would emerge from disparate collections of "I's."

Despite the renewed interest in schools as communities since Sergiovanni's 1993 address, little attention has been paid to defining community or examining its underlying norms and values. Many simply use the term, mixing descriptive and normative elements without defining how it is being used or without identifying the implicit claims of their concept of community. Many scholars and practitioners use the term *community* to describe a collection of people (classroom, school, school and neighborhood) who are bound together by common ties of experience and history, by shared norms, beliefs, values, and goals.

Sociologists and educators with sociological training have made much of Tönnies's (1957) distinction between gemeinschaft and gesellschaft communities. Many suggest that the former relates to a simpler, friendlier past era in which people knew and worked with their neighbors, respected tradition, emphasized kinship, and shared experiences. "Commitments between people in *Gemeinschaft* are taken for granted, rather than intentionally chosen" (Merz and Furman 1997, 13). Gemeinschaft is the model we traditionally think of as community, described by one of my friends who wrote the following:

I grew up in rural Alberta, in the house that my great-grandfather built and my grandfather and my father grew up in. This connection to my ancestors is important. The connection to the land is important. Our community was made up of neighbours, many of whom were relatives, whose families had farmed there for generations. Many of us went to the same small, local church. Many of my teachers were our neighbours who had gone to the same school. Later I became one of those local kids who came back to teach. There were many of those "traditional, mythical" community values enacted in many ways. When our barn caught fire in the middle of the night, one phone call brought dozens of neighbours within minutes. Everyone helped a farmer, who had been in a car accident, with his harvest.

This sense of community even extended to the small town where we shopped. When my mother accidentally left one of her five children at the co-op, the store clerks figured out who he looked like and called an aunt in town to come and pick him up.

My friend's reflection did not stop there. She continued:

It's only now that I can look back at that community and see the flaws. It was expected that everyone would be the same. Newcomers were welcomed—if they took part in our activities, looked and acted like us. Someone asked if you had to be related to go to church! (MH, personal journal, used with permission)

Gemeinschaft community, despite a nostalgic focus on its many attractive elements, is not a model to which school leaders may profitably turn. It is founded on an assumption of homogeneity that is inappropriate for schools today. As we saw in Marilyn's description, gemeinschaft tends to perpetuate a type of stereotypical recognition and labeling of others. Indeed, within a gemeinschaft community people were expected to perform in predictable ways: they had grown up together, they went to the same church and school; some were considered leaders, others undoubtedly were pegged as losers.

Gesellschaft is often thought to be the opposite of gemeinschaft. Based in an industrial, cosmopolitan, and urban way of life, its values, according to Tönnies, are expertise, financial wealth, and mutual advantage based on negotiation and bargaining. Merz and Furman explain: "In *Gemeinschaft*, an individual's status is determined by familial and cultural roles; in a *Gesellschaft*, status is determined by the job that a person does, based on competency and training as well as the place of the job-role in the organizational hierarchy" (1997, 16). In a gesellschaft community, people frequently do not know their neighbors; they mistrust people in authority until they have proven themselves; and they typically hop in their car to travel a few blocks to the store rather than drop in next door to borrow an egg or a cup of sugar. As the pace and complexity of life seem to increase each year, it is not surprising that we sometimes long for a return to gemeinschaft communities that were (in memory, at least), simpler, friendlier, and less complex.

Nevertheless, gemeinschaft and gesellschaft communities have more in common than has often been expressed. Neither embraces difference nor accommodates change easily. In the former, you know that if you need to borrow money, you may approach the school principal or mayor; in the latter, if you need to borrow money, you approach the bank. In gemeinschaft, if you need your plumbing fixed, you call Joe because he knows how to fix things. In a gesellschaft community, you look in the yellow pages to find someone who has a formal certification and knows how to fix things. To some extent, gesellschaft is simply gemeinschaft on a larger scale, with slightly different but similar rules of exchange and relationships to accommodate greater numbers of people.

We live in communities and societies largely constructed out of past experiences, traditions, and perceptions. As we construct the realities of organizational life—of schooling—for students of today, we need to pay attention to issues of inclusion and exclusion. If we want to use the term *community* at all, we need to clarify a concept of community robust enough to encompass the many purposes of schooling, including the purposes related to academic excellence and social justice for all participants.

Often the term is used with the assumption that everyone understands exactly what is meant. In his book *Improving Schools from Within,* Barth writes that community was central to his "conception of a good school and a healthy workplace" (1990, 9). Boyer expresses a similar sentiment: "Community is, without question, the glue that holds an effective school together" (1995, 15). In these instances, *community* is used normatively, as a quality to be desired, a norm to attain, but with little specific information about what it is and how it might be achieved.

Another reason for the confusion about the use of community in education is that there are two fundamentally different strands of thinking. One, sometimes called school-community relations, applies to schools *in* community and focuses on the school's relationships with its wider community as it makes contact with parents, engages in service projects, encourages business partnerships, and the like. The other refers to schools *as* communities—the creation of a sense of belonging, comfort, friendship, and security within the classroom or school building itself.

Not surprisingly, the boundaries of these two definitions are frequently blurred, as when Baber advocates multicultural education to help "students understand and affirm their community cultures and . . . to free them from cultural boundaries" (1995, 345). Just as it is difficult to attempt to develop relationships with parents without attending to the interactions with students, it is almost impossible to create an inclusive, caring, and respectful culture within the school without encouraging students to understand and incorporate their own identities and those of their families into their learning experiences. Perhaps we do not permit the boundaries between home and school to blur frequently enough.

While the focus of this book is the concept of schools as communities, that does not preclude discussion of parental and community involvement; indeed, it necessitates it, as we shall see in chapter 6. Even there I focus on how the wider community becomes part of the school community, not on formal partnerships or relationships that may be forged at an entrepreneurial or administrative level without affecting the central core of school life.

Community is more than the familiar relationships of gemeinschaft or the predictable rules and roles of gesellschaft. It involves what Martin Buber called *Beziehung* (encounter) in which people look for ways to engage fully with each other in order to meet with themselves (as cited in Smith 2001). Buber talks about a community of practice, a "narrow ridge" in which each participant is open to an "adventure in heightened awareness of living." This is what he means when he focuses on "I–thou" relationships. These, in contrast to the more distanced and impersonal "I–it" relationships, imply an existence that is intensely relational. Community seeks to embody "the idea of *e pluribus unum* within our nation and to create a society that recognizes and respects the cultures of its diverse people, people united within a framework of overarching democratic values" (as cited in Smith 2001, 345).

THE PLURALIST DILEMMA

While it is pleasant to think that a nation recognizes and respects the diverse cultures of its citizens, the history of many developed countries suggests that progress toward this end has been slow and difficult. Diverse groups have encountered difficulty in learning to live together peacefully in several countries. The following examples illustrate some typical historical dilemmas.

In the United States, for example, the Naturalization Act of 1790 extended citizenship to immigrants who were white and male. In 1924 the Asian Exclusion Act (in force until 1965) "barred all but a trickle of Asian immigrants for permanent residence" (Minnich 1995, xi). In Canada, finding that an increasingly large head tax had been ineffective in stemming the flow of Chinese immigrants, legislators passed a Chinese Immigration Act in 1923, virtually excluding all Chinese from Canada. Immigration from India was quelled in a different way, with a federal order-in-council declaring that "all immigrants must arrive via a continuous journey from their country of origin" (Walker 1989, 5). In New Zealand, despite the Treaty of Waitangi (1840), which provided equal status to Maori and New Zealand European settlers, it was not until the Education Reform Act in 1989 that steps were taken to equalize educational opportunities as well as outcomes and to facilitate some curricular modification that has the potential to increase the relevance of the students' educational experiences (Rae 1996). In Australia, settled under a false claim of *terra nullius* (land belonging to no one), European settlers took control of the land and its governance, quickly passing laws in every territory that required the segregation of Aborigines, always with the explicit rationale that segregation was for their protection. In 1982, with the successful action of Eddie Mabo, Australian Aboriginals and Torres Strait Islanders were granted a degree of native land title, thus providing a legal basis for some reconciliation between Aboriginal and non-Aboriginal Australians. In Fiji, citizens of Indian origin are not permitted to own land, while native Fijians are.

In these and many other nations that have struggled to overcome past injustices, it is little wonder that one frequently finds a belief that diversity both tests and challenges the core commitments of democracy. These countries have been confronted by what Brian Bullivant (1984) calls "the pluralist dilemma" the problem of reconciling diverse claims of constituent groups with the claims of a nation as a whole. If we replace the word *nation* with *school,* the dilemma is equally compelling and challenging for educators. How can we maintain cohesion in schools or society while at the same time responsibly acknowledging and incorporating ethnic, linguistic, cultural, and other kinds of diversity? How can we acknowledge difference and at the same time live together in community?

For some, the problem seems so complex that resolution appears impossible. Yet I believe strongly that it is possible, as well as essential. I concur with the sense of paradox that Tierney describes:

> Democratic community revolves around contradictions. We search for commonalities while encouraging difference. We seek community through conflict. We act as leaders by following. We develop voice by listening. We learn about ourselves by trying to understand ot[(1993, 143)

Although we cannot eliminate conflict and contradiction, we need to balance tensions and learn to live with paradox and ambiguity.

SCHOOLS AS HOMOGENEOUS COMMUNITIES

The most common approach to conceptualizing schools as communities is not to embrace tensions and difference, but to take a relatively homogeneous notion of community, assuming a fixed core of norms, beliefs, and values into which to socialize others. This is consistent with attempts in many countries to use education primarily to socialize immigrant children to the norms and values of their new country and society and to help them develop facility with a new language (Tyack 1974).

Describing the rise of public education about the middle of the nineteenth century in North America, Tyack writes that along with a strong police force, public education was seen a means of maintaining social order and "stringent legislation [was passed] to force truants to go to school" and remove them from the decadent influence of "the streets" (1974, p. 68). In the 1880s, the state superintendent in California wrote that "citizens should support compulsory education to save themselves from the rapidly increasing herd of non-producers . . . to save themselves from the wretches who prey upon society like wild beasts" (p. 69). Some educators today act as if society has not changed, as if the goal of education were still to socialize newcomers into the norms and values of the existing institution.

Some theorists have written that good secondary schools are those in which all participants "have common understandings and are in agreement about what should be happening" (Knozal 1997, 1). Knozal identifies two types of communities that facilitate consensus: functional or valuational communities. Functional communities occur when people live in "close proximity and have social connections . . . so that common expectations for children are reinforced by all adults within the community" (p. 2). Valuational communities occur "where people have similar value systems, but are not necessarily connected socially" (p. 2), for example, when shareholders meet annually to ensure the security and profitability of their investments.

Schools that are composed largely of either functional or valuational communities are likely to have common understandings and to find agreement about common goals relatively easy to achieve. The problem is, of course, that in most schools in developed countries with high rates of mobility and/or immigration, there are neither homogeneous functional nor valuational communities. Educational leaders, therefore, need to find ways to bring people together.

Knozal goes on to suggest that "a more productive stance for educational leaders is one where together professionals and parents construct notions of what goes on in good schools" (1997, 24).

The first way of thinking assumes that participants have common understandings, not that they develop or construct them. The second requires coconstructing an understanding of the desired day-to-day activities of schooling. This is one way to ensure that various perspectives are represented in the absence of functional or valuational communities; however, the process is difficult and messy.

In 1992 Vadasy and Maddox conducted a study to investigate the educational conditions for success of migrant, Hispanic, and Native American students in the Yakima Valley. They found "abundant adaptation, yet little fundamental change" (Vadasy and Maddox 1992, 1). They describe how schools adjusted and modified existing systems to accommodate students from different cultures, languages, and lifestyles, but failed to "address or reflect how children's culture determines their school experience" (p. 1). Vadasy and Maddox found that educators spent time trying to help children succeed in traditional academic ways, without modifying the structures or school curriculum to include the cultures and life experiences of the students. For example, they report that there were many parent advisory councils (PACs) but little parental involvement, in part because parents had not been taught to overcome their lack of familiarity with, or fear of, schools, but had been expected to accommodate themselves to school expectations.

Unfortunately, these findings are still the norm in many multicultural schools today. Sending home newsletters in students' home languages or providing translators for parent-teacher evenings are examples of accommodation. In these and many other ways, school communities believe that it is enough to reach out to students and their families. Educators expect that, in response, parents will become more involved in activities like PAC, which in turn will help students fit in to existing norms and activities. Adaptation by parents is expected to result in better student achievement. If students still fail to become integrated into the life of the school, educators tend to blame them or their families and rarely turn a critical gaze on the education system as a whole.

Vadasy and Maddox are careful to point out that the educators in their study "really want to do the right thing" (1992, 2). They explain that "planning for educational quality for all children is not like ordering a Chinese meal—you can't pick and choose willy-nilly and end up with a good product" (p. 2). Yet too often we keep the menu as it is, adding items (such as hamburgers to accommodate different tastes) or subtracting a few items or a few ingredients (like MSG to adapt to different needs) and then we wonder why children are still feeling marginalized and failing to succeed academically.

Vadasy and Maddox report finding a common understanding about minority parents. They suggest that educators frequently believe implicitly that "'they' can become more like 'us' after 'we' convince 'them' that it is there for the seeking" (1992, 16). May notes the irony of trying to make others like us: "In short, attempting to enforce ethnic, linguistic, and/or religious homogeneity is far more likely to foster disunity than to ameliorate it" (2000, 5). In Kafkaesque fashion, educators offer an image of community that is always beyond the reach of those to whom it is offered, for *they* (as my Newfoundland experience showed) may never truly belong and will constantly be frustrated by the image of reality presented to them. To make matters worse, parents and students are then criticized for being unable to attain the unattainable.

I believe attempts to create homogeneous communities out of diversity have caused considerable frustration and disillusionment with the concept of community itself. Strodl and Johnson note, "The potential for conflict may be expected when people of dissimilar backgrounds, different cognitive predilections come together to make decisions for the larger pluralistic community served by a school" (1994, 3). In a homogeneous concept of community, however, many problems and issues are not addressed if they cannot be commonly defined among members of the community. Tensions and conflicts simmer beneath the surface as superficial changes rather than significant and fundamental improvements are introduced. (The well-known metaphor of rearranging the deck chairs on the Titanic while it is sinking reminds us of the inefficacy of changes that are too little and too late.) Yet the potential for conflict is real and must be addressed.

CHALLENGES TO COMMUNITY

Because educators have frequently attempted to implement homogeneous concepts of community in heterogeneous schools, there has been considerable frustration and disillusionment with the idea of schools as communities. Maxine Greene (1993) reminds us that community has its dark side, excluding some people as well as including others. She urges clarity and caution in adopting the ideal of community.

Some reject the ideal of community altogether, believing it is simply a quest for unity and sameness. Outside of the educational community, Iris Marion Young has rejected the notion of community because she sees in it "a desire for the fusion of subjects with one another which in practice operates to exclude those with whom the group does not identify" (Young 1990, 227). She goes on to assert: "It denies and represses social difference" (p. 227). Young then advocates rejecting the ideal of community and replacing it with the metaphor of the "city." She writes, "I propose to construct a normative ideal of city life as an alternative to both the ideal of community and the liberal individualism it criticizes as asocial" (p. 237). City life, as Young describes it, is composed of clusters of people who do not know each other but venture beyond familiar enclaves to meet and interact (p. 237). Young's proposal to use the city as a normative metaphor emphasizes civil interaction by strangers; my concept of a community of difference goes much further. Nevertheless, it needs to be carefully defined.

The paradox of using the term *community* as a normative concept to describe a desired change, but at the same time continuing to use it in a way that emphasizes homogeneity and implicit shared values, has been noted by several writers who have proposed various solutions to address the complex and diverse contexts of public schooling. Strike, for example, addresses the problem of whether there can be a resolution to the tension between shared values and inclusion of diverse perspectives. He concludes that constitutive values—values that "generate a conception of the ends of a good education" (1999, 47)—and liberal inclusiveness are incompatible "*at the conceptual level*" (p. 67). Hence schools as communities must take a middle ground, perhaps by instituting degrees of differentiation and choice within the public spaces that are schools. He suggests that approaches such as "house plans," schools within schools, or charter schools sharing buildings or classes with traditional schools might create "more space for constitutive values within public schools" (p. 68).

The wide diversity in public schooling in most countries shows that creating spaces for various constitutive values through the introduction of choice and alternative structures is, at best, a partial solution that may fragment, rather than build, community. It may also entrench old and exclusionary norms rather than foster the creation of new ones.

I fear that, as in the past with schools segregated by race, alternative structures to accommodate various constitutive values may perpetuate inequality in the name of school choice. This does not mean there is no room for separate structures, but their purpose must be clarified and the shared values made explicit. It may be appropriate, for example, to support the demands of some aboriginal groups to oversee their own schools when public schools are failing their children. In fact, such separation may be an essential, if temporary, step as aboriginal groups in many countries move from dependence (and subjugation) to independence and then to interdependence.

Although I acknowledge that there may be a place for separate structures to accommodate various constituent values, I am more comfortable if structures designed to achieve alternative purposes are open to people of different persuasions who hold different values and beliefs. Hence, a school district might develop magnet schools for math, science, foreign languages, or the fine arts—on the condition that each school is open to all students, regardless of ethnic or social background or place of residence within the district.

I believe that a more robust concept of community, one that respects and understands diversity and difference and accommodates value differences, but also demonstrates cohesiveness, caring, and shared goals, is necessary to move us forward. This is the concept of a community of difference.

SCHOOLS AS COMMUNITIES OF DIFFERENCE

In 1999 Furman-Brown expressed concern about the dilemma or paradox of "community building in public schools with diverse populations, given that a widely held assumption about community is that it is based in commonalities such as shared values" (1999, 7). At that time, she used the term *community of otherness* as a new way of thinking about community.

I prefer the term *community of difference* to emphasize the need for educational leaders to take account of difference in fundamental ways. Others (Fine, Weis, and Powell 1997; Furman and Starratt 2001; Murtadha-Watts 1999a; Shields and Seltzer 1997) have used the term *community of difference* to encourage dialogue about a new kind of community, one that does not try to homogenize or assimilate its members into an established set of shared values, common beliefs, and preferred practices. It is not necessary to accept the status quo as a model for social cohesion or to move to a relativistic position in which there are no agreed-on norms or values. Hence, I use the term in both a descriptive and a normative way, trying to describe its essential components and to recognize that more inclusive, respectful, mutually beneficial, and equitable schooling is not a neutral concept, but a deeply moral ideal to be achieved.

A community of difference, like other models of community, is a socially constructed concept. Because the membership of each community is different, reflecting a wide range of personal experiences as well as multiple and diverse values, hopes, and goals, each community develops differently. Accepting the norm of a community of difference means accepting that what diversity it values, what conduct it tolerates, and what actions it identifies as unacceptable are not predetermined. There are no prescriptions for community. Educational leaders cannot copy another version of community but recreate it in each new context. They may advise, like Freire, "You don't have to follow me. You have to reinvent me" (as cited in Torres 1998, 142).

In a homogeneous community, members generally exhibit a high degree of commonality. Its foundations are some taken-for-granted assumptions, some predetermined norms, beliefs, and values that members support and to which they give allegiance.

A community of difference has a different foundation. It is not based on the assumption of implicit common norms but is grounded in explicit, negotiated, and shared beliefs about fundamental principles, processes, and values. The starting points are neither rules about the acceptable belief system for the community nor the norms and customs of an already powerful or established group. A community of difference is grounded in strong personal commitments to dialogue, reflection, critique, and social justice, on the basic values of inclusion and respect. Collectively, members of a community of difference explore ways to achieve shared understandings about what the community will be like, subjecting all assumptions, even these inclusive starting points, to regular reexamination and renegotiation to best address the needs of all members. Members of a community of difference recognize the differences within the community and engage in dialogue to promote respect and understanding. In turn, this leads to a fluid and dynamic unity rather than a fixed and irrevocable one.

Creating a sense of community out of the increasing diversity of today's schools requires participants to willingly enter into negotiation and dialogue, change the predetermined center, and recenter the community in inclusive ways. Hill asserts that

> marginalization will be perpetuated if new voices and perspectives are added while the priorities and core of the organization remain unchanged. Marginalization ends, and conversations of respect begin when the curriculum is reconceived to be unimplementable without the central participation of the currently excluded and marginalized. (as cited in Tierney 1993, 25)

Thus a community of difference will develop new, explicit, and agreed-on understandings from the participation of all of its members. Out of the ongoing dialogue, a new center will emerge. "It is fostered," states Furman, "by processes that promote among its members the feelings of belonging, trust of others, and safety" (1998, 312). In such a community, people of diverse backgrounds, with differing beliefs, values, goals, and assumptions, come together to achieve cohesion through new understandings, positive relationships, and the negotiation of shared purposes and norms of behavior.

This notion of a community of difference applies to schools with students and teachers who are visibly different from each other in that it offers a way to include the myriad of perspectives and needs arising from diversity of race, gender, ethnicity, or home language (diversity that is sometimes referred to as multiculturalism). Less obvious, but equally important, is its applicability to schools that, at first glance, may seem relatively homogeneous but include diversity that may be invisible—differences of class, religion, sexual orientation, or ability. Schmuck, from her research in small rural schools, wrote that if people are unable to see difference and inequity, they are sticking their heads in the sand (1993, 5). In school communities where diversity is not readily apparent, it is important to acknowl edge its existence by seeing the invisible and by hearing silenced voices, whether they are voices of parents, students, or teachers. If educators fail to recognize diversity or to ensure that schools are respectful, equitable, and welcoming to all students, then many students will continue to be despondent, isolated, and marginalized by the institution whose role[3] (at least in part) is to prepare them to participate fully in democratic society.

Those who wish to establish a community of difference must be willing to take the time to understand each other, identify and work through differing perspectives, and listen carefully to each other. Giving people the opportunity to be heard is meaningless unless others are listening. Talking past each other adds to the frustration. In a community of difference, members are responsible to, and with, each other for the good of the community. They take seriously Seigfried's advice, "Until each person's perspective on a situation that includes her or him is heard and acknowledged, the complexity of the situation cannot be grasped, and possible relevant insights may be lost" (as cited in Green 1999, 45).

A COMMUNITY OF DIFFERENCE IS A LEARNING COMMUNITY

In 1990, in a work that has been widely referenced, Peter Senge identified five components, or disciplines, of what he called a learning organization. Although his work was not designed primarily for an educational audience[4] and does not have a specific critical or social justice focus, the disciplines provide a useful starting framework for thinking about becoming a community of difference.

Senge calls his first discipline *personal mastery*. He emphasizes that everyone in the organization (let us call it a school community) needs to *be* capable and *believe* he or she is proficient. As educators, we must feel empowered, knowing that we are on top of our subject matter. Students must know they can learn and understand what is expected of them. Personal mastery, Senge explains,

> goes beyond competence and skills, though it is grounded in competence and skills. It goes beyond spiritual unfolding or opening, although it requires spiritual growth. It means approaching one's life as a creative work, living life from a creative as opposed to reactive viewpoint. (1990, 141)

He continues, "people with a high level of personal mastery live in a continual learning mode" (p. 142); moreover, they have a strong sense of purpose that lies behind their visions and goals. Unless everyone in the community has a sense of personal mastery, it is difficult to work in inclusive, accepting, democratic, and equitable ways.

The second requirement for a learning community, according to Senge, is the identification of existing *mental models* and the creation of powerful new ones to guide our actions. Mental models are "deeply ingrained assumptions, generalizations, or even pictures or images that influence how we understand the world and how we take action" (1990, 8). Sometimes we need help to identify our powerful guiding models and uncover the gaps between our espoused theories and our current behaviors. The next step is to ask ourselves if we really value the espoused theory. If, for example, we say we value high expectations for all children but uncover mental models that discount the potential of poor children, then we need to first figure out what we really believe about all children and then begin to act accordingly. If we have mental models of schools as places of conflict, closed doors, and demoralized teachers (as several educators have recently described them to me), and if we want schools to be different, then we need to help educators develop more positive images of their ideal school. I propose, as a starting point, an image of a community of difference, a happy, caring, optimistic, purposeful place in which administrators, teachers, students, and parents from various backgrounds and multiple perspectives work, talk, and learn together in a mutually supportive environment. Helping people identify their existing mental models and create powerful, positive new ones is an important task for a transformative educational leader.

Becoming empowered with a clear vision of what is desirable is a starting point for Senge's next discipline, *shared vision*. A shared vision is

> not an idea. It is not even an important idea such as freedom. It is, rather, a force in people's hearts, a force of impressive power. . . . At its simplest level, a shared vision is the answer to the question, "What do we want to create?" (1990, 206)

A shared vision binds people together around a common identity and a sense of destiny. A shared vision does not happen as leaders go away on a retreat, develop a mission (or vision) statement, and bring it back to the organization for approval.

I once worked with a school staff to help teachers develop a sense of shared vision. I held up one statement I had found in a file called "mission" and asked what it was. "Oh, that was Jim's mission statement," they replied. "He was principal here ten years ago." I read out another, to be told it was "Ken's mission statement; he came after Jim." We repeated this procedure with several more statements.

If a vision is not shared, but is simply the statement of one person, its development is a futile exercise. The shared vision of a community of difference emerges as people talk about their own mental models of the organization, as they uncover images and goals that they hold in common, goals that "come from a common caring" (Senge 1990, 206). A shared vision is not simply a statement on paper; it is a dynamic vision that is created as people work together, share their ideas, and develop some common understandings. When a shared vision is the driving force behind an organization, inspiring action, acting as a benchmark for decision making, helping individuals and groups determine whether a suggested action or activity is consistent with and advances the mission of the community as a whole, then it provides the focus and energy for learning.

Team learning is the fourth of Senge's five disciplines. "Team learning is the process of aligning and developing the capacity of a team to create the results its members truly desire" (1990, 236). Team learning is a tool for raising the collective IQ of a group above that of anyone in it (p. 259). It recognizes that a group of talented individuals does not automatically constitute a team (as professional athletes readily acknowledge). A team needs people who perform different functions and take different roles, while being cognizant of what others are doing and working toward the same end. A community cannot emerge if individuals are seeking glory or recognition for themselves rather than the good of the group. There is a need in a community of difference to continue to work, to learn, to challenge, never becoming complacent or believing that the final goal has been achieved.

It is the role of the transformative educational leader to make sure that both the overall good of the community and the good of its individual members are carefully considered when decisions are made. Team learning acknowledges that in a community of difference, every member of the team is important. No teacher may refuse to admit a student into a class simply because the student may not perform as quickly or as well as other students and might bring down the class average. Nor will a teacher be expected to keep a child in class who is so disruptive that the learning environment for the rest of the children is endangered. In a community of difference, achieving the desired academic goals, and attaining justice and democracy, depends on the collective wisdom of a school community and not just on the thinking of a small group of powerful people who have always held the power.

Senge's fifth discipline is *systems thinking,* a "discipline for seeing wholes . . . a framework for seeing interrelationships rather than things, patterns of change rather than static 'snapshots'" (Senge 1990, 68). It is therefore critically important to examine and understand the community as a whole, to reflect the demographic composition of the students in meaningful ways, to enlarge one's conception of school community to include parents and other caring and supportive adults, and to understand that the community is composed of multiple cultures and realities.

The lack of success (in many countries) of students of aboriginal origin clearly exemplifies the need to think systemically, to understand patterns of interrelatedness. Lack of student success is frequently attributed to low motivation, poor attendance, behaviors requiring disciplinary intervention, and lack of supportive conditions in the home. In turn, these explanations contribute to increased frustration in the aboriginal community, increased difficulty communicating, a lack of trust, and name-calling on both sides. Nonaboriginal students and their parents are often relieved to see the misbehaving students either suspended or drop out and, once again, the aboriginal community is blamed and marginalized. The cycle resumes. Lack of student success continues; parents who themselves may have been marginalized or oppressed by formal mechanisms of schooling continue to oppose the well-intentioned efforts of educators representing a system that failed them; commitment to work together wanes. Thinking systemically would require us to address previous oppressive practices before we can expect marginalized parents to consider developing trusting partnership relationships with their children's schools.

Senge asserts that a learning organization develops a shared vision among competent individuals who are engaged in personal growth and self-reflection, who acknowledge that the community is more than the sum of its parts, who believe that there can be a synergy that helps it move toward its goal, taking into account its unique position in a wider social, economic, and political system.

Thinking about how to move Senge's ideas forward to help create a community of difference, I have suggested that an educational leader might help members of his or her community develop a sense of personal mastery, a commitment to lifelong learning and continuous inquiry. An important step is also the development of strong mental models and images—in this case images of a just, democratic, empathetic, and optimistic community, how it would feel, what its attributes would be. Out of these individual images would grow, as people shared their hopes and dreams, a sense of common vision, of the "possibilities" for the community. Then, building on the synergy of the group and connecting it to the wider systems in which it is embedded, the community would continue to grow and develop.

MARCO POLO SCHOOL: AN ILLUSTRATION

A few years ago, I conducted an ongoing research project in a small inner-city school I'll call Marco Polo Elementary School, located in the heart of an area of high crime, prostitution, alcohol and drug abuse, and extreme poverty. Children came from approximately thirty different ethnic groups; many were urban aboriginal students. One September, to celebrate school opening, the new principal and his staff decided to hold a dinner for parents and students. From one perspective, the evening was a great success as many neighborhood parents showed up.

Yet, when I spoke with the principal and one of the multicultural workers, they told me they had abandoned plans to welcome the parents and introduce new teachers. "They couldn't handle it," one said. "These parents aren't used to structure; we couldn't do it."

Later in the same conversation, I commented on the purchase of several new couches located in the school foyer and said how nice they looked. Again, I was surprised by the response. "We aren't sure we should have bought new couches. They are likely better than anyone has at home and they may make people feel bad; besides, they won't know how to take care of them, so they'll probably get wrecked."

The educational leaders of the school were well intentioned; they had planned and paid for dinner and had purchased new furniture; they cared about their students. But their mental models were flawed and their vision was limited. Their good intentions were not enough. There was little respect shown for the parents' ability or willingness to meet the new teachers; there was no attempt to engage them in dialogue over whether the purchase of new couches would be desirable, reasonable, or acceptable expenditures of school funds. Rather, assumptions were made about the parents' abilities, their attitudes, and their involvement in the life of the school. And those assumptions were based on educators' beliefs about the parents—convictions that they were somehow deficient, unable to contribute in meaningful ways to their children's education. Hence the educators adopted a stance of *doing for* the parents and children, rather than *doing with* them. They unknowingly rejected the discipline of systems thinking and restricted the potential team; only teachers were deemed qualified to participate in educational decision making and activities.

Parents in Marco Polo School have a wide range of educational backgrounds and life experiences. Apart from occasional attendance for free meals or visits to the food or clothing banks, many have had predominantly negative experiences with school. Most have no idea of how they might become actively involved in their children's education. Few have graduated from high school, but some have completed university and engage in professional careers. Overall, these parents have not been asked what they want for their children nor invited to suggest ways the school could meet their needs. The school offers services: educational upgrading, after-school groups, language training. But educators appear to have overlooked the importance of relationships—of mutuality in the creation of school communities. No one has recognized the strengths and capabilities that exist in the parent group. In this instance, a transformative leader would help parents and teachers together develop a sense of personal mastery and become part of a new and vibrant learning community.

RETHINKING THE WALL

To return to the metaphor of Frost's poem, in Marco Polo Elementary School, stones continue to be replaced and walls reconstructed likely higher than before because the only communication is ritualized and superficial. The neighbors have said it all before. In a community of difference, the rules and customs need to be negotiated through the meaningful dialogue of all participants—students, whose voices are typically silenced; parents, including those whose attitudes may be colored by their own unpleasant school experiences; professional educators, who represent many subject areas; and other interested citizens. Without the norms and values of dialogue, respect, or inclusion, a community of difference will be an elusive goal in schools like this one.

In a community of difference, shared goals and vision emerge from team learning, from the best thinking and ongoing interactions of all members. As people explore ideas together, the mental models and meanings associated with some customary understandings will be challenged. Together members of the community will learn that traditions are not objective realities carved in stone, but have been constructed over time by people with the power and authority to do so. As others engage in the dialogue, including low SES parents who are too often excluded, some traditional power structures will be destabilized. A new sense of personal mastery and new understandings will emerge because the group will become more inclusive.

I stress that in a community of difference there will always be disagreements and tensions. Dissenting voices should not be silenced and conflict cannot be suppressed. Moreover, conflict and differing opinions will always be held in a tenuous dynamic balance, one that is constantly being renegotiated. At the same time, it is important to acknowledge that inclusiveness does not mean that anything goes. Indeed, one of the tasks of the community will be to determine its bounds of tolerance and intolerance; there is no room in community for ethical relativism that diminishes the importance of moral discourse.

One teacher studying to complete her master's degree in education told me that her school and teachers' federation had instituted what she called a "policy of tolerance" in which educators were urged to tolerate varied perspectives. They were particularly focused on creating an environment in which both homosexual and heterosexual lifestyles were accepted. Shortly after the communication of this policy, the teacher received a letter from a parent who stated that because she did not believe in homosexuality, she wanted the school to know that she condoned her child's teasing of a classmate. In the name of tolerance, her child's homophobic behavior was to be accepted. The teacher consulted with her principal and, together, they agreed to support the parent's right to hold an intolerant, homophobic position. The teacher seemed surprised when I rejected the parent's version of tolerance as well as her own convoluted explanation. Tolerance of an explicitly intolerant position is not tolerance at all. Tearing down walls does not provide a license for unjust or uncaring behaviors.

The contrast between beliefs and behavior is important. In fact, it represents one cornerstone of Weissberg's discussion of political tolerance. He writes, "Insisting that everybody agree to 'be tolerant' to ensure harmony is nonsensical, even delusional. . . . unrestricted tolerance is an impossibility despite our infatuation with endless argumentation" (Weissberg 1998, 2–3). Weissberg makes an extremely important distinction between personal tolerance and public and political tolerance. He advocates that organizations should focus on the need to adopt a view of tolerance as a systemic characteristic rather than one based on personal psychological traits. Regardless of the parent's or student's *belief* about the rightness or wrongness of homosexuality, permitting its expression *in action* that results in teasing, taunting, or rejecting a child based on his or her parent's lifestyle is intolerant *behavior* and should not be accepted in the guise of one's right to hold a differing opinion. Failing to differentiate between opinion and behavior will lead to schools being uninviting and unwelcoming places for many children and adults.[5]

Figure 2.1 illustrates the concept of schools as communities of difference that has been described in this chapter. Instead of making

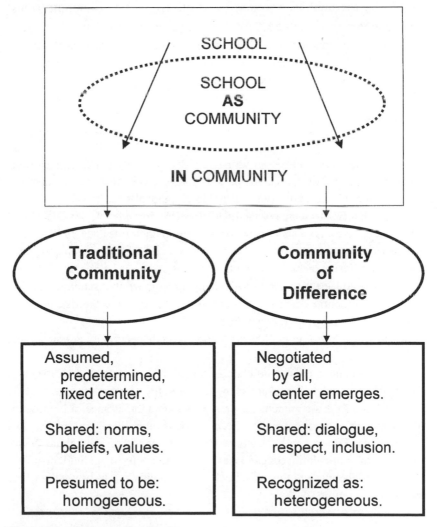

Figure 2.1. School as Community

assumptions of homogeneity and starting with implicit shared norms, beliefs, and values that constitute a predetermined center, a community of difference starts with the premise of heterogeneity and a commitment to engage respectfully in extensive dialogue with all participants, to discuss norms of behavior, and to negotiate shared values on which the life and work of the school will be based.

My claim is that in a community of difference, the community as a whole, through dialogue and negotiation and the exercise of collective wisdom, comes to a moral judgment about its boundaries. In order for this to be accomplished morally and ethically, the community must have adopted some agreed-on values and guiding criteria.

In the next chapter, I propose some values that may be useful as building blocks for the new community and some criteria against which to assess progress toward the creation of a community of difference.

NOTES

1. The New Zealand school year is divided into four ten-week terms, divided by three two-week vacation periods and a longer Christmas/summer vacation. More will be said about scheduling in chapter 8.

2. A recent (2000) search of the ERIC database, for example, revealed 1,479 items with the words *community* or *communities* in their title and a further 5,842 in which *community* was either a descriptor or an identifier. (Amazon.com listed 28,881 books using the words as part of their title.)

3. Although I identify one purpose here, I recognize that schooling fulfills many, and sometimes competing, purposes in society. See the discussion in chapter 3 about purposes of schooling.

4. However, Senge et al. 2000 is a book aimed specifically at educational organizations.

5. Unfortunately, those who choose to read Weissberg's book (1998) will find that in the concluding chapters, he falls into his own trap, fails to provide a moral basis for his comments, expresses personal intolerance of homosexuality and multiculturalism, and neglects to focus on political and institutional perspectives. For example, he characterizes the work of Banks and Nieto, well-known multicultural educators, as "radical collectivist egalitarianism" (p. 247). After labeling it in this way, he dismisses their work as unworthy of serious consideration.

CHAPTER 3

Criteria for Excellence and Social Justice

Marco Polo Elementary School, the school I introduced in chapter 2, has gained a measure of local renown for its diverse and very poor student population and for its location in the postal code area with the lowest per capita income in Canada. During the third year of my study, a school-based educator spoke in the following terms.

> We have been making considerable progress. Marco Polo School is much safer now than it was before. Incidents of hostility and violence have been reduced. This is largely due to some programs in behavior control and self-esteem. We have been working hard on self-esteem, as we believe that without it kids can't learn. It's now April and I am finally ready to start the fifth-grade curriculum.

I asked each new teacher and administrator about the school's philosophy and each, in turn, repeated the same idea. We need to establish a safe and caring climate first, work on self-esteem, and only then worry about academics. "Don't academic self-esteem and academic achievement go hand in hand?" I asked repeatedly. "You don't understand," they answered, "you need to know the kind of kids we have in this school. They just are not ready to learn."

I thought I did know them. I had spent time in the school on a regular basis for over two years; I knew about the numerous special programs, English language support and instruction, social welfare activities (meals, food, and clothing banks), pullout programs for learning assistance, aboriginal programs, and after-school programs. I knew that there was a one-to-four adult-student ratio in the school, and that some teachers were frustrated by the concomitant fragmentation of the school program. Some were even calling for a new mentoring program, to ensure that each child had a meaningful interaction with one adult every day. Surely something was wrong!

Almost five years after the conclusion of my study, some educators from Marco Polo Elementary School have begun to acknowledge that something was wrong and they report that school programs are slowly changing.

But what of the decades of working from a deficit mentality that did little to validate or empower either students or their community? How were the students affected? What are appropriate goals for schools serving diverse and challenging populations? Are there criteria that might help us to assess progress toward our goals? What values and norms might educators use to guide our actions? Are some values bedrock values and others negotiable? These are the questions to be addressed in this chapter.

In responding to these and other questions, I suggest some criteria that might form the basis for thinking about whether a school has indeed become a community of difference, one in which educators strive for both academic excellence and social justice for all children. In chapter 1, I argued for transformative cross-cultural leadership and in chapter 2, for schools as communities of difference. I believe both are useful concepts for heterogeneous schools in this half of the twenty-first century.

Educational leaders in most developed countries are working in environments of intense pressure for accountability. Whatever changes they initiate must take account of context, including political and fiscal realities. Thus, in the United States, high-stakes testing seems to drive much educational reform and funding. In Canada, provincial examinations and published reports by the Ministries of Education or by independent agencies such as the Fraser Institute raise public awareness about school performance. In Britain, published league tables perform the same function. In New Zealand, new performance appraisal requirements from the Educational Accountability Office exert additional pressure for accountability and high achievement. Throughout most of the developed world, educational accountability has been raised to a new level. But the questions still remain: Accountability for what? To whom? For what purpose? Once these questions have been addressed, then criteria may be established and progress toward them assessed.

In this chapter, I examine some broad purposes of education, discuss commonly held goals of schooling, and finally suggest criteria to help educators assess progress or lack of it.

AIMS AND PURPOSES OF EDUCATION

My purpose here is not to review the many debates over the aims and purposes of education that have existed throughout history but to signal that ideologies (both implicit and explicit) drive how we think about education and what actually happens in schools. I am not suggesting that there is only one purpose for schools. I am proposing that the complex and multiple purposes to be fulfilled by schooling should be debated and made public in order to guide both planning for educational excellence and equity and the day-to-day reality of schooling.

In the Marco Polo School illustration, when the goal of education was conceived as providing a safe and supportive environment—without reference to academic achievement and educational goals—then the focus became a misplaced emphasis on feeling good and interacting positively. If a young man was striving to become a hockey player, the coach would not consider keeping him on the bench during practice until he was good enough to score goals. If a young woman had determined to become a musician, the teacher would not suggest that she refrain from practice until she was good enough to play flawlessly. Separating the achievement of educational goals from self-concept and self-esteem in schools is similar to these ridiculous scenarios. How can students attain academic self-confidence if they do not engage in challenging academic activities?

Academic Preparation

A primary purpose of schooling is academic preparation. In many developed countries, schools also provide support for children whose families are in need of help for many different reasons. Schools are often called on to provide counseling, legal advice, social work, or medical support for children and their families. Each of these is an essential function, enabling the students who receive these services to better focus on the educational activities of the school. It is critical, however, for educators to recognize that there is no other institution in today's society whose primary function is education. Only schools are charged with the responsibility for the academic preparation of citizens. YWCAs, community programs, church groups, government agencies—all provide recreational, social, and welfare functions for children and adults. But only schooling is intended to provide the academic instruction that supports, and prepares students for participation in, democratic processes.

Regardless of the multitude of other needs children bring to schools, and of how stretched educators may feel, they cannot afford to relegate academic functions to the back burner. If schools do not provide the education that helps people change their life circumstances and offers hope for a better future, what institution will fill that gap?

The problem, however, is that academic preparation is often defined in narrow terms related only to preparation for university programs or professional training. While this is one important academic function, it is not the only one. Many students who hope to enter trades or engage in entrepreneurial activities also need appropriate academic preparation. This does not mean that they need a watered-down curriculum, but that they may need a different academic emphasis. The fact that each student has unique needs requires educators to spend time reflecting on and discussing what constitutes an appropriate education for each child. The academic needs of students talented in the fine arts or in mechanical ability must be deemed worthy scholarly pursuits rather than as extraneous to the central purposes of schooling. If we broaden our definition of academic instruction, then during times of fiscal constraint, vocational or fine arts programs (sometimes perceived to be siphoning needed funds away from core academic preparation for higher education) would perhaps be in less jeopardy.

I think of Chad, the Métis[1] administrator I have known for several years. His mother was a British war bride who followed her soldier husband to his trap lines in the northern Canadian bush before moving to an urban center. They raised their family in an urban ghetto situation, in a home with no running water. From a young age, Chad saw education as offering the way out of the poverty in which he was raised.

Despite his family's status as a welfare family, Chad was identified for a gifted program, offered a place in a summer drama school, and shown repeatedly that he had the ability to change his life situation. Although he often felt out of place, Chad persisted, convinced that education was his "ticket out." Had Chad not had opportunities to participate in the summer drama program, and encouragement from his teachers to pursue an academic program, it is unlikely he would be an educational leader today. Schools cannot abrogate their responsibility to provide opportunities for social mobility for students.

Training for the Workforce

A second commonly identified purpose for public schooling is training for the workforce. Educational mission statements developed by many American states and Canadian provinces make this goal abundantly clear. In 2002 in Utah, for example, the mission of education was "to provide the opportunity for each student to be literate and possess the basic knowledge and life skills necessary to become a contributing citizen in today's society" (Utah State Board of Education, 2002). In the same year, the Government of British Columbia Ministry of Education (2002) stated that "the purpose of the British Columbia school system is to enable all learners to develop their individual potential and to acquire the knowledge, skills and attitudes needed to contribute to a healthy, democratic and pluralistic society and a prosperous and sustainable economy."

No one is likely to state that students do not need to know how to seek and hold a job in the future, or that society would be better off with students liberally schooled but living on welfare. However, some people fear (and experience has confirmed) that if education systems are too heavily focused on job training and responding to the needs of the workforce, then other purposes of schooling and the potential for a well-educated citizenry may be constrained.

Balance is needed. Educators should not focus too strongly on preparing students for university or for direct transition to the workforce. Being a productive citizen does not require a university education and does not necessitate leaving school and immediately finding a job. When we stress these polarized positions, many students who may be well suited to other careers seem to fall through the cracks.

My own son, now a successful welder, talks with some bitterness about how he was encouraged to consider university but was never presented, even during school job fairs, with opportunities to investigate skilled trades. His schooling did not open a vista of possibilities to him, but rather instilled a sense of frustration and despair. He knew he did not want to proceed to university, yet he did not see any viable alternatives. Educators must carefully consider how schools of our time can fulfill both academic and economic functions, opening rather than narrowing students' life choices and opportunities.

Socialization Functions

Socialization is a third commonly identified purpose of school, one that has been explicit from the beginning of the nineteenth century. Indeed, some claim that the primary purpose of schooling is to help students become acquainted with the linguistic and cultural norms of the society within which they live. I believe that we need to help people from other cultures understand how to navigate the bureaucracies and conventions of our present society. However, I am also firmly convinced that it is counterproductive and hegemonic to attempt to socialize students into existing norms without consideration of their own backgrounds and identities.

Sometimes the term *socialization* is used in a generic way to imply teaching students appropriate social (as opposed to antisocial) behaviors. Thus we socialize students not to hit, cheat, lie, steal, and so forth. Yet *socialization* is also used to mean helping students accommodate to the mores of our society, and in this sense includes cultural norms and traditions as well. Words like *socialization, accommodation, assimilation,* and *acculturation* are often used in vague and almost synonymous ways.

Jane Roland Martin provides a useful differentiation between assimilation and acculturation: "Assimilation is a one-way process. The alternative is acculturation—active cultural membership—in which both parties to the transaction are affected" (1995, 1). Although *acculturation* is not always used in this way, the distinction is essential. Unfortunately in schools we too often speak of acculturation but practice assimilation.

I think about the teacher in a small Navajo school in the United States who, ignoring the students' own history and culture, believed they should be taught that Columbus *discovered* America. She claimed that despite the presence of American Indians, it was still appropriate to say that "Columbus *discovered* America for Europe and for the rest of the world." There was no need, therefore, to examine what kind of society Columbus found when he arrived in 1492, how his arrival affected it, or how it might have developed differently had Columbus arrived two hundred years earlier or a hundred years later. Despite teaching in a predominantly American Indian school, she did not integrate the perspectives of her students or include their historical realities in her instruction. She was not concerned about learning from her students or their families, only about communicating her Eurocentric perspectives to them.

Following the curriculum as laid out in texts or guidebooks may seem natural, but it too often occurs at the expense of meaningful and relevant instruction. Sometimes it reflects narrow assumptions about what counts and does not count as legitimate knowledge. At other times it may reflect fear and uncertainty on the part of the teacher. It is important, however, to recognize that society and culture are not static but dynamic.

As times and contexts change, so too do norms, beliefs, and behaviors. Regardless of how cursory one's knowledge of history, no one would deny that times have changed. Citizenship is no longer limited to white males; women, aboriginals, and people of color now have the right to vote. Increased opportunities for intercontinental travel, international communication, space exploration, new technological advances, innovative photographic techniques—all remind us, as the Greek philosopher Heroclitus said in 475 B.C., that we can never stand in the same river twice, so constant is the state of change in which we find ourselves.

When we talk about the purposes of schooling, we must not only consider where we have come from and what our society is like now, but what kind of society we want to create for the future. If we want to ensure that schools do not require making everyone fit the same mold, we need to ask how we can help young people envision and create a just, diverse, and multicultural society. Instead of trying to hold on to a romanticized past that is no longer viable, educators need to become proactive.

Social Justice

A fourth purpose of schooling, undergirding the other three, is the creation of a just society. Such a society, Minnich says, helps us "acknowledge, affirm, and find strength in our singularities while at the same time maintaining connections with others in intersecting circles of community, large and small" (1995, xxi). Schooling can therefore help students understand their uniqueness and individual strengths, their own circles of community, and the attributes of other social groups as well.

Some might say that helping students build circles of connections as a way of creating or recreating society is not a goal for publicly funded schooling. Others may object that it is too ambitious an undertaking to commit to individual teachers and administrators in classrooms and schools throughout our nations. Yet it is in schools where the immediate, day-to-day closeness of the interactions provides an outstanding opportunity for what Green describes as "local face-to-face communities of democratic struggle" (1999, 163). Just as leaders must reflect critically and act morally, one of the primary purposes of schools is to teach students to reflect carefully and critically about the society in which they live and to make careful and caring decisions about the legacy they wish to leave for future generations.

Educators would do well to take seriously the seven-generation precept[2] of some Native American groups who believe that during a single lifetime, one has the possibility of knowing seven generations: great-grandparents, grandparents, parents, self and spouse, children, grandchildren, and perhaps great-grandchildren. Thus, when making decisions, it is appropriate, at a minimum, to consider the potential effect on the seventh generation. This wise tradition is graphically depicted in a beautiful, life-size stone sculpture of a native woman erected in one community by a Mohawk stone sculptor. The school principal explains:

There are seven white doves spiraling around her, the uppermost is just leaving her fingertips. The seven doves represent the seven generations idea in Mohawk culture. According to this idea, all decisions must be made in a sustainable way so the impact of actions will allow for respect and honour for seven generations. The seventh generation hence must inherit an environment where they can thrive. If each generation takes this approach, sustainability is achieved. (personal communication)

Some people might suggest that emphasizing social justice and the creation of an inclusive community contradicts the academic goals of schooling I have previously outlined. I see no such fundamental contradiction; instead, I believe that improving the environment in which children learn and enhancing their learning outcomes must go together. Sometimes the social justice purpose is critiqued as being too narrow and too limited a form of justice, excluding distributive justice, moral, legal, or political justice. If social justice is interpreted narrowly in relation to the isms—racism, classism, sexism, and so on—then it is definitely too narrow to accommodate all of the issues that need to be considered in public schools. If it is interpreted more broadly as providing a benchmark (like the seven-generation concept) against which to assess all educational decisions, it offers a comprehensive way to address the marginalization and oppression of individuals and groups in social institutions such as schools, as well as to ensure consideration of the wider context within which students and their families live. Considered in this way, taking a social justice perspective does not simply improve the educational experience for current students but may help them exert a lasting impact on future generations.

A UNIFIED VISION

Schools simultaneously fulfill complex and multiple purposes related to preparing students to be productive citizens, equipping them for lifelong learning and further academic studies, acculturating them by helping them to both understand existing social norms and to create new norms, teaching them to challenge injustice. Thus educators may find the enormity of the task overwhelming. But making these purposes explicit is the first step to ensuring that we direct our efforts to their accomplishment.

Being explicit about our purposes also helps us define words that are currently used glibly in political and educational circles, meaning different things to different people, often too vague to constitute realizable goals for practice. Terms like *equity, excellence, success, efficiency, effectiveness, high standards, social justice* come to mind. Although it is beyond the scope of this chapter to discuss each word in a comprehensive way, it is important for me to clarify how I use them in the rest of this book.

Again, I do not find these goals to be in conflict with one another. Indeed, I hope to show that there is no necessity for equity and excellence or efficiency and effectiveness to be seen as competing goals; nor is the notion of holding students to high academic and social standards contradictory to an emphasis on social justice. When I envisage a successful school, it is successful because it considers each of these aspects, ensuring that they are simultaneously addressed in all decisions taken by the school community.

Equity and Excellence

How could a school claim excellence if only students from upper-middle-class backgrounds achieved high grades on either norm-referenced or criterion-referenced tests? Or if an achievement gap existed between children from different ethnic groups represented in the school? Or if only children from higher socioeconomic families were represented in advanced, enriched, or college preparatory classes, while those from welfare or low-income families were disproportionately represented in alternative dead-end programs?

I once visited a school with great diversity in its student body and a wide range of programs designed to meet student needs. When I looked around the classrooms, the academic program classes appeared to have students who were predominantly white or East Asian, while programs that were less demanding academically had high proportions of South Asian, aboriginal, and other minority children. I asked the coordinator of the gifted program whether students from different social and ethnic groups were proportionally represented in the class.

She replied, "No, we just take those who apply and the program simply doesn't seem to attract some of those children."

I persisted, "Do you make any attempt to modify your admissions criteria or to advertise the program in such a way as to make it appeal to various ethnic groups?" Again, the reply was negative.

I tried once more, "Have you ever had any aboriginal children in the gifted program?"

"Oh yes, there was one once. But she only lasted until October. I never did figure out what the problem was!"

Despite the avowed excellence of the gifted program in that school and the strong academic performance of students enrolled in it, my contention is that when excellence exists at the expense of equity, it is not excellence at all, but elitism. Note, I am not arguing against gifted programs as others do (see Oakes 1985; Smith 1995). Rather I support academically challenging content, even gifted programs (see Shields 1995, 1996), if they do not exclude children prima facie on the basis of ethnicity or social background. Excellence and equity must go hand in hand.

Effectiveness and Efficiency

Efficiency and *effectiveness* are problematic terms for several reasons. Efficiency has come to be associated with a reduction of fiscal or academic support for schools or a business takeover of education services. Despite some unsuccessful American experiments during the 1990s, school districts are increasingly beguiled by the appeal of reduced costs and increased success offered by large corporations. In the United States, Educational Management Organizations (EMOs) such as the Leona Group (offering public charter schools in Arizona), New Visions Schools in New York, and Edison Schools in Philadelphia are prospering. Using clever marketing techniques to suggest that they offer a contrast to what one finds in public schools, they claim, for example, to be "very conscientious" or to "offer an intimate, rigorous, and community-based education."

In 1999 the first such British experiment was reported when Cambridge Education Associates (CEA), a small educational consultancy, was put in charge of schools in the borough of Islington in North London. Not only was the company expected to run the schools, but to make a profit estimated at about £500,000 a year (BBC 1999). In Australia, in

August 2000, the federal Labor government announced a plan designed to take over disadvantaged schools. The multimillion-dollar program was intended to create dozens of "education priority zones" around Australia and raise literacy and numeracy levels.

This trend toward commercializing educational services is one reason for a pervasive suspicion of efficiency among many educators. Additionally, as budgets are cut and curriculum consultants and academic support people are often the first to lose their positions, fiscal efficiency is sometimes seen as operating on the backs of students and teachers. Although neither I, nor any other responsible taxpayer, would argue for wastefulness or overspending in education, extravagance and basic support are quite different.

The public is often not prepared to allocate more funding to schools despite indications of real need. In the last few years, many American jurisdictions (including California, Florida, Missouri, and Washington) have been unsuccessful in attempts to pass education bond issues or raise taxes by even a fraction of a cent to support educational expenditures. The discourse of efficiency and the perception, often perpetuated by stories in the media, that schools are failing despite large amounts of public funding are contributory factors.

Effectiveness is often opposed to efficiency. A common argument among teachers is that schools cannot be effective, given the need for teachers to respond to students' physical, social, emotional, and educational needs, if there is no additional funding allocated to provide needed services. This is largely a topic for another scholar and perhaps another book, in that it begs an exploration that goes well beyond the scope of this discussion, of how public funding is allocated and how educational institutions provide accountability. Here it is sufficient to state my belief that providing needed services is a fundamental mandate of schools and governments and that adequate funds must be provided for that purpose. However, I am also firmly convinced that sometimes educators use lack of funding as an excuse for failing to meet the needs of students. Educators must find ways for schools to be effective and help students achieve academic success even in times of fiscal restraint.

Effectiveness is often too narrowly defined in terms that reflect a body of literature known as "school effectiveness research." Models of school effectiveness generally include a focus on well-defined goals, staff training on a school-wide basis, control by staff over instructional decisions, a sense of order, a system for monitoring student progress, and good discipline (Purkey and Smith 1986, 47). While these are important, I contend that a school can achieve clear expectations and consistent practices without meeting the social justice criteria I believe are critically important.

The Academy is a highly rated academic public secondary school, located in a predominantly high-income and high-status area, with a small number of students from a neighboring Indian reserve and a few lower-income families. At one point, teachers from the school stated that when students did not fit into the norms and mandate of the school, they were moved out to a school in which they were more likely to achieve success and feel a sense of belonging. The teachers gave the rationale that the practice was efficient, effective, and for the good of all students. Although these educators insisted that the policy worked, they seemed unaware that the implicit negative messages given to the transfer students were that they were stupid, deficient, and undesirable. In this case, efficiency was achieved at the expense of offering all students an effective educational experience in their neighborhood school.

Such action is contradictory to the creation of inclusive school communities and sends the message that membership in public schools is exclusive. Students are only entitled to attend their local public schools if they are smart enough or hold the right academic inclinations and university orientations.

High Standards and Social Justice

The way in which the Academy defined high standards was oppositional to what I call social justice goals. Maintaining its reputation as a high-performing academic school was essential to the sense of efficacy and self-esteem of teachers and administrators alike. Yet the two do not need to be contradictory. It is not only possible but essential for public schools to implement a variety of programs to meet differing student needs and abilities, to hold all students to high standards within these programs, and to find ways to ensure that all students contribute to the sense of school community. However, in a public school, there must always be alternative ways for students to achieve success in their respective classes and programs.

Noddings, in her advocacy for both caring and competence, suggests that "it may not be possible to attain high levels of achievement without attending to the needs of students as persons; that is, the establishment of caring relations may be essential to the development of student competence" (1999, 217). Her comment supports the thesis of this book that developing a new kind of community in schools is both morally right in itself and a way of supporting the academic purposes of schools.

Green described participants in democratic community as having a "lively recognition of their *continuing valuable diversity*, so as to direct cooperative actions in the directions of shared hopes, and to guide and support the ongoing self-recreation of its members toward their shared and yet deeply personal ethical goals" (1999, 154). Helping students with diverse needs and talents and deeply personal goals to find ways to come together in cooperative action and shared hopes is one task of the socially just community of difference I am advocating.

Policy makers may argue that accountability for academic outcomes is the goal of many of the high-stakes testing programs so prevalent in the United States. Some educators claim that high test scores are only attained by inappropriately narrowing the curriculum and expecting all children to become conversant with white middle-class cultural experiences. Yet requiring schools to disaggregate their data and report student achievement by socioeconomic or ethnic group may also fulfill a social justice goal. Some states, for example, require that schools and districts disaggregate results for students who participate in free and reduced lunch programs, as well as for African American, Hispanic, and white youth. Despite the many, and often valid, criticisms levied against these testing programs,[3] the goal of achieving high standards for all children is laudatory. Skrla and Scheurich, for example, state that as a result of some of the heightened awareness and accountability within the past five years,

a very few examples of sustained district wide academic success for children of color and children from low-income homes have begun to emerge in the research literature. These examples have appeared in states

that have highly developed, stable accountability systems with equity-oriented components, such as New York, North Carolina, and Texas . . ,
Preliminary research in some of these districts points to the possibility that the superintendents have found ways to resist deficit thinking and, thus, to make strong, demonstrable progress toward educational equity in their districts. (Skrla and Scheurich 2001, 5)

In contrast, the "school report cards" constructed by a conservative Canadian think tank, the Fraser Institute, are simply a compilation of the rate of student success on provincial exams for examinable subjects (normally those that entitle students to university admission). These school rankings, in the name of public accountability and parents' right to know, do little to demonstrate how schools are achieving the concomitant goals of excellence and social justice. I asked an official from the Fraser Institute if it would have made any difference to the rank ordering of schools had he known that all of the aboriginal students from the top-ranked public secondary school had dropped out prior to the final year of high school. His data, which had been collected at a single fixed point in time, did not reflect that fact. His response was that it would not have changed his perception of the school's success. Moreover, he believed, the public has a right to available data, regardless of how partial or distorted the data may be. I disagree. High standards and social justice must be inseparable, and distorted data are simply not just.

Interpreting Data Intelligently

Educators must be careful not to perpetuate dichotomous thinking that places worthwhile goals in opposition to each other. It is important to collect and interpret data as a basis for accountability and decision making, but we must do so responsibly. We often hear statements like, "nine out of ten doctors recommend" or "80 percent prefer" such and such a product. Such statements mislead us, providing partial information at best, in the hope of persuading us to buy a certain product. Yet if we knew that nine out of ten doctors in a specific clinic were given a product to distribute as a free sample and then recommended it, in no way implying preference or a superior product, we might be less likely to buy the product. Likewise, advocates of using car seat belts all the time and not just on long trips often quote the statistic that "most fatal crashes occur within twenty-five miles of home, at moderate speeds and on roads that are familiar to the driver." When we consider that most trips begin or end at home and involve daily activities also near home, we might realize that the statistic reflects driving patterns and is not necessarily a rationale for seat belt use.

We may be persuaded by distorted information, but when it is intended to shape policy, we need to be cautious. Moreover, educators must be proactive in ensuring that the necessary data are available. In Canada, New Zealand, and many other countries, often in the name of privacy, many school records do not include reference to ethnicity or home language. Frequently there is not enough information to permit disaggregation of data to identify patterns that might be indicative of particular problems or successes. Perhaps, as the social-worker wife of a senior district administrator cynically remarked, "If we don't disaggregate the data, we will not uncover information that suggests there are problems, and we can perpetuate the myth that our institutions are socially just!" I am not in any way implying that disaggregated data ensure either social justice or high academic standards. I do, however, suggest that if we do not take explicit measures to determine whether all children and groups of children are achieving to similar high levels, it is difficult to take steps to eliminate inequalities and to promote socially just education.

A transformative leader recognizes that educational systems and programs need to be carefully balanced. Each of the foregoing components is essential. School systems need to strive for excellence in ways that neither exclude certain groups of students nor leave them behind. Publicly funded education systems must be accountable and must operate efficiently, but that cannot be permitted to outweigh effectiveness and the need to offer a range of programs and activities to meet varied student needs. High academic standards are laudable but must be real. It is not enough to focus only on the students who can most readily achieve high test scores. Instead, the academic success of all students must be considered if an emphasis on outcomes is to be just and equitable.

SOME USEFUL CRITERIA

There are several ways of thinking about leadership for social justice in schools that may help us move toward schools as communities of difference. Kincheloe and Steinberg, in their introduction to their book *Thirteen Questions,* state that systems of meaning which help us identify what type of schools we want to create or how we decide what we need to know should be "just, optimistic, empathetic, and democratic" (1995, 2). These four words, summarized in figure 3.1, provide useful evaluative criteria to assess progress toward the multiple educational goals we must strive to achieve in public schools. But they must be considered carefully and holistically. *Justice* implies *equity* and *equality,* terms carefully explicated by Farrell (1999). *Democracy* relates to both presence and participation—the right to have one's voice heard and understood. *Empathy* is similar in some ways to Noddings's robust notion of caring and requires that all students are respected, feel accepted, and believe they are understood. *Optimism* refers to providing students with hopeful chances and choices beyond school. Educators may learn that these criteria,

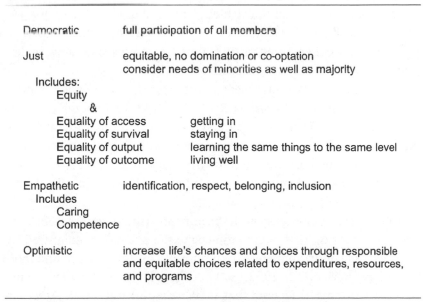

Democratic	full participation of all members
Just	equitable, no domination or co-optation
	consider needs of minorities as well as majority
Includes:	
Equity	
&	
Equality of access	getting in
Equality of survival	staying in
Equality of output	learning the same things to the same level
Equality of outcome	living well
Empathetic	identification, respect, belonging, inclusion
Includes	
Caring	
Competence	
Optimistic	increase life's chances and choices through responsible and equitable choices related to expenditures, resources, and programs

Figure 3.1.   Criteria for Developing Schools as Communities of Difference

taken together, help them to provide programs in which students find belonging and acceptance in the present, and hopeful opportunities for the good life, both individually and collectively, for the future. I examine each term more carefully in the next few pages.

Democratic

Democratic is a term frequently applied to schools. It is often presented as an ideal, a normative concept designed to increase equity and ensure the participation of all members of the school community. As we saw in chapter 1, *democratic* may also be misinterpreted and misused to perpetuate the status quo. When accompanied by appropriate checks and balances, it is one important criterion to assess practice. To what extent are all members able to participate in decision making that directly affects them? Who makes what decisions within the school? Whose voices are heard and whose may be silent?

Jefferson's statement that an "enlightened citizenry is indispensable for the proper functioning of a republic" is often quoted in support of the need for democratic education. Dewey, whose name is frequently linked with democratic education, appeals for a renewed understanding of democracy as a way of life "which provides a moral standard for personal conduct" (2001, 175). He believed that although the founders of American democracy often made claims for democracy, a new understanding of democracy was needed.

Democracy, at its roots, means "the government of the people," coming from the Greek words *demos* (people) and *kratos* (government or power). There are rich and varied traditions of democratic thought, including liberal ideology, socialist thought, and economic liberalism in the form of capitalism (Macridis 1992, 22–23), such that any appeal to democratic principles in education needs clarification.

If one traces democracy to its origins in Athens roughly between 450 and 350 B.C., one might emphasize the principles identified by Pericles: "participation, equality before the law, pluralism, and individualism" (Macridis 1992, 22). Although the principles sound good, we often fail to note that they were not universal. Athenian law guaranteed equality for everyone, but *everyone* was defined narrowly as "educated males" and excluded, among others, women and slaves.

Even as modern democracy has developed, its tenets of full participation and equality have almost always been qualified in some way. Participation has been limited to those who know how to gain access to political systems, own land, or have other legal and material qualifications. Until quite recently, for example, one could not be an elected member of a local school board in some jurisdictions in Canada and the United States unless one owned property within the district's boundaries.[4] This regulation effectively eliminated newer immigrants or lower-income residents from having their positions directly represented.

Ample examples exist to support the position that, in and of itself, a criterion of democratic is insufficient. Promoting either representative democracy or participatory democracy as a way of enhancing decision making and enlarging the group that exercises voice to determine the outcomes of a governance process, unfortunately, offers no guarantee that all perspectives will be adequately represented. Democracy requires a deliberate effort to encourage and facilitate the participation of those who have, for too long, been excluded from the processes and decision-making forums. As Schmuck says,

> We need to listen to the voices of students in our schools, of lesbian and gay students who deal with assaults, of young women and young men in lower-class communities who struggle for an identity and a job in a transforming global capitalist economy. . . . If we deeply believe that schools are the democratic sphere of our society, that in them and through them we will continually build toward greater democracy, a greater sharing of privilege, we need to move to the margins. We need to make visible the invisible, and we need to hear the silenced voices of students in our schools. (1993, 18)

Transformative cross-cultural leaders will take seriously the need for democracy to both move to the margins and to protect those at the margins, as they assess the dominant values and goals of their schools.

Just

To ensure that the often marginalized voices of students, teachers, and parents are heard, I add the second criterion: education should be *just*. Justice requires that we attend to invisible norms and power imbalances. It demands equitable processes, free from domination or co-optation, and considers the needs of individuals as well as groups, of minorities as well as majorities.

Farrell proposes four facets of equality as ways to think about the extent to which a given practice may enhance justice or alternatively may operate as a "selective social screening mechanism" (1999, 159): equality of access, survival, output, and outcomes. *Equality of access* refers to the ability of children from all social groups to be accepted into a given program, school, or system. *Equality of survival* represents the probability that all children will complete the program, without either dropping out or being pushed out. *Equality of output* assesses the extent to which all children "will learn the same things to the same levels at a defined point in the schooling system" (p. 159). If outputs are equal, then deficit thinking will not be evident and similar high standards and expectations will be in effect for all students. *Equality of outcomes* relates, I think, to the criterion of optimism proposed by Kincheloe and Steinberg (1995). Farrell recognizes that looking at what happens in school is not enough. We need to examine the potential of children from various groups to benefit equally from schooling in their later lives (whether in terms of income, type of job, ability to hold political power, etc.).

In a powerful examination of the ways in which the dominant culture has repressed Maori rights in New Zealand, Bishop and Glynn write about the need for justice, for the redress of hegemonic practices, to enable the full participation of all members. They claim that unless primary imbalanced relationships are rectified, current practices will continue to "dominate the way in which cultural diversity is understood and discussed" (1999, 52). Justice requires an opening up even of democratic processes to ensure that minority perspectives will be heard and understood. We cannot assume that change will occur because we have identified a need for it. Educators must overturn inequities where they exist to enable every person to be able to come as an equal to the conversation about a recentered community.

Justice has sometimes acquired a reputation for cruelty and harshness, for legalistic responses rather than empathetic ones. Gilligan (1993), for example, talks about the contrasting ethics of justice and care in which it is sometimes thought necessary to subordinate relationships to rules. The practices of due process, appropriate notice, and formal hearings are generally associated with justice. Although they may be conducted with empathy, their primary purpose is to ensure that an individual's legal rights are protected. Educational processes must be conducted with justice, with appropriate regard for checks and balances to prevent inappropriate action, coercion, or harassment directed against individuals or groups. Yet justice without caring must not be the norm in a community of difference. Educators should stop pretending that they are separable and begin to see them as inextricably united.   *Justice + caring*

Empathetic

The participation inherent in the concept of democracy and the equitable treatment assured by justice must be tempered by *empathy*. *Empathy* is defined in one dictionary as "the intellectual identification with or vicarious experiencing of the feelings, thoughts, or attitudes of another." Sometimes we interpret *empathy* to mean that we must share in other people's experiences, but this is often unreasonable and frequently impossible. The concept of *intellectual* identification is important. We do not even need to like another person in order to care. What is essential is a commitment of the will to enter into relationship, to act in caring and empathetic ways, with the other. The dictionary stresses that empathy is an enduring value. Empathetic education therefore requires an ongoing identification with, and an understanding of, the perspectives of others in our educational community.

Noddings interprets caring in a particularly helpful way that includes both intellectual and emotional aspects, and not simply as a feel-good concept. Caring, as Noddings understands it, is fundamentally *relational*.

It forces us to look at both parties. We can't evaluate a relation or encounter as caring simply on the basis of acts performed by the carer or of

[handwritten annotation: leitmotiv — definite & recurring theme, as in a novel —]

intentions proclaimed by the carer. . . . But, more important, when the relation fails to be one of caring because the cared-for denies that he or she has been cared for, we must probe more deeply. (1999, 207)

Educators in empathetic schools would emphasize the relational aspects of school communities and focus on creating schools in which every individual and group felt accepted. Programming for the specific needs of students would not occur apart from considerations of social integration, friendship, and support. Students whose home languages are not English would not be shunted off (in the name of efficiency) into separate classes with little meaningful instruction and minimal interaction with mainstream peers.

During a recent visit to an ESL class in which students had been placed for three to five years, I was dismayed to hear very limited facility with English. Moreover, as I observed the class, I found students spent most of their time working individually on worksheets (designed to facilitate individual progress). Following up later, I found that none of these students had English-speaking friends; none participated in other school activities. *There must be a better way* became a personal leitmotiv.

Indeed there are better ways, as the ESL teacher in another urban high school demonstrates. Rather than provide a protective classroom shell for her students, she requires, as part of their instructional program, that each student participate in at least one school activity. By instituting this requirement and helping them fulfill it, she is facilitating their integration into the wider school community.

I have asked a number of teachers about their own experiences as minority students when they first attended school in North America (see Shields 2002b). Repeatedly, they told of feeling ostracized in ESL classes, of making minimal progress either in English language acquisition or in academic concepts when they were placed in restricted classes with peers who also knew neither the language nor the culture. One teacher whose first language was Mandarin told me that she overcame her lack of progress in her ESL class by going home every day after school to share a glass of milk and watch a television show with her grandfather, who then insisted she discuss the show with him in English.

Empathetic schools do not marginalize children in the name of appropriate educational programming. They do not place so much importance on academic achievement, as evidenced by high ranking on test scores, that they move students to other schools. Neither do empathic schools confine students to segregated classes in the interests of effectiveness.

In empathetic schools, educators and students find ways to support each other, demonstrate respect for individuals within the community, value the lived experiences of each person, and make meaningful interpersonal connections with those with whom they interact each day. Regardless of students' needs for special support for learning or adaptations of academic programs, educators find ways to ensure that students are integrated as fully participating and valued citizens into the life of the community.

Optimistic

Encouraging participation, ensuring justice, and emphasizing caring might facilitate the creation of schools that are pleasant and inviting places in which to work, but there is still a piece missing: the criterion of *optimistic*. Schools that are optimistic do not neglect their primary academic purposes; they do not focus so single-mindedly on safety or self-esteem or belonging that they neglect issues of curriculum and pedagogy. Schools that are optimistic ultimately attend to outcomes. They make conscious and deliberate choices related to fiscal expenditures, curricular choices, personnel, and student assignment to classes and programs. They make decisions that will increase life choices and opportunities for all students—not just those who enter school with advantages of birth and privileged family backgrounds. As Farrell (1999) suggested, without attention to outcomes, there is no real equality or justice. A Texas superintendent expressed the same idea when talking about his district's need to go beyond looking at student performance on basic skills tests: "I can't lay claim to being an excellent district until such time as I've closed the gap with AP, with SAT, with ACT,[5] with all those 'beyond' indicators" (Skrla and Scheurich 2001, 16). Optimism involves attending to the beyond for all students.

Making optimistic choices might, for example, mean that not all students are provided with equal computer access during the school day because those who have no access at home require differential access at school. We might ensure that sports and other extracurricular activities a open to all students, not just those who excel in specific ways. We might offer summer school or intersession programs free to those who need supplemental attention—adding to their life experiences (taking them to the post office, bank, or beach), providing academic support, or offering intensive language instruction.

Maxine Greene describes, from a different starting point, what optimism means. She asks, "What does it mean to be a citizen of the free world?" She concludes that it is "having the capacity to choose, the power to act to attain one's purposes, and the ability to help transform a world lived in common with others" (as cited in Banks 1991, 32). What a nice summary of some of the outcomes of an optimistic education!

A HOLISTIC APPROACH: PUTTING IT TOGETHER

A transformative educational leader realizes that balance is needed in selecting and applying the criteria against which the success of a school or program will be judged. Emphasizing democracy while neglecting justice may mean that the majority makes inappropriate decisions for minorities. Focusing on empathy without thinking about the need for optimistic outcomes may help students feel safe and happy in school, but not adequately prepare them for life beyond. Together the criteria begin to provide an image of a community of difference, one in which educators attend to the multiple goals and purposes of education as well as to complex criteria for achieving negotiated, shared, and desired goals.

To create such a school, an educational leader must consider all four criteria with their explanatory subcomponents. She constantly asks herself such questions as whether her students are becoming citizens of the free world, and how the school is helping them have the capacity to choose, act, and transform their own lives as well as their communities. She develops a set of probing questions and keeps them constantly in front of staff and students to guide large and small decisions. Such questions might include:

- Who benefits; who is disadvantaged?
- Who is included; who excluded?
- Who is marginalized; who privileged?
- Who is legitimated; who devalued?
- How do we know; to whom are we listening?
- What data are we using for our decision making?

Diversity is not new. In reality, it has always been an inescapable aspect of society and social institutions. What may be new today is that our daily exposure to both the presence and the significance of diversity seems heightened, more intense, more extensive. Diversity is in our faces (so to speak). To meet the changing social and academic needs of our students, educational leaders need to create school communities in which students, compelled by respect and high expectations, learn to live and study together in peace and justice, as well as prepare for life in diverse and global communities beyond school.

In chapter 1, I outlined a concept of cross-cultural leadership that I believe can be transformative; in chapter 2, I delineated a normative context for cross-cultural leadership: schools as communities of difference. In this chapter, I have focused on criteria—ways to think about the goals, aims, and purposes of schooling that will help us to achieve *success*—schools that are equitable, democratic, excellent, and socially just. All of these ideas are summarized in figure 3.2.

The model integrates the components of transformative cross-cultural leadership with the idea of schools as communities of difference—communities that are heterogeneous rather than homogeneous. It offers four criteria that, taken together, may serve to guide our thinking, help in our decision making, and offer benchmarks for accountability and evaluation of our movement toward schools as communities of difference. The framework is not intended to be prescriptive but to form a starting point for educators who catch the vision of transforming schools for a more deeply democratic and just society.

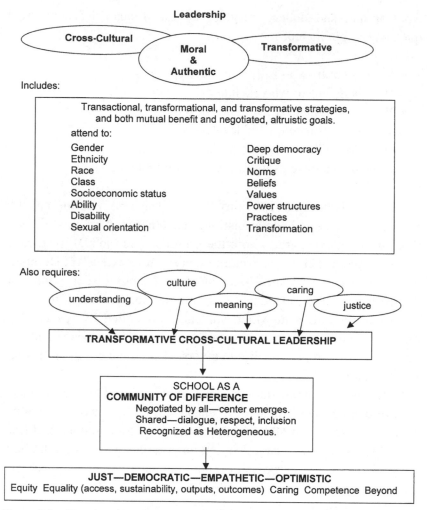

Figure 3.2. Transformative Cross-Cultural Leadership for Communities of Difference

NOTES

1. A Canadian term used to indicate mixed heritage of Indian and French origins.

2. The ideas behind the seventh-generation concept of stewardship are outlined at "L' Initiative de la septième genération," at www.cyberus.ca/choose .sustain/mb-e/7em-g.shtml.

3. For more complete discussions of these programs, see for example, Adams and Karabenick (2000) regarding Michigan; Raivetz (1992) for New

Jersey; Brewer, Feifs, and Kaase (2001) for North Carolina; and Kannapel et al. (2000) for Kentucky.

4. Until the late twentieth century, most support for education came from property taxes; using the rationale of no taxation without representation, people who did not pay school (that is, property) taxes were not eligible for election to school boards.

5. AP (advanced placement), SAT (Scholastic Aptitude Test), and ACT, (American College Testing [www.act.org]) are all used for college admissions and placement in the United States.

PART 2

Learning from Experience

Something there is that doesn't love a wall,
That sends the frozen-ground-swell under it
And spills the upper boulders in the sun,
And makes gaps even two can pass abreast.
. . . .
We keep the wall between us as we go.
To each the boulders that have fallen to each.
And some are loaves and some so nearly balls
We have to use a spell to make them balance:
"Stay where you are until our backs are turned!"
We wear our fingers rough with handling them.
Oh, just another kind of outdoor game,
One on a side. It comes to little more:
There where it is we do not need the wall.

In part 1, I stated that good intentions are not enough. Despite the fact that we do not necessarily love the walls we have created—walls of tradition, of security, of failed attempts at educational reform, we tend to rebuild them. We create gaps big enough for two to walk together yet quickly close them, re-using the same stones, although perhaps not placed as securely as they were, willing them to balance, just for a time, until we can figure out another ending to the game.

In the five chapters of part 2, I introduce schools and educators who are in the process of tearing down the walls and recreating schooling in ways that are more inclusive, respectful, open, caring, and just. They are educators who struggle to find answers, who are humble, willing to take risks, fail, and try again.

The experiences of these educators and schools are drawn from ten years of research in schools in Canada and the United States and briefer periods spent in schools in other English-speaking countries, primarily Oceania (Australia, New Zealand, and Fiji). I have spent time in each school, visiting, observing, asking questions. I have drawers of tapes, interview transcripts, coded data, and documents that form the basis of these chapters. However, it is not my purpose in these chapters to develop an academic report complete with methodological descriptions, but to try to make the ideas come alive, to startle and challenge and inspire you. The schools range from large urban high schools to small rural elementary schools—from elaborate new structures with curved glass sides and skylights, well equipped with the latest high-tech innovations, to tiny four-room schools made from cinder block, lacking what many would consider even the most basic school supplies. They have in common dedicated teachers and administrators striving earnestly (although they might not articulate it in this way) to create schools that are democratic, just, empathetic, and optimistic.

Each chapter in this section begins with practice—an overview of a school, an educator's personal story, some vignettes of daily life. Each chapter introduces literature that I believe helps us expand our horizons and overcome some of the entrenched approaches to schooling, reflected in the refrains so often heard in school corridors and staff rooms, "We've always done it that way" or "They won't let us . . ."

In 1990 Senge, whose five disciplines of learning organizations were described in chapter 2, expressed the opinion that our institutions, including schools, have learning disabilities that must be overcome. He identified various manifestations of these disabilities that educators should take seriously. We mistakenly believe, for example, that we are our positions, confusing loyalty to the job with our own identities. We develop a kind of "the enemy is out there" syndrome (1990, 19) that precludes taking responsibility for the successful accomplishment of organizational goals, and we engage in finger pointing and blaming. We delight in what Senge calls "the illusion of taking charge" (p. 20) without recognizing that before we take action, we need to thoroughly understand the challenges at hand. We become fixated on events—a playground brawl, the adoption of a new curriculum, a specific test score—rather than attempting to understand the longer term, more pervasive processes (the press for accountability or changing demographics) that threaten our organizations' health (pp. 21–22).

These disabilities lead to some relatively complacent attitudes and behavior, sometimes illustrated by using the parable of the boiled frog. Allegedly, if a frog is placed in a pan of boiling water, it will jump out; on the other hand, if it is placed in a pan of lukewarm water and the temperature is gradually raised, it will sit there and ultimately boil to death, oblivious to small but continuous changes in its environment. So it is with organizational life. The parable suggests that if individuals do not pay attention to small changes in their environment and respond in appropriate ways, there will come a point where the changes will kill us, preventing goal attainment and restricting any possibility of success.

Finally Senge identifies "the delusion of learning from experience" (1990, 23) and the "myth of the management team" (p. 24) as learning disabilities that prevent the creation of successful learning communities. When we rely on past experience or on those in charge to provide guidance for the future, we are abrogating our individual and collective responsibility to learn how to go beyond mere survival to become part of a learning organization, one that "is continually expanding its capacity to create its future" (p. 14).

A vision of educational leadership needs to be grounded in our vision of a desirable future, but also in our moral principles and our understanding of socially just practice. Reflecting carefully on the literature presented here, letting it challenge us, applying it to our practice, opening our hearts and minds to what these educators can teach us will help us overcome our disabilities and our paralysis, and hopefully dream new dreams and invent new models of schooling where we are. The ideas in these chapters are not presented as prescriptions but as examples of schools that demonstrate what might be described as more healthy learning environments. They are intended to help us begin the dialogue right here, right now. Whether we are in university classrooms or in K–12 schools, we must initiate and facilitate discourse about our social, political, and cultural contexts and how to introduce changes that will work for us—not just the mainstream educator "us" but the whole community of which we are a part.

Gardner states that "leaders cannot be thought of apart from the historic context in which they arise, the setting in which they function . . . and the system over which they preside" (1990, 1). The three are critical. What works in the legislative framework in the United States with such funded programs as Title I may not be possible in a different country where at-risk factors are defined or funded differently. What is feasible in a large urban organization with many specialists may be impractical for a small rural school (and vice versa). What is appropriate in a reservation (or reserve) school setting with a relatively homogeneous student population may not be transferable to a school with twenty-seven different ethnic groups. Setting and context are critically important in understanding how current practices have developed and what changes are possible.

I urge you not to reject out of hand the changes that have been introduced in these schools. While they may not be either transferable or generalizable, I believe that the experiences of these schools and educators have much to teach each of us. Examine and understand your context; engage in dialogue with your school community. The kernel of a good idea may be here, but its full development is yours to determine. Do not think that because something worked in the United States or in Australia, it will work for you. Conversely, do not assume that because an idea originated in New Zealand or Fiji that it has nothing to teach you, whether you are in North America, Britain, or elsewhere.

There is a rough order to the following chapters in that I have chosen what may be some of the easier topics to understand and deal with first—but that is just my interpretation, where I am today. You may choose to deal with the chapters sequentially, examining the ideas in them, considering how they might be applicable in your setting, and then engaging in dialogue about how to address similar issues in your workplace. But you may start anywhere. These are not linear or sequential concepts. Structural change, as we shall see, often acts as a catalyst for other changes. Changes in power relationships, as Bishop and Glynn (1999) assert, are fundamental to implementing more democratic and just decision-making processes. Understanding culture is critical for examining identity, but one cannot understand identity without considering culture (and so on).

In chapter 4, "Making Culture(s) Visible and Meaningful," I examine how principals in two secondary schools have begun to more clearly represent the cultures of their students in the physical appearance and structures of their buildings and to incorporate it in meaningful ways into the curriculum. Chapter 5, "Identity Crisis," examines in more detail how schools can negatively or positively affect the self-concepts and identities of children. Chapter 6, "Breaking the Boundaries," examines ways to broaden the conception of community by opening schools up to new forms of community involvement. In chapter 7, "Critique, Carnival, and Consciousness," the focus is on new ways of thinking about relationships in schooling. This part concludes with chapter 8, "Walls, Fences, and Other Structural Changes," a chapter on structures and how they may inhibit or facilitate needed and lasting educational change and act as a catalyst for improved student learning.

The discerning reader may ask, how can you move us toward a concept of transformative cross-cultural leadership and propose a new normative concept for schools as communities of difference without addressing power? Clearly the answer is, I can't. I wrestled with whether or not to have a chapter dealing explicitly with power but decided that because power is so integral to everything that happens in schools, it would be both artificial and counterproductive to relegate it to a separate chapter. The topics of power, privilege, and hegemony are woven throughout each chapter. In one sense, all of the chapter divisions are arbitrary; there are many other ways to organize the material in this book. Nevertheless, I hope that each reader will take seriously the need to reflect on the relationships among power and culture, power and identity formation, power and structures, power and everything that is under consideration, asking questions like: Who has the power here? How does privilege work to confer power? What power relationships perpetuate this inequity? What kind of positive power is operating here? How do power structures and power relationships need to be transformed in order to make this change?

McLaren, when asked about the basis for his "arch of social dreaming" replied, "You could say my arch of social dreaming is built upon the strength and power of the imagination and the courage to face the real" (as cited in Borg, Mayo, and Sultana 1998, 360).

Educational leaders wanting to be transformative will need both imagination and courage. So, gird yourselves, open your hearts and minds, prepare for conversation and dialogue, let yourself be challenged and stimulated. Let the change begin!

CHAPTER 4

Making Culture(s) Visible and Meaningful

Canyon Collegiate is a small, modern secondary school, located in one of the most remote and beautiful settings of the four corners area in the intermountain United States. Visitors often come to the school wanting to help the poor Indian students, only to leave amazed at the wealth of resources, physical, technical, and human, they have found in the school and community.[1]

Regal High School is typical of secondary schools in New Zealand: an expansive complex of buildings, classroom blocks, an administrative wing, a swimming pool, and a tennis court, as well as a marae, where traditional Maori ceremonies are held. Situated in a small town in close proximity to the third-largest city in New Zealand, the school has struggled to overcome a reputation of being "tough."

Entering each school takes one into a culture that is visibly different from the mainstream white European or Anglo culture within which it is situated and away from the sterile environment of many secondary schools. But it has not always been that way. Each school principal has worked in different ways to make the cultures of her students visible and meaningful. Before we enter the schools, however, some general comments about culture are in order.

As I indicated in chapter 1, *culture* is a very complex term and many disciplines and subdisciplines (cultural studies, cultural anthropology, feminist cultural studies, postmodern approaches to culture, etc.) have developed around attempts to explain and understand it. In education, *culture* is used to refer to many different things—students' home backgrounds, school climate, specific subject matter, or beliefs students bring with them to school. According to one dictionary definition, *culture* refers to the "sum total of ways of living built up by a group of human beings and transmitted from one generation to another."

Each of us holds deeply ingrained assumptions about culture that need to be made explicit so they may be examined, challenged where necessary, and changed as appropriate. People who share one common characteristic, such as religious affiliation, ethnicity, or geographic location, are often thought to have a shared culture. But as we go about our daily lives and move from home, to work, to recreation, to worship, the cultures in which we find ourselves change. Additionally, as people move from one group to another, perhaps because of geographic relocation, changes in the wider society, religious conversion, or mixed marriages, the sum total of their experiences changes, as do the beliefs, values, and assumptions that are passed down. Sometimes cultures change as one group adapts to, is subjugated to, or is dominated by another group in the wider culture.

It is important to note that we all belong to more than one culture and frequently cross the borders from one cultural community to another. Each experience shapes us. We cannot and must not assume that because people live in the same place, speak the same language, or share a particular social or educational background, they will think the same way. I once spoke with the principal of an elementary school who was planning a goal-setting activity with a group of parents, many of whom came from a single ethnic group that was different from his own. As we chatted about what we hoped the activity might accomplish, we spoke about criteria for success. The principal suddenly said, "I wonder if they will all think the same thing?"

To this, I quickly responded, "Why should they? Do we?"

He looked sheepish and then expressed surprise that, after years of living in the community, he could ever have articulated such a question. I have since heard him ask my question several times of others in his school, both of teachers and visitors from outside the community.

What is apparent is that everyone has culture. Indeed, everyone represents aspects of many cultures and participates in intersecting and overlapping cultural groups and activities.

Every organization also has a dominant culture. Sometimes it is an unrecognized reflection of some aspect of the wider society; at other times, it may reflect the values and beliefs of a smaller segment of the population. Organizations also, through their diverse membership and multiple subgroups, are not cultural monoliths. Rather, organizations and institutions often exhibit complex and sometimes conflicting or competing cultural norms and values.

One task of a cross-cultural school leader is to attempt to make visible, in meaningful ways, the various cultures represented in her school. This necessitates a careful examination of the competing cultural norms and values as well as recognition of those that are dominant.

In the two schools we now visit, educators have focused primarily on cultural representation of ethnicity. I remind you that the discussion needs to be applied, as well, to the many other aspects of cultural diversity you find in your workplaces.

CANYON COLLEGIATE: A SCHOOL NOT LIKE ANY OTHER

Red Rock School District and the county with which it shares its boundaries is a vast, sparsely populated area, in which approximately 16,000 people live in an area of roughly 8,400 hundred square miles. Locals talk colloquially about how the district is divided into the "north" and the "south," code for Anglo and Navajo territory respectively. In the north are the towns, district offices, and government and social services. The reservation is in the south, a vast expanse of semidesert and red rock mesas that hides indigenous dwellings, a desert resort with a grocery store and gas station, and several trading posts. Overall, there is little economic development and students, particularly in the south, are faced with the dilemma that success in school likely leads to a decision to leave the area for work or further study.

It is difficult to adequately describe the rugged beauty of the countryside. Imposing red rock monuments, many considered sacred sites by the Navajo, rise on all sides in striking shapes and various sizes from the desert floor. Canyon Collegiate is amid these monuments, as far south as you can get in the district. The school, located on the Navajo reservation, serves a predominantly Navajo student body of approximately 225 students in grades 7–12.

Most students live amid the landscape in traditional family clusters (many without running water, some without electricity). Their lives are full of apparent contradictions: while many of their grandparents speak little or no English and still engage in traditional activities such as sheepherding or weaving, they may also have cell phones for regular communication. While many practice traditional Navajo ceremonies, some hire limousines from as far as 120 miles away to drive them to their high school graduation celebrations. New technologies and traditional practices coexist easily, reminding the careful observer that the absence of so-called modern conveniences should not be equated with discomfort or unfamiliarity with technological innovation. Similarly, one should not assume that the perpetuation of traditional practices implies a lack of sophistication.

The school stands in stark contrast to the small, almost invisible homes scattered throughout the imposing landscape. It is a modern, sprawling, brick structure, with a grass playing field, an asphalt track, and extensive technological resources (three computer labs, interactive television studios, media capabilities, weight room, industrial shops, and drama, music, and art rooms). The teaching staff is fully certified and relatively stable, the majority having been there for more than ten years. More than one-fourth of the teachers and all of the aides are Navajo.

Alicia, the principal, has been in her present position for ten years, although she has been in the school for over twenty, first as an English teacher and then as a guidance counselor. An Anglo and, until 2001, the only female school principal in the district, she is the principal I introduced in chapter 1 as the recipient of the prestigious Milken Award for Excellence in Education.

Canyon Collegiate is in a curious (but not uncommon) situation. Its student body is almost entirely Navajo (97 percent), and thus the students are in a numerical majority. Nevertheless, because the school comes under the jurisdiction of the county school board, uses the state-mandated core curriculum, and is subject to state control and mandate, the legislative and pedagogical context is that of the dominant cultural group in the state. Decisions tend to be made away from the reservation by white, generally LDS,[2] legislators and educators, who often have little familiarity with the day-to-day realities of the reservation. Hence the school finds itself in the paradoxical position of being homogeneous ethnically but of being considered by many people as a minority school. Because the white population in the district retains most of the political and fiscal power, with the power and control of the Navajo remaining largely confined to reservation governance issues, the majority school population has less influence in educational decisions than one might expect. The power imbalances of the wider community are located beyond the control of the school and its immediate community, yet they still influence school activities.

The fact that most students are Navajo might suggest that they are homogeneous in culture, lifestyle, and outlook. However, as I have already suggested, there is incredible diversity among the Navajo people, even in small communities: diversity of religious belief, cultural practice, and in some instances, even in dialect and language use. Many of these differences have deep historical roots, some of them stemming from what has become known as the Long Walk.[3] There are four major Navajo religious traditions[4] mixed with the dominant Anglo religions of the area as well as a variety of other influences. Differences in educational philosophy are also evident. Many of the Navajo people want their children to learn "white ways" and become proficient in English, while others are anxious to retain and enhance their cultural and linguistic proficiency in Navajo. Some people fear that there is too little economic development and little to enable young people to remain in the area and prosper. Others are concerned that change is too rapid and will destroy the traditional lifestyle.

Alicia told me that shortly after her appointment as principal of Canyon Collegiate, two women from the state capital visited the school. As they left, they thanked and complimented her. Alicia recalled, somewhat indignantly, "One lady commented that you walk into these doors and you would think you were in any school in Salt Lake City. And I remember thinking clearly then, 'That's not what we want; we don't want people to walk into the school and think they are in any school.'"

Alicia immediately set out to make changes to reflect the Navajo population and cultures. The pillars in front of the school are now painted with Navajo themes, while Navajo art, baskets, rugs, and posters decorate the school walls. Examples of student artwork and historic objects are prominently displayed in glass cases in the foyer and media center. One of the small portable buildings at the side of the school has become the Navajo Culture Center—full of artifacts, instructional materials, books, and models. Outside, the evidence that this is not a school like any other is inescapable. As one approaches the school, one sees a large, well-kept vegetable garden and, on closer inspection, an ethnobotany area where students are learning about indigenous plants. Behind the school, an arch stretching between two aluminum-sided portable trailers proclaims, *Ndahoo'aah* (relearning/new learning). An antique wagon is parked beside the gate. Through the gate, a large hogan (a traditional circular, log and red earth structure) dominates the foreground. In front of the hogan is an outdoor amphitheater; beside it, a smaller "male" hogan. Behind it, one sees a small sweat lodge, and still farther back, a sheep paddock with traditional Churro sheep and a (nontraditional) llama purchased to help guard the sheep.

These buildings are not, however, a monument to traditional lifestyles of times past, but vibrant parts of the instructional program that reflect current realities. Classes and meetings are held in the hogan; visiting students may even sleep there. Other visitors join with local students to sing or dance in the amphitheater; students look after the sheep and the gardens, learning both traditional and modern agricultural methods.

Implementing an Empowerment Model

Shortly after Alicia became principal, she, along with most of her teaching staff, enrolled in classes designed to help them acquire bilingual certification. Having already completed her master's degree and administrative certification, Alicia did not need to gain this qualification. But she believed that if it was good for her staff, she needed to acquire it too. This example of the leader learning with a group of teachers is fundamental to many of the changes that occurred in Canyon Collegiate. Because she was participating in the courses, she was able to encourage the discussion of some course materials during school staff meetings.

One of the first articles teachers chose to talk about was one by Cummins (1989) in which he outlines his "empowerment model" for minority students. Cummins asserts that interactions with educators in schools have the potential to either empower or disable children; this is particularly true for dominated groups that tend to be assimilated, homogenized, or marginalized by the dominant power group. This occurs, he states, through the use of subtractive and exclusionary practices oriented toward transmission and legitimation:

> Minority students are disabled or disempowered by schools in very much the same way that their communities are disempowered by interactions with societal institutions. Since equality of opportunity is believed to be a given, it is assumed that individuals are responsible for their own failure and are, therefore, made to feel that they have failed because of their own inferiority, despite the best efforts of dominant-group institutions and individuals to help them. (1989, 23)

Cummins therefore proposes four areas in which educators need to work in additive, collaborative, reciprocal, interactive, and advocacy-oriented ways to empower, rather than disable, minority students. Interactions with students, he writes, are mediated by the

> role definitions that educators assume in relation to four institutional characteristics of schools. These characteristics reflect the extent to which
> 1) minority students' language and culture are incorporated into the school program,
> 2) minority community participation is encouraged as an integral element of children's education,
> 3) the pedagogy promotes intrinsic motivation on the part of students to use language actively in order to generate their own knowledge, and
> 4) professionals involved in assessment become advocates for minority students rather than legitimizing the location of the "problem" in the students. (p. 21)

Community Participation

Alicia and the staff at Canyon Collegiate began to address each component of this model, in part through the Ndahoo'aah program. The word is written in large letters on the arch leading from the paved driveway to the yard behind the portables. Alicia describes the genesis of the project:

> I was approached by a math professor from the University of Utah with an idea that actually originated at the University of Alaska. A professor there had developed a geometry support program using LOGO computer programming combined with Native Alaskan geometric designs. She was interested in trying her program out on the Navajo reservation because of the interest she had in Navajo rug patterns. . . . No one she had talked to yet was very excited about it, but I thought it was a great idea. We set up a summer program with the Navajo elders teaching the weaving part and university graduates teaching the LOGO part. We recruited students from the high school and middle school age groups. The program has been great! Besides enriching the math and technology skills of the young people, the program has become a forum for enhancing relationships between the youth and the elders. While they are sitting around the weaving looms, they share stories and converse. The young people teach the elders about the computers and the elders teach the young people how to weave the patterns they create. We have shared this program with schools all over the reservation and continue to offer it each June. The program has expanded to include beadwork and basket-making as well as rug-weaving. Not only do the elders teach the children how to make their artifacts, they also share stories about the symbolism of the patterns, the shapes and colors, and about traditional ways to gather and prepare the materials.

Alicia's description is understated and she is unduly modest about her role in overcoming the challenges and making the program a reality. She has shared it not only on the reservation but throughout the district and, through invitations to present information at conferences and on television, across the United States. The original conception of the program included translators because many of the elders do not speak fluent English and many of the students have never learned to speak Navajo. A side benefit of the interaction around the shared activity was that the translators soon were not needed as children and elders learned to communicate with each other.

Ndahoo'aah has become a centerpiece of bringing the community into the school and incorporating cultural knowledge into aspects of the school curriculum. Its success demonstrates the importance of persistence and of catching a glimmer of possibility in an idea implemented elsewhere. Yet Alicia muses that she would like to do more. Although the program has forged new bonds of friendship and support for the school that persist throughout the year, the central elements of the program are largely confined to the summer. She would like to see similar concepts infused into the daily instructional program.

Despite her desire to do more, there is little doubt that Alicia has succeeded in changing the physical appearance of her school to reflect the Navajo cultures in meaningful ways. While some district principals have followed her lead and introduced changes reflective of student cultures, others have not. In fact, one principal appointed in 2001 stated clearly, "It is not my job to display cultural artifacts in the school."

Consider how different Alicia's initiatives are from what one finds in many schools with large non-English-speaking populations. Many educators take pride in translating their materials for parents in order to communicate rules and goals with them. They rarely invite parents and community to share in programs like Ndahoo'aah that relate to the central teaching and learning activities of the school.

Cultural and Linguistic Incorporation

Cultural and linguistic incorporation is an important component of Cummins's model. He states, "It should be noted that an additive orientation does not require the actual teaching of the minority language" (1989, 25). This is a significant point. What is imperative, he believes, is that students receive powerful messages affirming the value and validity of their home language and culture. In Canyon Collegiate, not only are the students' cultures visible in the decorations, signage, and schoolyard, but for several years, one of the Navajo teachers has been assigned to help teachers develop ways to integrate the Navajo culture into the daily curriculum. Teachers have gradually decided that another way to value their home languages is to permit students to speak Navajo with their peers in class. Although this would not be the dominant approach, there are times when it may be desirable for students to discuss a particular assignment in Navajo before tackling it in English. Indeed, this may actually enhance their understanding in both languages.

As a result of a recent legal decision, Canyon Collegiate, like all other schools in the district,[5] offers classes in the students' predominant heritage language (Ute, Spanish, Navajo). Schools on the reservation offer classes in both Navajo language and Navajo culture. In Canyon Collegiate, all students, whether Navajo or not (unless their parents request exemption), are required to develop basic proficiency in Navajo language and to take a Navajo culture class at both the junior and senior high level. At this point, a small number of academic courses are also offered completely in Navajo. The goal is to gradually increase the number of classes available in Navajo.

Offering classes in Navajo in a small school like Canyon Collegiate poses several administrative challenges. If students have to take Navajo language and culture, what courses must be eliminated to create space? If there are only one or two teachers capable of teaching a senior subject area class in Navajo, the potential offerings are necessarily limited, and not all students will choose what may be offered. Offering a class such as American history in Navajo may be beneficial and attractive to some students, but it may also exclude others, with the result that some students may not be able to take the course they want in the language of their choice. While the agreement related to the court settlement places some constraints on scheduling and presents some staffing challenges, Alicia and her staff are committed to its success.

Interactive Pedagogy

To foster the academic achievement of minority students, Cummins advocates an appropriate and interactive pedagogy rather than reliance on typical transmissive modes of instruction. The basis for the reciprocal interaction model is a firm belief that talking and writing are essential to learning and, hence, that a language-rich pedagogy is particularly beneficial to students from what Cummins (1989) and Ogbu (1992) identify as dominated groups. Here, too, the staff have been seeking training, learning, for example, about sheltered English and cooperative learning strategies.

I spoke with a science teacher who had come from class frustrated at the students' inability to understand the periodic table, despite his efforts to explain each word in the textbook definition. I asked, "What is the periodic table?" He began to explain that it is a table that gives the atomic numbers and relative positions of various chemical elements. I asked again, "But what is the periodic table?" After he had made several attempts to describe the chemical and physical properties the table presents, I asked him if it might best be described as a way of classifying or organizing the chemical elements and wondered if it could be introduced by exercises in which students were asked to organize or classify objects with which they were familiar. Using language-rich instruction does not simply require defining isolated words but finding ways to make technical language and new concepts come alive for students.

Perhaps the most unique aspect of the pedagogical program at Canyon Collegiate is the combination of traditional pedagogy, cultural incorporation, and technology instruction. The students have access to approximately 175 computers, many with Internet access, multimedia equipment, and several classrooms designed for distance education. Because so few of the students (approximately 15 percent) have computer access at home, the labs remain open from 7:00 A.M. until 6:00 P.M. All students in seventh through ninth grades must take a technology course. Others take advantage of the Accelerated Reader, remedial math and language programs, and the Plato lab, all offering computerized, self-paced units of instruction in virtually every core area.

In addition to these conventional programs, teachers have developed creative and innovative ways to combine technology with aspects of the curriculum to address community needs. Some students take care of the Churro sheep, attend to the ethno-botany project, and work in the school's garden—another project that receives enthusiastic support from the wider community, especially when people receive news that fresh produce is on sale or free packets of seeds are available.

One group of students made an award-winning film, *Hear Our Voices,* about the uranium mining conducted on the reservation between 1940 and 1970.[6] The film highlighted the lasting and devastating effects of the mining, not only high cancer rates but also the ongoing mistrust between Navajo and non-Navajo.

One year, to fulfill the construction requirements of the core curriculum, the senior woodworking class designed and built outhouses. Students learned the requisite elements of construction and also provided an important service to several elders in the community whose toilets needed repair or replacement. The next year, a more ambitious construction project was undertaken as students designed and built a modern octagonal hogan. The octagon project was subsequently funded by a school-to-work project included in a district grant from the federal government that permitted the school to provide some wages to participating students. The project serves several functions. There is a waiting list of people in the community who want to buy and live in an octagon; students have gained valuable construction experience and a small amount of remuneration; at the same time, they have been encouraged to complete their schooling. Clearly, in Canyon Collegiate, Alicia has created an almost seamless interface between promoting a school culture in which students see themselves reflected on a daily basis and developing broader school-community relations.

Assessment for Advocacy

The assessment component of Cummins's (1989) empowerment model is one that Alicia and her staff are still struggling to implement. Despite the fact that students' culture is reflected in the school, graduates have high levels of technological proficiency, and students' fluency in both English and Navajo has improved, student test scores on statewide norm-referenced tests are still well below acceptable levels.

Part of the explanation is likely the inappropriateness and bias of norm-referenced tests for minority students. Questions that are culturally based, such as "Who is the son of your uncle—your nephew, brother, cousin, or father?"—will almost always be answered incorrectly by Navajo children who respond that the correct answer, in their culture at least, is brother. Another explanation, it seems to me, lies in some deep-seated deficit attitudes and educational traditions that are discussed in the next chapter.

Still another aspect is how scores are reported, what they mean, and what people believe they mean—in terms of the legitimation of the schools, programs, and students' performance. For example, overall school test scores are reported in the press without any indication of the number or percentage of students who are, or are not, proficient English-language speakers. If schools that have the lowest test scores are also the

schools with higher proportions of students with limited English proficiency, they are automatically perceived to be performing poorly. This
use of test scores leads to inappropriate conclusions about the academic
performance of individual schools as well as invalid comparisons between and among schools.

Cummins states that we often use assessment in ways that legitimate
traditional Western knowledge and practices and that marginalize and
pathologize the experiences of minority students in our schools. Asking
all students to respond to the nuances of a comprehension passage
about a ski vacation in a mountain chalet may show less about some
students' abilities to read and write than about their social and economic circumstances. Cummins says that educators need to become advocates for students. We need to critically scrutinize the societal and
educational contexts within which the child has developed and then
identify ways in which these contexts may have located the problem
within the lived experiences of the students rather than in the inequitable power relations between school and community that are reflected in biased questions on standardized tests.

Larson and Murtadha express the same idea in different words. They
say that educators need to delineate how inequality in achievement is
inextricably related to inequalities in freedom to achieve (2001, 29). If
students do not know how do perform a specific task or answer a given
question, we need to distinguish between what they have had the opportunity to learn and what they have had the opportunity to experience. Reducing disparities in "freedoms" will, they suggest, be accompanied by a reduction in disparities in achievement.

The principal and staff of Canyon Collegiate have begun to take this
idea seriously. Each year they try to determine what they might change
to help raise student test scores. They have worked with a researcher
(this author) to survey and interview each student in the school to determine whether there were patterns related to home experience, background, school experiences, travel, extracurricular participation, and so
forth, that might help predict success (there weren't). They have
worked with another researcher to understand whether students were
taking the tests seriously (they were). They have focused on helping
students understand how to take tests and why they are important. The
staff has also begun a process of examining school data, including test

results, as a basis for reconsidering school goals and programs and for thinking about student opportunities and freedoms.

All students in the state are required to have a student educational and occupational plan (SEOP), developed in collaboration with their teachers and parents and intended to guide their academic planning. The teachers in Canyon Collegiate have recognized that although some students have had opportunities to participate in school trips that help them explore the world beyond their homes, not all have. While some students have visited postsecondary institutions and inquired about career opportunities, others have not. Teachers have now devised a format for the SEOP that includes listing some of the freedoms they want students to experience before leaving high school. For example, each student will identify and participate in a certain number of experiences beyond the local area that may help him or her with personal goal attainment; each will attend a specified number of cultural activities, and each will visit several tertiary educational institutions. In these ways, consistent with Cummins's (1989) approach to empowering all students, the educators at Canyon Collegiate have begun to use data, including assessment information, for advocacy purposes.

The principal's comment as we concluded one interview sums up her dedication. I asked whether, after twenty years at Canyon Collegiate, she was ready to retire or move to another school. She replied, "I want to stay here until we figure this out. I do!" Figuring it out goes beyond making the cultures in her school visible to creating meaningful educational experiences for all students.

REGAL HIGH SCHOOL: CHANGING REPUTATIONS

Figuring out what needs to be done to empower students is a continuous process requiring patience, dedication, sacrifice, and love. Brenda, principal of Regal High School in New Zealand, is another cross-cultural leader with transformative goals. She too has made a difference in the lives of her students. Regal High School is typical of secondary schools in New Zealand. It consists of an expansive campus with many different buildings, including classroom blocks, an administrative wing, a swimming pool, and a tennis court. The school serves approximately

450 students; 70 percent are Maori and the rest are of predominantly white European ancestry, or Pakeja, as they are called locally.

The school is situated in a small town in close proximity to the third-largest city in New Zealand. The town, which serves a large, predominantly rural and Maori population, is somewhat economically depressed, perhaps due to the lingering effects of the historic dispossession and capture of Maori lands. Most of the Maori there have strong connections to their traditional culture, in part because their community is near the marae of the Maori queen. Although this would not always have been the case, the presence of the queen has been an important cultural influence in the area since the revitalization of the Maori king movement in the 1920s (Rae 1996, 4).

In addition to the buildings and recreational facilities mentioned above, the school has a beautifully crafted *marae*. The *marae* is a Maori spiritual place, a place for learning, a place for meeting, and a symbol of identity. The traditional Maori meeting house, with paintings and carvings symbolic of Maori historical and spiritual traditions, is used by the school for many ceremonial and social purposes. It is the location of the school opening ceremonies each year, assemblies, and cultural events, as well as the point of welcome for visitors to the school. *Marae* ceremonies make extensive use of Maori protocols for bringing people together, recognizing each other, and validating each other's identity.

Structurally, Regal High School's *marae* resembles many others around the country, with its high-peaked facade, large porch, and impressive meeting room, all painted in traditional red, white, and brown patterns, and displaying intricately carved and highly symbolic designs. Like the hogan of Canyon Collegiate, Regal High School's *marae* is not just an artifact of bygone traditions; it is the center of school life, serving as a meeting and teaching place and perpetuating Maori cultural traditions. The *marae* is also a dramatic reminder that the school is on traditional Maori land.

Many of the students at the school are children of previous students. Two of the teachers have also been students at the school. Nine of the twenty-eight teachers are Maori—a higher proportion, I was told, than in most New Zealand schools. Many of the nonteaching faculty in charge of special programs are also Maori. In Regal High School, both deputy principals and two department heads are Maori. As in Canyon Collegiate, teachers and administrators are there because they want to be, not because it is the only job available. They are concerned, caring, and dedicated educators whose anxiety over the gaps in achievement between Maori students and New Zealand European students have led to the introduction of numerous new programs and educational initiatives.

When I met her, Brenda, the principal, had been in her position for four years, having moved from another secondary school where she was a senior English teacher. She has a deep understanding of, and respect for, the traditions and culture of her majority school population.

In this school, diversity is primarily a function of having two dominant cultures (Maori and Pakeja) that are also to some extent aligned along socioeconomic lines, with the Pakeja generally better off economically than the Maori. These alignments create some tensions between the two groups that reflect historic policies of assimilation and unequal power as well as racism and other present realities.

The site-based governance structures introduced as part of New Zealand's Education Reform Act in 1989 permit considerable local control by school councils and school staff. Thus there is the potential to introduce curricular, programmatic, and structural modifications that may increase the relevance of the students' educational experiences.

The most striking feature of the school is the artwork that grips you as you walk in the door. Large wood, metal, and ceramic sculptures, some decorated with bright colors, feathers, buttons, and other objects, stand in corners in the foyer. On the walls, in the foyer, the offices, the halls—everywhere—are large frames containing student artwork, including some of the panels that they created for the senior art exam from the previous year.

Although Brenda did not explicitly identify a goal of ensuring that Regal High School did not look like any other school, I caught my breath at the beauty and power of the artwork. I walked into the gym to find, in addition to banners signaling athletic success, that the walls were also lined with framed student paintings.

In Regal High School, the art is not just for decoration. It is not used here as a superficial representation of the other, or as an attempt to capture something of the Maori identity or traditions. Rather, it is a means of expressing students' understandings of eternal themes: life, death, identity, and relationships. As with Canyon Collegiate, the art serves the purpose of helping students see both Maori and Pakeja cultures reflected in their school. Teachers sometimes use it as a basis for discussions about various cultural themes. The art does not just represent Maori culture but reflects the core curriculum themes in ways chosen by the students themselves.

Brenda told me the art teacher hired three years before had worked wonders; students had begun to take many awards, and a tradition had developed of producing an annual calendar[7] showcasing student art. Brenda encouraged them to leave their work at school, with the promise that the school would buy frames and exhibit it. That way, she explained, the work would not be hidden away in a closet at home but displayed for the students' own children in future years. The students' art is put on view along with other art and wall hangings reflective of traditional Pacific Island cultures and European traditions. The acclaim that the students and school have received as a result of their success in art has prompted a new sense of pride and achievement among the student body, sometimes to the envy of educators from other schools. They often express both surprise and reluctant praise for the standard of excellence now being set by Regal High School.

As in Canyon Collegiate, evidence may be seen of each component of Cummins's (1989) empowerment model (although here the congruence is more coincidental than explicit). Community involvement, attention to pedagogy and assessment, and linguistic incorporation are clearly evident here. Many students, for example, avail themselves of elective Maori classes, while 15 percent of the student body is enrolled in a Maori immersion program.

Brenda and her staff have worked hard to involve parents in the academic life of the school through numerous special initiatives. Sometimes letters of invitation were sent to parents, asking for their participation; and sometimes, as one of her coordinators stated, "Home visits are the only way to get parents involved." Brenda described annually setting up her program by "inviting parents to barbecues, and having an open place for them to come and see the work and discuss the program." Participation and success seem to follow. Brenda indicated that one of the "problems" with the parent volunteer programs is that through their involvement in the school, unemployed or undereducated parents often discover a new sense of capability and confidence to take further training. With newfound skills and increased self-esteem, they then leave the cadre of school volunteers because they have found full-time employment elsewhere. And Brenda's recruitment and training begin again.

To facilitate the success of all students, parents and school staff to-gether have instituted a transition program (for students who had dropped out of school and who agreed to return), a truancy program run by parents, and what Brenda calls "a lovely alternative program . . . where Maori parents take responsibility for their kids." In the latter pro-gram, Maori parents volunteer to act as school-community liaison workers, making contact with homes, sitting with children in class, and generally providing support for academic success.

The strong belief of all adults in the school community is that "kids have got to see alternatives." Thus Regal High School has in-stituted a series of varied curricular offerings: academic, fine arts and performing arts, and a bilingual Maori program, as well as alter-native classes designed to offer extra support and assistance to those who need them. As one might expect, teaching strategies and peda-gogy vary. Although some use very traditional and transmissive ap-proaches, others have developed highly student-centered, interactive pedagogies, strategies Brenda encourages as much as possible and employs whenever she teaches.

Academic achievement is important for the staff at Regal High School, who clearly share Brenda's goal of ensuring that "every student will leave school with a meaningful national qualification." Brenda re-flects on their concerns:

> Our exam marks are sometimes really low. And you get quite despondent about it, but look at the man who just came in who has grandchildren who are Maori. One of his grandchildren did not do well at all academi-cally, but was a strong presence in the school. She's just been accepted to teachers' college because they've got the New Start Program at uni-versity for Maori students. Quite a few of our kids go there. They've got that transition year—they always need a year to catch up. A year in the New Start Program and they learn all of the skills they need for being at

university, including research skills. And then they go to teachers' college after that. So we've got a lot of success.

Brenda is concerned that Pakeja children still outperform Maori children based on measures of school certificates and bursary (university entrance–type) exams and the percentage of students going on to higher education. She states that the "statistics are shocking for Maori students," but that they are also misleading, in that many students do subsequently attend college or university. Brenda is convinced that many of their "ex-students are stunning young people, but are not showing up on the statistics at all." She believes that although they may not continue directly after high school to university, labeling their certificate as terminal is inaccurate, especially when one learns, a few years down the road, that not only have they completed further studies but "suddenly, they are teaching." Hence Brenda would like to "subtract the kids further down the line."

The assumption, in New Zealand as well as North America, that students who do not continue to tertiary education in the year in which they complete high school never go on to further study is inaccurate. This narrow and often erroneous definition of school leaving creates a statistical picture that is especially disadvantageous to many young people from minority backgrounds.

Although Regal High School has not yet attained a fully equitable situation in terms of academic outcomes, students have begun to close the gap, to experience increased equality not only of access and sustainability (or retention), but also with respect to a more optimistic beyond.

TRANSFORMATIVE LEADERSHIP: MAKING DIFFICULT DECISIONS

I had several lengthy conversations with both Brenda and Alicia about what it meant to include students' home cultures in meaningful ways in the daily life of the school. Alicia talked about the place of traditional Navajo ceremonies in school activities. Sometimes members of the community wanted ceremonies performed—to ensure the success of sports teams or to cleanse an area that had been contaminated by accident or injury. She explained,

> We have never done a ceremony that we have paid for or required people to attend . . . that would be a complete violation of school and state policy, but we have allowed ceremonies on occasion, such as one to cleanse the building following the killing of a snake in the gymnasium.

Thus she permits such ceremonies to be performed in the school but does not allow them to disrupt academic activities or become central to the life of the school. Alicia described incorporating traditional Navajo beliefs in this way as "interesting, but not difficult and not intrusive."

Brenda seemed to wrestle more with the appropriateness of incorporating Maori culture into the center of school life, and with the extent to which it was possible and desirable. She described how all visitors are, for example, welcomed to the school in a traditional *marae* ritual that includes speeches, songs, and prayers. I asked her whether there was any problem incorporating elements of the Maori traditions that might seem to be religious—elements that in some places would raise concerns about the separation of church and state. Her lengthy response ended with the statement: "As far as I'm concerned, you have to decide what you're going to do. You can't . . . embrace the Maori culture in school, but then say, 'we don't want that bit.' If you're going to do it, do it. I just don't have tolerance for anything else."[8]

For Brenda, personal sacrifices are involved in ensuring a place for *Maori* culture. As a woman she is not allowed to speak during Maori *marae* ceremonies and hence has to cede her place as school leader to the male vice principal of the school. Brenda has been willing to display congruence of belief, stated goals, and behavior—attributes of an authentic leader—in that she has been willing to give up some of her power to accept the rules of the culture she wants to respect and include. She explains:

> There are lots of things we have to accept. There are a lot of issues around welcoming students onto the marae. Women can't speak on the marae. I don't speak out there, but if we come inside I make a point of

speaking. From a feminist point of view it is quite a difficult thing to manage. But I just let it go because I have too much respect for the Maori teachers. That's really what it boils down to.

I've had a lot of experience with Maori things. I thought that I would be fine at this school, but it's like being with a pretty different culture. And I feel at times alienated from it. And that's as it should be. I'm Pakeja and I'm different from them. I never had a problem with that.

If I have a problem in the school, I ring up one of the Maori teachers and say this is what I've been asked to do and what do you think? What's your opinion? And she tells me. She's the expert. I don't have to be an expert. And I think when you start to, you've got a real problem.

Brenda has articulated some important principles of transformative cross-cultural leadership. It will not always be easy; indeed, it may not even be comfortable, and some personal sacrifices may be necessary. You cannot and will not always be the expert. The transformative leader will recognize that being respectful of different cultures requires a level of knowledge, empathy, and understanding, but that the expertise always remains with those from that culture.

Learning the "Rules" of Power

Although making cultures visible in meaningful ways is not always comfortable, it must be done wholeheartedly and with integrity. Brenda exemplifies the cross-cultural leader who, in her desire to be transformative, is willing to change the center, to accept her discomfort and frustration and let others be the experts. This does not mean that Brenda is a passive or unprincipled leader. Rather, she chooses her battles in terms of what is good for her students in order to create an inclusive, excellent, and just school. While Brenda is prepared to accept some things she does not fully understand or agree with, she is also determined to help her students understand the rules and demands of the majority New Zealand European culture so that they may decide for themselves what to accept and what not to.

One of the cardinal rules for making cultures visible in meaningful ways is to make them explicit. Lisa Delpit has written at length about this. Delpit maintains that every organization operates on the basis of

...y) unwritten rules that coincide with the rules of the dominant power group. She argues that there are five aspects to a "culture of power" that educators need to understand (Delpit 1990, 86–88). First, Delpit asserts, issues of power are enacted in classrooms. These include such issues as the power of the teacher over the students, the power of the curriculum to determine what counts as knowledge, and the power of legislators to determine normalcy. Second, we need to recognize that the codes or rules for participating in power relate to how we (the dominant groups) talk, write, dress, and interact. Moreover, the rules of the culture of power reflect the rules of those who already have power. In other words, middle- and upper-class English-speaking children are advantaged because the rules of the classroom are the rules they experience on a daily basis, while children from other cultures may learn a different set of rules at home and in their communities. Fourth, being told explicitly the rules of the culture of power makes both participation and acquiring power easier. Too often well-intentioned educators try to overlook students' lack of understanding of the rules in an attempt to minimize discomfort, all the while hoping they will soon "get it." Yet Delpit is clear that being told the rules is kinder and easier than being left to figure things out for yourself—as anyone who has struggled in a foreign culture will acknowledge. Finally, she asserts that those with power are the least aware of and least willing to acknowledge its existence, while those without power are the most aware of its presence.

As an invited participant to an educational symposium during my sabbatical in New Zealand, I learned firsthand the value of making rules explicit. I had just finished talking to a group about Delpit's concept of cultural power, when we broke for morning tea. As I spoke informally with some members of the group, I did what I often do at home and perched on the edge of the table as I spoke. My hostess quickly came up behind me and whispered, "Off the table." Later she said, "I hope you didn't mind me telling you, but sitting on a surface where there might be food is considered rude in Maori culture." What an irony! I had been talking about making rules explicit and had my hostess not been willing to do so for me, I might have continued causing offense for some time. In fact, I wonder if I would ever have discovered the rule for myself if the person who knew the culture had waited for me to figure it out rather than tell me directly how to behave appropriately.

Delpit's point is that we must help people learn to communicate across cultures, while at the same time eliminating the power differentials and barriers that silence and marginalize some children and continue to privilege others. While she recognizes that everyone must bear some responsibility, she is clear that it is "those with the most power, those in the majority, who must take the greater responsibility for initiating the process" (Delpit 1990, 101). Making rules explicit is not enough. Where such rules perpetuate power differentials that privilege some people and marginalize others, educators must also work to change the cultures within which they work. Transformative leadership requires working on two power fronts: changing the fundamental power imbalances and teaching those not in power the rules to enable them to participate in organizational life.

Brenda and her staff take this task seriously. Brenda spoke, for example, of the need to "teach young people how to behave" at public events like concerts. The faculty all teach students such things as how to handle disappointment when they don't receive an award for which they are nominated, the skills needed to speak in public, and the necessity of being active participants when they represent the school at various functions.

Alicia followed the same precept. She recalled that at an early parent-council meeting, she held a training session in Robert's Rules of Order. She was not suggesting that all people need to know these rules for conducting a meeting but was offering it as an example of how providing training and guidance can empower people who are unfamiliar with the rules. She believed that parents, as well as students, sometimes have to be taught whatever skills they feel they lack in order for them to be willing to participate or take on leadership roles. Otherwise, she asserted, "If you've never been taught, you just don't know how to do it." As another example, Alicia reflected on the need to teach parenting skills to many adults in her community because many people who either had attended boarding school themselves or had parents who attended "didn't know how to be good supportive parents of public school children." Helping people acquire specific skills is one way to empower members of the community, and one outcome may be that they are willing and able to participate more fully in the life of the school community.

Teaching students the rules of the dominant culture is one thing. Ensuring that people in power from the dominant culture do not use the rules in prejudicial ways to mask racist behavior is the other side of the coin. When others acted on inappropriate assumptions, expecting, for example, that aboriginal students would automatically behave inappropriately, both principals were indignant. Brenda recounted one incident when she had taken students to the theater.

> We were sitting in the front row, quietly, and the kids were really excited about going. . . . The manager came out and blasted the kids. "Don't you do this and don't you do that." . . .
>
> I let it go and then at the end I asked if I could speak to her for a minute. And I just said, "Tell me what that was about. . . . Have you ever had a problem with Regal High School students?"
>
> She said, "No. But it's such a rough place."
>
> I said, "Well, did you look at any of the students? Did any of them look rough?"
>
> She said, "Have I really messed up?"
>
> And I said, "You really have."
>
> So she apologized. She was sorry and she realized that she had been wrong.

TRANSFORMING WITH MORAL OUTRAGE

Part of making culture(s) visible and meaningful is knowing when and how to be an advocate. Sergiovanni talks about this type of response as "leadership by outrage." He writes, "It is the leader's responsibility to be outraged when empowerment is abused and when purposes are ignored. Moreover, all members of the school community are obliged to show outrage when the standard falls" (Sergiovanni 2000, 277). Leadership that includes a healthy dose of moral outrage is an essential component of a transformative leader. Power was abused by the theater manager and Brenda demonstrated outrage. She was ready and willing to take a stand on behalf of her students, combat inappropriate stereotypes, and address racism.

Reflecting on the situation she had just recounted, she stated, "It's to do with racism. . . . Mostly to do with racism." She is, however, one of the rare educational leaders I have encountered who was willing to identify racist behavior in her school and use the term *racism*. Too often racially motivated behavior is masked with other explanations or labels, or dismissed as simply "kids will be kids." At the same time, name-calling and physical scuffles, even when they occur between students from different ethnic groups, do sometimes represent simple misunderstandings.

Delpit provides some important insight into the dialogue that may permit leaders to address difficult issues like racism. She writes,

> To do so takes a very special kind of listening, listening that requires not only open eyes and ears, but open hearts and minds. We do not really see through our eyes or hear through our ears, but through our beliefs. To put our beliefs on hold is to cease to exist as ourselves for a moment—and that is not easy. It is painful as well, because it means turning yourself inside out, giving up your own sense of who you are, and being willing to see yourself in the unflattering light of another's angry gaze. It is not easy but it is the only way to learn what it might feel like to be someone else and the only way to start the dialogue. (Delpit 1990, 101)

If dialogue about culture(s) is an integral part of the daily life of the school, it will be easier to identify the cause of inappropriate behavior and address it. This will be particularly effective if the transformative leader accompanies a sense of moral outrage at injustice with the empathy described by Delpit.

MAKING CULTURE(S) MEANINGFUL

Because of the nature of the student bodies in these two schools, this chapter has focused primarily on ethnicity as a reflection of culture. Some may feel that this discussion is not particularly relevant to their more ethnically heterogeneous student bodies. Educators whose primary responsibilities are in urban schools with large numbers of students from many ethnic groups may be tempted to dismiss the attempts of Alicia and Brenda to make the cultures of their schools visible as a first step toward creating inclusive communities of difference.

Let me reiterate that I recognize that diversity manifests itself in various ways in our educational institutions. Where I have talked about ethnicity, one may as easily talk about gender or social class, physical or mental abilities or disabilities. In the case of these two schools, each principal has made concerted efforts to ensure that the students *in her school* are represented through visible symbols and artifacts. I believe it is possible for each educator wanting to create a community of difference to do the same.

Does that mean that we need to affix posters of each ethnic group represented in our school to walls throughout the building? Perhaps, but not necessarily. Does it mean that every language should be given equal time, separate instructional periods, and cultural-awareness classes?[9] Not likely. It may simply require educators to permit students to converse at times in their home languages; but it may also necessitate some additional linguistic instruction.

To make cultures visible, students, teachers, administrators, and parents in each school should come together to discuss ways to make sure that their school does not look just like any other. Having students create symbolic multicolored murals might be one approach. Asking each student to decorate a ceiling tile with a personally significant symbol is another. Rotating the responsibility for displays in various parts of the school may be meaningful. Ensuring that every classroom is equipped with an up-to-date map of the world or a globe is a necessity. The key is not to try to cover the student body in superficial ways, but to find meaningful approaches to reflect who the students are. In Canyon Collegiate, the use of Navajo artifacts was important. In Regal High School, despite the 70 percent Maori population, the artwork covering the school walls and filling the halls became a focal point for both Maori and Pakeja cultures as students selected artistic traditions that helped them represent universal themes (life and death, sadness and joy, friendship and alienation) in highly personal ways.

We are reminded once again that as each of us lives in, and moves among, multiple overlapping and intersecting communities, so our cultural identity is constructed from multiple sources. Those who have spent time tracing their genealogies are often surprised by the richness and variety of their own cultural backgrounds. As we will see in chapter 5, "Identity Crisis," we need to exercise caution not to label people or essentialize them because of any one characteristic, including cthnicity.

UNDERSTANDING CULTURE(S)

In a study I conducted of the perceptions of teachers, parents, and students in Red Rock School District, I asked some questions about the place of culture in schools. Participants were asked about how well students understood their home cultures, what languages they spoke, how much Navajo should be taught at their school, whether they supported the district's bilingual plan, and what they saw as the major challenges in the district. While their responses were varied, there were two aspects of the data that I found both surprising and disturbing. What is perhaps even more troubling is that similar responses have been frequently found by other researchers.

In my study, many white students, when asked about their home culture, indicated that the question did not apply to them. They felt that thinking about whether they had been taught the beliefs and values of their culture at home, and whether there were important elements of the culture that they wanted to pass on to their own children, might apply to their classmates who were Ute, Navajo, or Hispanic, but not to them. Taylor (1999) reported that white tenth-grade girls in her study, when asked about their race or culture, tended to respond, "That has nothing to do with me." Other researchers and scholars (Roman 1993; Sleeter 2000) have identified similar responses.

Some parents and teachers indicated that they were supportive of teaching about other cultures in the school. However, the comments of many parents about culture and schools reflected an attitude similar to that of the students. Statements like "Culture belongs at home" or "It is not the school's job to teach culture" were common.

When people indicate that culture belongs at home or that the school has no right to teach culture, they are implying, rather than stating, that the school has no right to teach about a minority culture. They are forgetting that whether stated or not, schools do teach culture. In fact, they are overlooking the fact that traditionally (as discussed in chapter 3), one of the school's major roles has been societal acculturation. The attitude of these parents is another indication that educators may have too often interpreted the task as assimilation and downplayed all but the majority culture.

Both responses, that a discussion of culture does not apply to oneself and the belief that culture or cultures should not be taught or discussed in schools, are problematic. These stances reflect an unexamined belief that the dominant cultural position does not need to be examined, and that if others want to belong and be accepted, they need to conform. They imply that the school does not need to consider, talk about, or teach culture because its culture is the correct one, and no other matters. I am not implying that particular cultures should be taught directly in school, although there are cases where this might be the most appropriate decision. I am arguing that people must talk explicitly about what the dominant culture is, identify its rules, and discover how to make schools more inclusive and respectful, if we are to end the cultural exclusion of some children from the school community.

It may well be important for all students in Red Rock School District to have a sense of the historical realities, the horrors of the Navajo Long Walk, the political designation of certain areas as reservation lands, and so on. It may be even more important to create spaces for discussion about the relationship of hegemony and culture. How do the core curriculum and authorized textbooks portray any given situation? In what ways are the players represented? Ignored? Misrepresented? Whose knowledge is being presented and how does that shape the ways in which the material is interpreted? Only when such conversations are encouraged in schools, whether about math or science or literature,[10] can students begin to understand that everyone has culture, but that some cultures have historically been more privileged than others.

At its extreme, the notion that culture belongs at home implies that minority cultures belong at home and should not be seen or discussed in public institutions such as schools. Few people, when pushed, are likely to support this extreme position. But, in order to determine what the culture of the school should be like, and how it may best and most appropriately reflect and value people from all social, economic, and cultural groups in society, these issues must be examined. It is therefore necessary to find ways to facilitate, in classrooms, schools, and district meetings, conversations about the relationships between and among the cultures represented in a community. What are the characteristics of the majority culture, and what are the main features of the minority cultures? What does it mean to be white? Is there such a thing as white power and privilege? What about Navajo power or Asian power? What docs it mean to be Navajo, Hispanic, or Ute or any other ethnicity?

How do they fit together? What changes in belief or practice might result in improved relationships and more relevant instruction? These discussions cannot be left to chance.

It is unacceptable for any students in today's society to graduate from high school believing that they have neither culture nor ethnicity. Making the cultures represented in a school visible is a starting point that helps all children recognize and value their own heritage. But changing the appearance of a school does not guarantee that people learn to challenge their own deep-seated assumptions and traditions. Changing the appearance does not automatically make students understand culture and cultures in meaningful ways. Including artifacts of other cultures does not mean that white children begin to understand, for example, how the Navajo culture enriches them or vice versa. For that, considerable effort and dialogue are needed.

Making the cultures of the school visible in the decor, the buildings, the artifacts, and the curriculum is a starting point for dealing with cultural differences in a meaningful way. Changing the appearance of a school is one way to help students feel less alienated and more a part of a building for whose appearance they are, in part, responsible. But unless physical changes are accompanied by ongoing discussion about the reality and meaning of culture, the changes will remain superficial

SEEING THE INVISIBLE

In Canyon Collegiate, Alicia ensured that the decor of the school, its structures, and its programs included elements of the dominant (Navajo) cultures of her students. She developed extensive relationships with community members, spoke with community leaders, attended council meetings at the Chapter House, and collected data on which to base decisions about the equality of her students' opportunities. She looked both to past traditions and meanings and to the future, incorporating high standards and innovative technological programs to ensure that her students faced an optimistic beyond.

At Regal High School, Brenda, while extremely proud of the new artistic prowess of her students, was never willing to stop there. She used the displays as an entry to dialogue about barriers and opportunities, about racism and privilege, about the need for those in power to sometimes give it up in order to empower those from other cultural groups with different beliefs (about the role of women, for example).

Both principals have taken firm stands for their students. They have recognized that reflecting students' cultures does not simply mean perpetuating the frozen images of bygone days often seen in magazines or textbooks (Indians in hogans or tepees; Maori semidressed and holding spears). They have incorporated elements of culture as dynamic and intrinsic features of student life. Technology and traditional artifacts go hand in hand in the education of students in Canyon Collegiate. Modern artistic technique and traditional themes are combined in the exemplary art program of Regal High School. But the educators in these schools must not, and have not, stopped there.

Making cultures visible *and* meaningful requires ongoing advocacy, risk, and sometimes discomfort. It necessitates understanding how to help marginalized groups to recognize the power they have and to find ways to use it productively.[11] It requires creating opportunities for faculty, students, and the wider community to reflect on the issues related to power, domination, social control, and marginalization that are inherent in interactions between and among cultural groups. It demands that we reject the implication that some groups are inherently more able to learn, more intrinsically suited to hold power, more adept at making decisions, or more concerned about the welfare of the school community than others. Moreover, we must explore why and how people, including ourselves, have come to hold such beliefs. We must make explicit our underlying assumptions in order to clearly explain the basis and rationale for our critique.

Good intentions are not enough. Making cultures visible without dealing with them in meaningful ways may make schools more attractive, but it will not help them to become just, democratic, empathetic, and optimistic communities of difference. Brenda and Alicia have made tremendous strides and provide many illustrations of ways in which transformative cross-cultural leaders may begin the journey. But there is much left to be done. The next chapter, "Identity Crisis," deals explicitly with beliefs and attitudes that undergird some of our educational practices.

NOTES

1. Although I use the present tense to describe the schools in this chapter, you are reminded that schools change annually; although they were accurate as I wrote, the details (for example, the number of teachers on staff from a particular ethnic group) may be different as you read. This in no way diminishes the value of hearing about, and learning from, these schools.

2. Members of the dominant church, the Church of Jesus Christ of Latter Day Saints.

3. Between 1859 and 1868, disputes over land between the Navajo, New Mexico, and the U.S. government resulted in eviction, death, and relocation for many Navajo. Some, however, did not participate, and their descendants now wonder whether the treaty, signed in 1868, should pertain to them (Locke 1992).

4. The religious influences in the area are diverse and complex. Typically the Navajo belong to one of the following groups: Native American Church, Traditional Navajo, Episcopalian, or Revivalist; while the religions of the Anglo groups involved in district governance and social service agencies are, for the most part, LDS, Seventh-Day Adventist, and Jehovah's Witness.

5. In the 1970s, a court case alleging discriminatory educational practices was settled out of court, with the agreement that new schools would be built in the southern part of the district to better serve Navajo children, and new culturally and linguistically based programs would be introduced. Following a negative review from the Office of Civil Rights in 1991, the court case was reopened and again settled out of court in 1997, with provisions for Navajo (and other) culture and language classes to be offered, depending on the proportions of student populations from different linguistic and ethnic groups in each school.

6. A publicly available, award-winning film, *The Return of Navajo Boy,* also documents the mining. It explains that children played in the rocks left over from the mining and that people often used the rocks, striped with uranium ore, to build homes.

7. The calendar is professionally produced and is similar in quality to art calendars displayed, at least in North America, in art gallery gift shops.

8. In her New Zealand context, each school is required to develop its own charter, and there is considerable encouragement for the incorporation of Maori culture. Elsewhere, for example in North America, trying to incorporate traditional elements of various cultures might bring the school principal in conflict with policy or legislation. At that point, of course, the leader would have to work on several fronts, engaging in dialogue to broaden the possible interpretations of the rules while also working to bring about necessary change.

9. As mentioned previously, Cummins (1989) explicitly states that educators must differentiate between valuing home language and permitting students to make use of multiple languages at school, and the impossible task of attempting to teach every home language. Teaching all languages is not necessary; valuing them is.

10. For an excellent discussion of how math, science, and literature have been tools of colonialism and repression, see Kumashiro (2001).

11. This is in fact one of the guiding principles of civil rights movements or the kind of development work conducted by people like Paolo Freire. Sometimes people need to learn that although they may not recognize it they have power; hence it is important that they identify it and learn to use it.

CHAPTER 5

Identity Crisis

In the previous chapter, we examined how to make various cultures more visible and meaningful in a school context. Throughout that discussion, although we recognized that the idea of culture is socially constructed, the emphasis was on collective meanings and constructions. In this chapter, I want to focus more specifically on individuals and on how we often, unknowingly, engage in behaviors that exclude and marginalize the very people we want to include. Understanding how the concept of identity relates to a community of difference will help educators to move beyond good intentions to more equitable practice.

I had the privilege of gaining some insight into issues of identity, exclusion, inclusion, and the role played by others when one of my graduate students shared some writing with me. He was reflecting on how well-intentioned teachers had tried to acknowledge his difference through multicultural activities. Here he talks about the often used strategy, "Bring something that represents your culture."

And the tiger's eye rosary, made up of ninety-nine beads, is called a *tasbih*. I chose the tasbih as a symbol for my religion—the Shia Imami Ismaili sect of Islam—because it captures so many layers of personal meaning and interpretation of my faith. Aside from the five pillars of Islam we talked about in class . . . there are other aspects of Islam that I feel the tasbih represents for me. Each bead signifies one of Allah's ninety-nine beautiful names. The circular shape of the tasbih and each bead reminds me of the perfect unity of Allah. . . . The Ugandan flag and the ebony makonde curio represent the African in me. My grandfather emigrated from India to Mityana, a small town in Uganda, when he was a young boy . . .

After my presentation in class, I reflected on how hypocritical and irrelevant it had been.

How could I explain that as a devout and practising Muslim, I attend prayers in JamatKhana almost every day, I had to look up the meaning of the five pillars of Islam? . . . Is this heretical? How could I explain that I very rarely use a tasbih when saying my prayers? . . . I feel fraudulent claiming anything from Africa except my birthplace. Although I feel a deep spiritual resonance about that continent, I feel a similar resonance every time I think of Russia, a country I have never been to. How then can I represent Africa? . . . How could a curio available commercially possibly represent the "Africanness" in me? The regal crested crane, centering the yellow and black striped Ugandan flag, not only represents Uganda's emancipation from years of colonial rule but her aspiration for self-sufficiency, independence and grace: bullshit! I made all of that up . . .

I've never been to India . . . How could samosas and incense sticks . . . convey to anyone my imaginings and fantasies of Indian life? And if it did, is it legitimate Indian culture? What is distinctly Indian about me? What traditions am I preserving? . . .

No matter how fertile the soil is, can anything grow without the water of love and encouragement? I ached to tell some of the students in my class that although Canada, for me, is a pot of fertile soil, my seeds could not flourish in it. . . . How could I possibly explain that more than the traditions and customs of Indian or African culture, it is the experiences of alienation, poverty, racism, and marginalization that have forged the lenses through which I see life.

In an attempt to understand the alienation that I feel from mainstream society, I can catalogue many indignities that I have suffered. From being pegged in the side of my head by a stone disguised as a snowball to being excluded from drinking out of the same Coke bottle that was passed around in the boys' changing room. From being ridiculed for wearing Sears jeans instead of Jordache, to being humiliated for bringing samosas at lunchtime in grade eleven. From not being able to accompany my class ice-skating on Wednesday afternoons, to not being able to afford even the cheapest school photo that ensured my inclusion in the school annual. These experiences have influenced my perceptions and personality far more than any Indian or African ceremony I have ever celebrated or performed. (Sayani 2001, 24–27)

This man is my friend—this beautiful, articulate, sensitive educator who wrote these words for a term paper in my class. I read and reread his words, and my heart and mind and soul scream, "No!" How could I, we—our school system, my peers, my fellow educators, have so devastated him and so many like him? How could we let clothes or skin color hide the depth of insight and feeling so eloquently expressed in these words?

We do it unintentionally. Slowly, surely, carefully. Little by little, we tear down his self-esteem, we alienate him, marginalize him, let him believe he has nothing to offer us. Then we hit him! Yes, hit him while he is down—keeping him apart, building walls of his poverty, his ethnicity, his religion. We don't mean to. We think we are tolerant, multicultural, color-blind. Oh how careful we are to bury any hint of prejudice or racism—to keep it hidden from ourselves, since from his adult perspective Anish knows only too well who and what we are.

In this chapter, I begin to examine some of the beliefs and attitudes we hold that, despite our best efforts and good intentions, we wield like swords, destroying those whom we claim we serve. As we open ourselves to the truth, clarify our beliefs, and challenge some pervasive assumptions, we recognize that our words, our interactions always have an effect on other people. Although we frequently fail to understand what a profound and lasting impact we really have, the truth of Temes's assertion that leaders operate on the souls of their followers (1996, 80) becomes evident.

IDENTITY AND SELF-CONCEPT
IN STUDENT EDUCATIONAL EXPERIENCES

Researchers have, for some time, recognized that positive self-esteem is associated with success in life. Educators recognize that positive academic self-concept is also associated with success in school. For that reason, considerable research has been conducted into ways to enhance students' self-esteem. Many of the conclusions are well-known: facilitate positive relationships with other students, encourage participation in an extracurricular activity, and provide opportunities for a consistent relationship with at least one caring adult in the school.

Some writers extend this notion and suggest that it is not just direct relationships with others, but a perception of how others represent us that also affects our sense of self. For example, Giroux states that "how we understand and come to know ourselves cannot be separated from how we are represented and how we imagine ourselves" (1997, 14). Giroux suggests that "youth and racial identity are constituted within and across a plurality of partly disjunctive and overlapping communities" (p. 15). In other words, youth learn to understand who they are in relationship to a number of different, overlapping, and sometimes conflicting and contradictory communities related to home, school, and wider society.

Taubman (1993) has identified what he calls "registers" that help us understand how identity is constructed, what it means, and how it functions: *fictional, communal, and autobiographical.* Although his model (like any other) may be critiqued for creating artificial categories and perhaps for omitting crucial aspects, it may help us better understand Anish's reflections.

Taubman's fictional register is one that "imprisons the subject" (1993, 291) in an identity created by language and the perceptions of others. Because of its tendency to portray identity as fixed, this register is both alienating and objectifying. This is the register often used implicitly by teachers who ask students to bring something to represent themselves or their culture, without attending to the interplay of the other two registers. This register explains why, when we see Anish's brown skin, we identify him as East Indian, without thinking about how his Islamic religious heritage, his home language, his Ugandan birthplace, and his Canadian citizenship interact in complex ways to create his sense of identity.

This is the register we are using when we say that someone is gay or poor or gifted. Our label focuses attention on a specific characteristic, gives it undue prominence, and clearly shows the other how we are constructing him or her. We create a fictionalized identity around that characteristic as if is the truth. Hence, in the past, one heard statements like, "Gifted kids are small, not athletic, wear glasses, and spend their time reading." Such a constructed identity becomes so real in our minds that when we are asked to select students for an athletic competition, the child labeled gifted is unlikely to be considered.

The communal register heightens our understanding of how group relations create identities for those both inside and outside the group. Taubman (1993) says "it is only in relation to group membership that such identity may be explored" in that connections with a group serve to promote both action and reflection about the meaning of identity and help to create our cultural literacy. Within a group, sharing cultural symbols, celebrations, and experiences helps give us a sense of affiliation. Through the sharing, we come to know who we are and where we belong. Yet being part of a group sometimes requires us to hide the parts of ourselves that may not fit the group's expectations. An aspiring quarterback who wants to gain the respect of his peers on the football team may, therefore, believe he must hide the fact that he also writes poetry and plays the violin.

In like manner, just as a group constructs its own identity, it may also construct its view of an outside group by focusing on some characteristics and behaviors and ignoring others. Irving Janis (1982) called this phenomenon "groupthink." I recently heard a group of teachers describing a specific action of their government as showing it was intentionally "out to get the teachers." These teachers were unwilling to consider that some of the legislators were married to teachers, had children in public schools, and had shown support for education in various ways. What Taubman calls the communal register helps explain not only how we affiliate with a group in creating our personal identity but also how one group may construct an incomplete or inaccurate image of another group that may marginalize and exclude, even vilify, its members.

Educators, generally through lack of knowledge, often ignore such complexities as intergroup differences, the historical development of group identity, and ways in which group membership and social identity interact with individual identity. Moreover, it is difficult to take account of multiple communal registers in a classroom where the collective classroom ethos overshadows individual voices or outside group affiliations.

Finally, Taubman's autobiographical register recognizes that each of us has many selves. It does not try to create an objective real self but permits us to recognize the complexity of identity formation. In this register, Taubman says, "identity emerges as a personally meaningful and continually developing aspect of one's Self" (1993, 288). It is the private self, the self that does not create one's experience but captures it. The autobiographical self permits agency and responsibility. It interacts with the fictional and communal register, supplementing, elaborating, critiquing, and problematizing them. It permits love of football, poetry, and music to coexist in meaningful ways in one individual.

When we examine identity from these three vantage points, Taubman claims, it becomes apparent that "individuals are always more than and are always capable of transforming their social identities. They are not *only* intersections formed by grids of gender, class, race, ethnicity, religion, or physicality" (Taubman 1993, 297). Anish wants us to know him as a whole, complex person, not to try to peg him or understand him through one classroom presentation or though a label someone affixes to one selected aspect of his cultural background or daily life.

Although difference and diversity and how they are perceived and portrayed have an impact on identity formation and expression, identity is more than a compilation of discrete identifiable factors. For the educator, this does not mean that we should eliminate activities in which students talk about their culture, multicultural fairs and activities, and the like. What it does mean is that we should take care that we do not assume any single object, item of food, national costume, song, dance, or the like *represents* the student. We should take care to use such activities as starting points for ongoing conversations about the creation of images of culture through representation in textbooks, in curriculum, in classroom discussions. We should make sure that if we have several students from a single ethnic group, we make room for them to talk about their differences in religious beliefs and practices, historical and social development, and patterns of immigration, as well as to identify similarities. The key is not to engage in activities that reduce a student to a static, simplistic, externally fixed identity.

A number of theorists remind us that self-esteem is not enhanced if we inappropriately treat all members of a social or cultural group as homogeneous—as if they are all the same because of a single, usually visible, characteristic (Omi and Winant 1986; Pinar 1993). Moreover, it is not only in educational *activities* that we perpetuate reductionist approaches; our *assumptions* are equally culpable. Educators are fond of claiming, for example, that Asian students are good at math, that aboriginal students will not look you in the eye, or that black students are the best athletes. When we talk in these terms, our discussions imply that all members of these groups possess "some innate and invariant set of characteristics that set them apart from each other and from 'whites'" (McCarthy and Crichlow 1993, xviii).

We need to remember, as Roman (1993) explained, "white is a color, too." It no more defines me than brownness defines Anish. It is part of who I am and it includes me in a historic collective, some of which I would like to deny or forget. It also reminds me that just as there are differences of interest and ability among the white population, so there are in every other group, lest one be tempted to essentialize.

WHAT IF WE MINIMIZE DIFFERENCE?

As already noted, identity formation emerges from a complex interplay of personal and social factors. While we sometimes essentialize others in an attempt to understand them, the opposite practice, minimizing difference, is often as destructive and as marginalizing. Sometimes educators attempt to minimize, downplay, or ignore differences in a well-intentioned attempt to promote unity and harmony. In the following section, a number of common practices are discussed.

Being Color-Blind

We frequently proclaim our tolerance, our innocence, ignoring Anish's brown skin and dark eyes, protesting that we are color-blind (see also Akintunde and Cooney 1998; Holcomb-McCoy 1999; Johnson 1999). I ask my graduate students, "What does it mean to say you are color-blind?" Their responses are illuminating. Invariably my white students—teachers and administrators—respond that they are "tolerant, don't see difference, treat everyone equally." But my nonwhite students have a different idea.

"I have a best friend I've grown up with," says one North American–born man of Asian descent. "My friend often says, 'Mike, we're just the same. I don't think of you as any different from me.'"

But, Mike states, with grace and humor, "I look in the mirror, I look at my skin. I notice my eyes. I think I look different. Don't I look different? I sometimes wonder what he is missing when he says we are just the same."

Across the table, another Mike, this one of aboriginal ancestry, explodes: "When someone tells me he or she is color-blind, I feel marginalized! Of course there is a difference. If we were all the same, my people would graduate from high school at the same rate as white students. We would not have the highest rates in the country of poverty, school dropouts, alcoholism, incarceration. What do you mean, we are just like you?"

Understanding the subtexts of common phrases is a difficult task. When we say that someone is just like us, we are expressing our desire and intent to accept the other on his or her own merits, to minimize difference and recognize common bonds of humanity. Yet when we ignore difference, we are also devaluing and marginalizing the person whose difference was the implicit impetus for the statement in the first place.

This color-blind approach, far from showing respect to the other, misrepresents the individual and ignores deeply rooted prejudices and inequities in our society. With the best of intentions, we ignore fundamental differences, pretending they don't exist and failing to talk about, recognize, or celebrate them. In so doing, even as we imagine others are just like us, we disregard the differences that could enhance each individual's sense of identity and enrich us as a community.

Kincheloe and Steinberg state, "The color-blind construct . . . only works if we assume that being white is no different from any other race or ethnicity" (1998, 15). Implying that only white people can claim to be, or feel the need to be, color-blind is another hegemonic practice that divides us. Think about it. Do white educators who move to a foreign country to teach expect that others will be color-blind, pretending that they are not white?

I have white friends to whom two daughters were born while they were teaching school in Papua New Guinea. Many of their treasured photos show their white toddlers surrounded by villagers of all ages who were exhibiting intense interest in their fair-skinned, blond-haired appearance. Not for a moment would Tim or Sally have expected the

Papua New Guineans to ignore the differences in color. Not for a moment would the villagers have expected Tim and Sally to ignore their European ancestry or to pretend to be like them. Why, then, do white educators, when the situation is reversed, believe that noticing difference is disrespectful?

In the North American context, I have a friend who responded with fear and horror when his three-year-old daughter asked him a question about a "brown" woman. His response was to talk to her about difference not being bad or good, only different, and to address the thorny topics of tolerance and prejudice. First, I wondered why he did not hear her words as simply descriptive. Then I wondered if a "brown" child had described someone as a "white" woman, whether her parents would have reacted in the same way. Would that have been seen as disrespectful in our culture? Rost's (1993) test of justice and fairness—that once a decision has been made or a statement uttered, we reverse the positions to see whether we would accept or reject it—provides a useful litmus test.

Interaction without open communication and accurate representation is superficial. It may lead to continued presumptions and assumptions about otherness that cannot form the basis for the creation of communities of difference. Alain Locke's approach provides a helpful foundation:

> Cross-difference conversations on the common ground of basic humane values can lead to tolerant understanding of the historical roots of each others' differing perspectives, to deeper respect, to reciprocal exchanges, to some areas of agreement and experience-founded trust, and eventually, to collaborative projects for mutual benefit. (as cited in Green 1999, 10)

The point is important. We need to both explore common human values and understand our differences in order to come together as equal members of a community. We cannot do this without being willing to see and acknowledge difference.

Being Class-Blind

In addition to being color-blind, white middle-class educators are often class-blind. We fail to acknowledge that our educational practices perpetuate an inequitable hierarchy of lived experiences. Children who have had the opportunity to travel widely, participate in cultural events, acquire proficiency in a musical instrument, or engage in other enriching activities are automatically expected to perform well and have an academic orientation to schooling. Other children bring into the school situation considerable savvy and practical knowledge—knowledge about how to survive on the streets and find their way alone around a busy city, how to get themselves ready for school without adult help, how to prepare meals for themselves and their younger siblings, or how to look after an alcoholic or dying parent. They have learned to be self-reliant and sometimes even work to provide financial support for their family.

Knapp and Woolverton indicate that class, although "hidden in schooling and elsewhere . . . is central to social inequality" (1995, 549). They claim that there is "an enduring correlation between social class and educational outcomes" (p. 551); these correlations hold true across cultures and over time such that, in general, higher class correlates with higher levels of educational attainment and achievement and lower class with higher dropout rates, less likelihood of attending postsecondary institutions, and greater probability of holding lower-status jobs. Moreover, Knapp and Woolverton assert that there is abundant evidence that the large majority of educators in developed countries come from what may loosely be called the middle class and hence may find it difficult to understand or communicate with the considerable number of students from lower classes, many living in relative poverty.

Knapp and Woolverton found in their studies that in most developed societies, people believe that schools are great societal equalizers. While we might hope that this is the case, not in terms of homogenizing cultures, but in equalizing life's chances, education is not always very successful in achieving this goal. Knapp and Woolverton go on to say that

> our ideologies are not our realities, and no amount of wishing will eliminate the pervasiveness of social class dynamics in the lives of teachers and learners. Educators and the educated alike need clarity and insight regarding the presence, interplay and power of social class in their encounters with one another. (1995, 548)

Moreover, they have found that issues of class are pervasive across time and cultures. Most teachers come from middle-class backgrounds; many students do not.

How can we find ways to value and build on the skills of all children, as well as offer the knowledge required to help all children move beyond their circumscribed situations to have a wider range of options? How can we find ways to acknowledge that despite dire circumstances, many of these children live in families who cherish them; or to recognize that despite economic well-being, some children still suffer from neglect and abuse? How can we ensure that material possessions and traditional middle-class lifestyles do not become equated, in our curricula, with happiness and success?

Often North American teachers talk freely about the organizations and institutions in their communities without realizing that many children do not have firsthand experience with them. Although most middle- and upper-class families take their infants and toddlers to places like banks, post offices, or libraries, many other children, especially from poor families, have never been inside them. Many teachers have been taught that it is essential to inform parents of the need for children to have a quiet, separate place to study. Yet how many teachers stop to consider the message being given to parents who struggle to survive, living in broken-down trailers or low-rent apartments that sometimes house multiple families. Indeed, we are implicitly telling them that despite their best efforts, they are once again failing their children.

Educators know, sometimes in vague ways, that it is useful to acknowledge that children come from various ethnic and linguistic backgrounds. We sometimes introduce units on multiculturalism or bring in speakers from community groups. We encourage students to sing or dance during school assemblies and public performances. We also need to ensure that other children, whose differences are based in class more than ethnicity, are also included.

Sometimes class differences seem particularly detrimental to students and less desirable in society as a whole, and so we deem it more appropriate to downplay them. We do not want to single out or embarrass a child in any way. How then can we ensure that class differences are addressed appropriately rather than ignored in the daily conversation of schooling? Educators may, for example, empathize with a child whose mother suffers from cancer, whose siblings are in a foster home, or who seems to have only one ragged school outfit. We may want to help the child who comes to school dressed in dirty clothing or wearing shoes with holes. But most commonly, we ignore their realities. In the guise of kindness, we fail to help all students understand the societal conditions that perpetuate differences of class and socioeconomic status.

The critique of early reading books that present images of traditional families (father working, mother remaining home to look after the two children and their pets) is well-known. Yet changing the color of the family, giving the mother a career, or depicting her as a single parent still tends to represent today's middle-class reality.

Where are the stories of families in crowded third-floor apartments, sharing bathrooms, coping with ants, noise, and smells that are foreign to most middle-class educators? Our history books often mention, in passing, the dislocation of people during political upheaval. But where in these accounts are the lived realities of refugees or boat people struggling to understand and gain acceptance in a new country depicted? In our health classes, we often discuss the dangers of smoking, unsafe sex, and alcohol and drug abuse; but where are the spaces that permit students to discuss the realities of living with a dying family member, the fear, the anger, and the awful reality of loss? And how do we help them cope with the shame and embarrassment if the death is not socially acceptable (murder, suicide, AIDS)?

I am not suggesting that we draw attention to the situation of a specific child or that we single children out, making them even more sensitive and perhaps even more ashamed of their family situation. Quite the contrary. I am suggesting that we broaden our curriculum and our sense of community. We need to find ways to help all children understand that, in any given community, there is a wide variety of life circumstances and complex causes for the diversity. Depending on the age and maturity of students, we can help them understand the role of political forces, some causes of unemployment, or the reasons why governments have social support programs. We may want to help them recognize that there are different kinds of poverty—emotional, financial, relational, for example. If we do not open our curriculum to include issues of class, we are guilty of class blindness, another way of marginalizing and excluding the experiences of large numbers of children.

Being Spiritually Blind

Sometimes my graduate students, themselves thoughtful educators, ask me what to do about the religious and spiritual differences that often surface when we address ethnic, cultural, and class differences in a classroom or school. Should we simply ignore spirituality and differences in belief? In some ways this is a more difficult difference to address, as evidenced in part by the persistent religious strife in many parts of the world.

We have been taught that we should keep our opinions to ourselves, eliminating bias from our instruction and relegating some of the most important elements of children's lives to an uncomfortable, silent space in our schools and classrooms. In much of Canada and the United States, school prayer has been forbidden, Christmas concerts have been renamed "winter concerts," and national holidays have been denuded of any religious or spiritual significance. We claim that our educational systems are value-free. And, once again, our intentions have been good.

We remain silent because we do not want to impose our beliefs on others or because we respect the need to separate church and state. We rename the concerts and carefully select music in order to be inclusive. We still close schools for Christmas and Easter but pretend the timing is coincidental.

Silencing religious and spiritual differences in order to be inclusive creates a superficial sense of harmony but denies deeply significant parts of people's lives. How can anything be value-free when it is embedded in the social, political, cultural, and ideological contexts of our lives? We have already said that educators wanting to move toward schooling that is just, democratic, empathetic, and optimistic will recognize that education is a deeply moral enterprise—one that is intricately linked to the moral and ethical values of the culture(s) within which it operates. Making these values explicit, examining them, and discussing them is a critically important part of being a transformative educator. Ignoring them is another way of pathologizing children for whom spiritual beliefs and alternate worldviews are an important and intrinsic part of daily life.

Acknowledging the spiritual dimension of human life is not necessarily synonymous with permitting religious discussion to occur in schools (although there may be some overlap). Overcoming spiritual blindness requires that we acknowledge the animating force that permits us to make meaning of our lives and understand our world. Starratt defines spirituality as "a way of being present in the deepest realities of one's world" (2002, 12).[1] His definition suggests, by implication, that if we overlook or repress spiritual conversations about deeply held beliefs and the meaning and value of life, then we are denying ourselves, our students, and our education system the possibilities that come from dialogue about our deepest realities. Suppressing spiritual conversations may result in an inability to think altruistically and justly, beyond our self-interest and material realities, and to transcend the inequities of our time.

Starratt is not alone. Other educational leaders have begun to call for an alternative to the objective, rational, technical approach to schooling by emphasizing a deeper life force. Some find in Cornel West's "prophetic spirituality" a way of engaging in "protracted and principled struggles against forms of personal despair, intellectual dogmatism, and socioeconomic oppression that foster communities of hope" (as cited in Dantley 2001, 3). Dantley suggests that acknowledging the spiritual dimension can "broaden our current conceptions regarding educational leadership and what our standards ought to be" (p. 4).

Murtadha-Watts writes about what she calls a "womanist spiritual leadership theory," one that holds the potential "for bringing about changes in historically oppressed communities" (1999b, 166). She states that because of a "belief in a powerful force in their lives [some black women] have acted as risk takers with a purpose beyond the oppressions of white people. . . [They] have sought the means to live rather than abandon hope. . ." (p. 155).

Rather than force educators and children to deny the power of deeply held beliefs, a transformative educational leader helps people from diverse religious and spiritual perspectives to bring these parts of themselves to the dialogue of the community.

Let me illustrate with another personal example. Anish, as he has told you, is an Ismaili Muslim. I am a Christian. On one occasion, shortly after the tragic events of September 11, 2001, we were to travel from Canada, with a group of scholars, to an academic conference in the United States. Anish expressed some concern about the difficulties he had previously encountered at the border and the heightened security, fear, and ethnic profiling that existed at that time. We took as many precautions as possible; he carried letters from his employer and from our academic dean indicating that he was employed, was a graduate student in good standing, and definitely intended to return to his family and teaching position following the conference. (They were never needed.) For various reasons, the check-in process and customs and immigration clearance were smooth and swift.

Once we had cleared the checkpoints and were sitting waiting at the gate, I breathed, "Thank you God. I prayed about that this morning."

Anish responded quickly, "I did too."

What a rich and touching experience! What an amazing way of coming together, Muslim and Christian, in celebration of the fact that we each believe in a power beyond ourselves. Sharing a sense of spiritual reality adds an additional layer to our friendship that exists in, because of, and in spite of our differences. Ignoring it would deny us that point of connection.

Note that neither of us tries to proselytize. We do not attempt to claim superiority of one belief system or persuade the other that his or her way is in error. No educational good could come from that.[2] We celebrate the shared spirituality of our lives, enriching both of us in the process.

I often wonder about the effect of renaming a Christmas concert a winter festival. Does it unite members of a community in new ways? What message is given to those whom we are trying to include? This is a delicate and tricky issue. In trying to be inclusive, are we giving the message that no spiritual beliefs are valued? Are we implying that the majority's beliefs are so unnecessary that they are willing to have them ignored? If this is true for the majority, then what message might we be sending about minority beliefs and values? When we refuse to recognize the beliefs of a majority culture, what hope can members of minority cultures have that their traditions may find acceptance within the

discourse and practices of the school? This seems to be a curious reversal of relativism, one that implies not that anything goes, but that
nothing goes. Insisting on silence about the deepest realities of children's lives makes connecting to other aspects of their lived experiences much more problematic. I believe that insisting on silence about
one set of beliefs virtually guarantees that recognition of traditional (religious) festivals of other groups will be superficial at best.

OTHER DIFFERENCES: ABILITY, SEX, AND GENDER

In the name of good intentions, we often remain silent, pretending that
differences are unimportant. I have chosen these three differences
(color, class, and spirituality) as illustrative of a range of differences
that exist in every school today, differences that are visible and invisible, genetic, social, and spiritual. These are not the only differences we
need to attend to in our schools.

Children who excel in mathematics, music, or linguistics are often
left to stagnate in classes in which the majority of students are neither
motivated nor particularly capable. We advocate inclusion in the name
of democracy while failing to recognize that treating everyone the same
fails to fulfill justice criteria. Indeed, it may represent another form of
blindness in our educational arrangements.

I am definitely not suggesting that we revert to the tracking practices
of the past that rewarded the children of white middle-class families
and marginalized and pathologized children from lower SES and non-
English-speaking families. I am suggesting that we need to find ways
to meet all children's academic and social needs without labeling or
pathologizing them, to identify those needs in appropriate and multiple
ways, and to ensure that practices we institute in the name of democracy are also just and empathetic and optimistic. What may be required
to achieve the development of children's full academic potential is
recognition of differences in academic interest and ability—in the same
way in which we need to recognize differences such as ethnicity, class,
spirituality. We may need challenging homogeneous groupings for
some; others will require extended first language instruction; still others may learn best in bilingual programs, or with support for visual or
hearing impairments, and so on. A teacher I know puts it this way:

"What we don't need is the tasteless pabulum of a diet that feeds all but appeals to none."

We also need to acknowledge that there are sex and gender differences in our schools. In what ways and in which programs are males advantaged over female students and vice versa? How are issues of access and sustainability assessed in each class, program, and extracurricular activity to ensure democratic and optimistic levels of output and outcome? What about students who are gay or lesbian or who come from nontraditional families in which their parents and caregivers may be gay or lesbian? How is our curriculum inclusive of their sexuality and gender, without singling them out or pathologizing them? What types of clubs and activities are permitted and encouraged and which are forbidden?

Although I have identified some of the differences that exist between and among students (and educators) in our schools, there are many others I might have addressed. Some differences may be temporary; others are permanent. Some children have parents who are incarcerated. How do we assuage or exacerbate their feelings of anxiety or shame? Some struggle with alcoholic or abusive parents. Some have famous (or infamous) parents who figure prominently and regularly in the public media. How do we acknowledge their realities without letting a specific factor define them? How can we help students deal with difficult situations without singling them out or making them feel embarrassed or ashamed? How can we effect change in our deeply rooted assumptions and long-standing patterns of discourse to achieve greater equity in our schools?

In the name of good intentions, we often remain silent, pretending that differences of color, class, or spirituality are unimportant. These practices, we are often told, promote a sense of unity, of common humanity. But I disagree. Remaining silent implies that something should be kept private, never to be seen or discussed in public. It makes people think that their experiences are abnormal and hence destroys rather than enhances a sense of common humanity.

PATHOLOGIZING THE LIVED EXPERIENCES OF OTHERS

In the foregoing section, I insisted that recognizing and talking about differences is valid. Indeed, a community of difference builds on an understanding of and respect for difference. The tendency to overlook or negate differences in an attempt to develop common bonds is a firmly rooted and pervasive attitude best described as deficit thinking, blaming the victim, or *pathologizing the lived experiences of students*. But such pathologizing is not always done in silence. Based on a stereotypical image, educators may, unknowingly and with the best of intentions, allocate blame to an essentialized group based, not on their personal qualifications, but on a generalization or a label.

I recall a discussion in my school's staff room shortly after my husband left me. I had been a member of the staff for four years and all of my colleagues knew of my recent, quite traumatic separation. One day, somewhat to my surprise, a group of my teacher-colleagues began talking about the lack of parental support experienced by children from single-parent families.

"Hey, be careful. I'm one of them now," I protested teasingly.

"You're different," one said, "We're not talking about you."

But the barbs went deeper. Because of my changed marital status, my children would now be stigmatized, and yet neither they nor I had changed. I was still privileged, economically and through my position as an educated white woman. They were still children of a teacher and a clergyman, grandchildren of people with university degrees, who enjoyed summers at the lake, private lessons, and community sports activities. Yet our circumstances had changed and I quickly learned about my new reality—as a single parent. It meant working later into the night, having no one with whom to divide the "taxi" duties for my children, and letting my cleaning lady go in order to continue to fund their music lessons. But for the next few years, the label "single-parent family" defined my children more than anything they (or I) could do or say.

As noted earlier, schools were instituted to fulfill multiple purposes, including a socialization or acculturation function. This has led to numerous educational strategies that first label and then homogenize students in terms of academic programs, goals, and outcomes. Sometimes we use labels to determine who should go into which program. Sometimes we generalize from our labels and use them to make academic decisions that affect not only children's identities but their long-term career options as well. We assume that children from single-parent families will not have high levels of parental support and advise them against selecting challenging academically oriented math or science classes. We assume that children whose home language is not English lack the intellectual ability to understand complex concepts and suggest that they avoid conceptual topics and enroll in hands-on classes like cooking or auto mechanics.

We often act as if there is an implied hierarchy of language in schools—English is best; some Western European languages such as French, Spanish, and German are highly desirable. But facility in other languages, such as Cree, Maori, Tagalog, or Punjabi, is less valued. We may claim that some languages have more instrumental value in that they are more widely spoken and hence more useful to learn. This does not mean, however, that they have more (or less) intrinsic value. It is unjust to reward those who speak English fluently at home and see no reason to expand their horizons by learning other languages while punishing children who speak other languages at home and are learning English as a second or third language. Yet this is often what happens in the name of academic effectiveness or efficiency.

Children who are recent immigrants, whose English is less than fluent but who speak a different language at home and are working hard to develop their skills in English are sometimes encumbered with detrimental labels that are very difficult to remove. When I was teaching an enriched high school English class, some of my students asked me if there was any possibility a friend could transfer into the class. Upon investigation and an informal conversation with the student, I learned that Grace had arrived in Canada when she was eleven and had been placed in a fifth-grade classroom. When she participated in the required standardized testing at the end of the fifth grade, her IQ was assessed at approximately 80. Although she learned English quickly, her home language was Mandarin, a point that was consistently overlooked when she was subsequently directed to low-level courses. Grace, however, was extremely bright, her English improved rapidly, and she gradually moved into "regular" classes. I quickly acceded to her friends' request that she transfer to the enriched English class. There, despite an initial lack of self-confidence, she demonstrated her keen academic ability. Unfortunately, as much as I would like to believe that Grace's story represents an isolated incident, whenever I tell her story, another educator has a similar incident to share in return.

We frequently hear teachers and administrators reciting a litany of what they perceive to be negative school statistics. They complain about the number of students whose home languages are other than English, who have been identified as low- or high-incidence special needs students,[3] or who have physical or mental limitations and may need classroom support or assistance. Sometimes the complaint is about children's home situations, the number of children who come from homes with single parents, or homes where there is alcoholism, poverty, or abuse. As teachers seek explanations for low achievement on standardized tests, they often resort to this litany as if it explains children's school performance. They complain that the children's parents don't speak English or don't value education, or that their homes do not contain books, magazines, and other enriching materials. And, of course, factually some of these statements may be true. But coexistence does not mean causation. One fact (that there are few books in the home) cannot be interpreted as a cause for another fact or assumption (that parents do not value reading).

For example, children who have grown up on an Indian reservation, enjoying the love and support of extended family relations and learning the oral traditions of their cultures, may come from linguistic traditions that have only recently been written and in which there are still very few print materials. The lack of reading materials may simply reflect a lack of availability and not a home that does not value education. Educators must be careful not to impute sinister motives or oppositional values to parents or to believe that certain circumstances predispose children to school failure. Of course, aboriginal children may also come from homes with extensive libraries where reading is a daily pastime. Moreover, children from both situations may be either highly successful or very unsuccessful in school. The difficulty comes when we make assumptions about children based on a generalization, in other words, when we pathologize the lived experiences of aboriginal children and make unwarranted assumptions about their home life, parental support, or academic ability.

Children whose parent or parents live below the poverty line, struggling to hold several jobs to make ends meet, may not have the advantages of travel or private lessons, but that does not mean they are less intelligent, less accomplished, less inquisitive, or less emotionally stable than their more affluent peers. Their lives may be different from the lives of most middle-class English-speaking children, but that does not mean that they are intrinsically less able.

When we act and speak as though some children's experiences are more valid than others, we are pathologizing and devaluing some and privileging others. We are sending the message that some children are normal and others are not. Too often we use the lived experiences of children as explanations for poor school rankings, as excuses for placing children in lower-level classes, or for expecting them to achieve at a lower standard than mainstream children. We pathologize their experiences when we treat their lives as abnormal and in need of treatment. Moreover, when we pathologize children's experiences, we are implying that their cultures are abnormal. When educators send children the message that certain lived experiences may not be talked about in school, they may develop a sense of shame and embarrassment. When these children do not see themselves or their experiences represented in any area of the curriculum, they come to believe not only that their experiences but that they themselves are somehow less important or less worthy than others. Often we ignore much of the experience that is at the center of children's daily existence as if it were an untouchable, dirty, and unacceptable secret. To equate children's abilities with the conditions of their daily lives is simply wrong.

LOVING, ENCOURAGING, AND NOURISHING: A BETTER WAY

As Anish closed the story with which this chapter began, he wrote, "How can anything grow without the water of love and encouragement?" The story of Ruth Simmons, first African American president of an Ivy League university, illustrates this clearly. Appointed in 2001 as the eighteenth president of Brown University, Ruth is the daughter of a sharecropper, one of twelve children.

Morley Safer, host of CBS television's *60 Minutes,* introduced Ruth's story with these words: "an African American child born into abject poverty rises through the ranks of academia to become a dean, a college president, and now president, of one of its most prestigious universities" (Simmons 2001). During her interview, Ruth Simmons described how she was particularly encouraged by some caring teachers:

> I'm in this dark house with a tin roof. That's my little world. And I go into this place that is bright and cheerful with this wonderful person called a teacher. And she's cheerful and she thinks I'm wonderful and she thinks I'm smart. So it was . . . like a veil lifting for me.

Ruth's teachers did not pathologize her experience of being a poor sharecropper's daughter. They did not single her out or shower her with pity. Instead, they encouraged her. They "went into their closets and took clothes out of their closets and gave me their clothes," Ruth said. "They gave me money. My teachers did. It's amazing. So that's how I got to college."

This is not the story of a poor black girl who pulled herself up by her bootstraps and made something of herself. Rather, it is the story of how caring teachers loved and nurtured her. She went on to study sixteenth-century French literature at Harvard. When asked why she chose something so esoteric, she replied, "Because everything belongs to me. There is nothing—there is nothing that is withheld from me simply because I'm poor. That's what children have to understand."

Ruth Simmons is right. It is important for children to understand that education can open the world. But educators also have to know that, to a large extent, they are the gatekeepers. It is educators who either open or close the doors—and unfortunately, for too many children, we slam them shut.

"Education does not exist to provide you with a job," Dr. Simmons asserted. "Education is here to nourish your soul." She and Anish have used a similar metaphor. The soil may be fertile, the seed may be good; but educators can choose either to kill or to nourish the souls of the students in their care.

High-Stakes Testing Is No Excuse

Esther is an African American principal in Florida who believes firmly in the intrinsic abilities of all children. She is the transformative leader of John Howard Elementary School, a school with a very heterogeneous student population and a high proportion of students (87 percent) on free or reduced lunch programs.[4] Many of her students are African American. A large number come from Spanish-speaking homes. Some live in trailer parks, others in low-income housing, while still others live in a comfortable suburban neighborhood. Many have parents who are migrant workers and hence are very transient.

Esther's leadership practice exemplifies the work of Wagstaff and Fusarelli (1995). They found that the single most important factor in the academic achievement of minority children is the *explicit rejection* of a model of cultural deficiency. When she took over as principal of John Howard School, Esther (using the same metaphor as Ruth and Anish) set out to prove that her students were as "warm and bright as any others, like flowers you plant and then watch grow and flourish." She says, "I share poetry with them. I get on the TV in the mornings and I try always to have a thought for the day to leave with the students, to get them going with their day. First I tell them how smart and bright they are."

Esther, like Ruth Simmons, comes from a large, relatively poor family. She says,

I learned to read when I was very young and I just took an interest in books because I could read about places that I hadn't been and was excited just to be able to read. So my parents instilled in me that education was the way up and out and we were poor but I did not realize it. We were also rich. We had such love in the family. We always had plenty to eat and clothes and shoes; so, you know, we were very poor but we didn't know it.

I guess I've always looked out for people who are less fortunate or disadvantaged. That's where my heart is because I know that this child that's sitting in this classroom today can be a doctor, lawyer, astronaut, president, whatever. And I want the children to know that they can be better—that they can have better, that they can go places, they can do things. It's up and out of poverty.

Her vision of children who are bright and curious, eager to learn and able to become anything to which they set their minds is in stark contrast to the mental images of educators who pathologize children of poverty, believing they have neither adequate resources nor appropriate home support to achieve to high academic levels. Moreover, Esther stipulates that when she talks about "up and out" she definitely does not mean "out of their culture, but simply out of poverty." She wants them to learn to "give back," to be creative, to see how much they will grow.

Esther's comments suggest another truth that educators often seem to forget. Poverty is relative and subjective. As teachers we can make students who don't have many material resources feel as if they have nothing to contribute to society in any way; yet one of the greatest gifts we may be able to give students is the sense that they can be poor in material goods but rich in human relationships, values, and personal attributes and abilities.

Esther does not stop with working on a personal and relational level with students. She tackles structures and policies that disadvantage her students. For example, she is convinced that too many children from minority groups are suspended from school. When teachers bring students to her for disciplinary action, she asks, "What's your job going to be if I kick all the kids out . . . who are you going to teach?" She tells them there are other ways to get children's attention and has her guidance counselor work with the kids who appear disruptive to find out what the underlying problem is. She does the same at the district level. Esther says she has gone to the district office or to a board meeting, where she has tried to demonstrate that too high a proportion of Hispanic or African American youth were either failing or being suspended from district schools and that something systemic needed to change.

Note that Esther does not assume that the problem lies in the students' class or ethnicity. She seeks to understand each child and the issues that drive him or her but she also tries to change the system. Pathologizing the lived experiences of children involves making assumptions based on some general characteristic. Working with children to identify their individual problems and to address their needs in meaningful ways is quite different.

Esther strives to use the high-stakes environment in Florida in which she works to advantage her students rather than simply comply with state regulations. Under her leadership, Jerico Elementary, her previous school, successfully moved off Florida's "critically low" list in just two years. The change was so dramatic that state officials ordered Esther to prove the legitimacy of her reported progress. She responded by taking school records and a video of the children to the state capitol. Esther had not, as officials seemed to believe, exempted large numbers of children or falsified the records in any way. Rather, she informed the legislative committee that just because an inordinately high percentage of students were on free or reduced lunch (94 percent), there was no reason to doubt their academic ability. Ultimately she convinced them that the improvement had actually occurred.

Using data as a basis for decisions about curriculum and instruction is second nature to Esther. She describes her starting point at her present school:

> First, we did some data analysis, looking at our data alone analyzing our curriculum. We looked at what was being tested and what we were teaching and we looked at how our curriculum was aligned to the standards and the benchmarks. We expect our students to master the standards and we examined whether we were teaching for mastery in the classroom. We try to find out what their skill deficits are and attempt to remediate; so if we're going to use the test, we need to find the kids that aren't going to do well on it and teach them. . . . We have a history of all our kids currently at the fourth grade level and all of their test scores. We are going to enter into our database the FCAT [Florida Comprehensive Achievement Test] scores in June or July whenever we get them.

Esther has no sense that students cannot succeed—just that educators at the school have to use the testing in a diagnostic way and to advocate for the achievement of all kids. Cummins (1989) would likely agree that Esther's approach exemplifies using assessment data for advocacy rather than legitimation.

Esther and her staff are determined not to let test preparation "water down the curriculum" or "push out all enrichment activities." She explained that they need to focus on improving learning, not on taking tests. She is convinced that a structured reading program (Success For All) has been good for her students. While many educators are seeking programs that are open-ended and creative, she has chosen a more structured reading program to meet the needs of her population. She clarifies:

> I think the structure is good for our children but I don't think the teachers necessarily like it. I think our children need it because there's not a lot of middle class structure at home and they come to school and they know what's expected. When we have a substitute in the classroom, the children can tell the sub what to do next, because the children have learned the procedure.

Esther's decision to use a structured reading program for this group of students is consistent with Delpit's (1990) insight that children from different cultural backgrounds may need more direct and more focused instructional programs to ensure that the expectations are made explicit. Both Delpit and Esther would agree that direct instruction should not be considered the only tool, simply one that may have a role to play in helping some children achieve success.

Esther consistently talks about putting the needs of the kids above those of the teachers, not only in choosing programs with enough structure but in creating a staff team that is willing to go the extra mile. "I think the most important thing probably is achieving some measure of success for every child everyday." She adds:

> I make sure we have excellent teachers in the classroom—people with a vision—a shared vision. People who are on a mission. People who are answering a calling and know that they are in the right place at the right time and working with the right kind of students [for them]. Once I get the staff that buys into the vision, and we have that shared vision, then the sky's the limit. Then we have students that believe in themselves and believe that they can achieve; we can do great things. . . . For teachers, that means staying late until 6 or 7 o'clock, participating in after school tutoring, doing whatever it takes to get the job done. . . . Those are the kind of people I want working for me.

Working with students from difficult home situations in a high-stakes environment demands a strong guiding vision, a deep conviction that the students can be successful, and a high level of commitment, described by Esther as "being on a mission." This image of teaching as going beyond the requirements of the contract recurs frequently in the discourse of principals whose low-income or minority student bodies achieve considerable academic success.

DIFFERENT, NOT DEFICIENT

Esther's approach to educational leadership clearly recognizes that children are unique and that their lived experiences differ from each other's—and often from those of their teachers. But she is equally unambiguous that different is not synonymous with deficient. This is the message she consistently delivers to staff, students, and anyone with whom she comes in contact. She openly discusses, confronts, and rejects both ethnocentric and middle-class beliefs and practices at all levels, classroom, school, and district.

Brenda, principal of Regal High School, whom we met in the previous chapter, talked about her relationships with students, saying that educators cannot develop good relationships with students without knowing who they are. She indicated that the need for a relationship goes two ways in that students also need to know their teachers. She described how new teachers are often surprised by the personal questions asked by the Maori students—questions like "Are you married? How many children do you have? Are you gay?" She indicated, "They demand a relationship." Unlike some teachers who are astounded at the boldness of the students and the "inappropriateness" of the personal questions they ask, Brenda recognizes that people use various strategies to become acquainted with others and to develop positive and trusting relationships. Although educators may be more comfortable with some approaches than others, it is important that we take every opportunity to make connections with our students.

Alicia, talking about the difficult economic situation of the Navajo reservation on which her school is located, states:

> Many of my students' parents have moved off the reservation to cities where they can work, leaving the youth with a single parent or with grandparents. This has caused a real breakdown in many of the families and the youth are feeling a real lack of support by the adults in their

world. There are few jobs in Red Rock. . . . The unemployment rate is about 88 percent. The jobs that are available are seasonal and low paying. Most of the youth have come to realize that receiving a good education will lead them to a choice that means moving away from home and family. The family ties are still quite strong and the decision to leave is not easy.

Pathologizing the experiences of the majority of the children because their parents are either absent or unemployed is not the answer. Educators need to understand that students' motivation to study may be adversely affected by frustration with the options open to them—succeed and leave, stay and be unemployed.

Moreover, the stories from Regal High School, Canyon Collegiate, and John Howard Elementary School remind us that issues of class are confounded with race, ethnicity, and gender both in our society and in common educational practices. Yet we rarely discuss how our perceptions and reactions work to advantage some children and disadvantage others, to build up the self-esteem and self-concept of some children and destroy those of others.

OVERCOMING THE IDENTITY CRISIS

This chapter has focused on the topic of identity and its relationship to educational practices. It has shown that educators who want to ensure an equitable education for all children need to create learning environments that do not advantage some children and disadvantage others simply because of ethnicity, home language, or family living conditions.

We have seen that although educators may not often overtly speak of students as the problem, we frequently speak of them as having problems with home, school, and adjusting to the mainstream, largely white society within which many of them will study or work following high school graduation. Sometimes it is children's ethnic or class or religious background that educators identify as the problem, at least within the safety of staff-room walls where such conversations usually take place.

Children whom we deem to be disadvantaged are often placed, for at least part of the day, in separate classes designed to teach them the academic skills they lack before we expect them to succeed in more academic courses. Yet, when educators respond differently, expecting children to be curious, to want to learn, and to achieve at high levels, the outcomes are dramatically different. No longer is it necessary to talk about achievement gaps between advantaged and disadvantaged students; we can begin to tell stories of success. We can and we must create spaces to discuss many kinds of problems, indeed to expand and enlarge the curriculum itself that so that it does not present middle-class experiences as the only reality.

Educators rarely take the opportunity to critically examine these typical responses. We fail to realize that problems and pathologies are not the same thing. Every individual faces challenges, obstacles, and problems. They are a normal part of living that we learn to handle. Pathologies, however, we treat; they are not normal, but alien. Sometimes we even need to quarantine or isolate them. And there is no doubt that some children (for example, those who experience sexual abuse) are subjected to behavior that is not only inappropriate but illegal, behavior that needs to be treated and also punished. Educators must distinguish between the two and deal with each appropriately. Problems must be addressed rather than ignored. Inappropriate treatment of children should be met with moral outrage—directed not at the children but at the perpetrators. But normal parts of daily living must be included.

Transformative leaders assist teachers to bring the lived experiences of all students into the classroom, help children develop more comprehensive understandings of experiences that are legitimate and normal (although not necessarily easy or desirable), and facilitate the development of positive self-images for all children. Just as ignoring visible differences is a way of marginalizing others, so is continuing silence about social differences. Some differences may be less visible than others, but certainly not less important to children's sense of self-worth and identity.

I have described ways in which educators make harmful assumptions about children and provided illustrations of ways in which transformative cross-cultural leaders have moved beyond pathologizing the lived experiences of children to ensure they may fully participate in a community of difference. I have stressed that in this community, children must not be made to feel ashamed of who they are or of their home experiences.

I have tried to show how educators can marginalize and disadvantage children by assuming that *our* social realities are the norm, by claiming to be color-, class-, or spiritually blind, and by pathologizing the experiences of children from different backgrounds with different lived experiences. Each of these common educational approaches can have devastating effects on children's self-esteem, self-confidence, and, most importantly, on the ways in which they construct and internalize their identity. When we permit difference to become deficiency—and pathologize all experience that is different from our own—we are preventing people like Anish from enriching our lives and, often, from realizing their full potential.

Good intentions are not enough. As educators striving to create school communities for which difference is foundational, we must ensure that we do not pathologize it, that the stories of our students are not stories of marginalization, separation, discrimination, and injustice. As transformative cross-cultural leaders, we will challenge our assumptions and expand our practices. And we will help teachers do the same. We will provide all students and staff, from all classes and cultures, opportunities based on the legitimacy of their lived experiences to participate fully in the educational experiences of our schools.

We must develop a critical consciousness, what Maxine Greene (1977) might call "wide-awakeness" to our own situation and that of others. As educational leaders, it is imperative that we both ask questions and tell our stories. Cronon states,

> It is undoubtedly true that we all constantly tell ourselves stories to remind ourselves who we are, how we got to be that person, and what we want to become. The same is true not just of individuals but of communities and societies: we use our histories to remember ourselves, just as we use our prophecies as tools for exploring what we do or do not wish to become. (1992, 1369)

The stories of Anish, Esther, and Ruth Simmons all speak eloquently to us. We also need to tell our own stories, for we each have a tale to tell. Some of my most memorable experiences as an educator have come through the use of narrative. On several occasions, Anish and I have told some of our personal stories in order to help school-based leaders understand the power of narrative and its relation to the development of a positive self-identity and to encourage them to share their own experiences. Following each presentation, we have had educators approach us, sometimes in tears, to tell us of the ways in which hearing our stories had liberated them from some past hurt and given them courage to share with us and with others.

By encouraging others and sharing their own stories, educators will learn that difference is normal, to be neither celebrated nor denigrated. It just is. The differences in our schools provide a rich tapestry of human existence that is the starting point for a deeply democratic, academically excellent, and socially just education. No one is defined by a single factor or characteristic. Indeed, individual and group identities are formed by continuous and dynamic interplays of social, political, and cultural factors as well as genetic and inherited characteristics.

Sharing stories is one way to begin to understand these differences. Then, to take appropriate account of these factors, educators and educational leaders must adopt a set of guiding criteria, perhaps the ones I suggested in chapter 3, to act as benchmarks for the development of just, empathetic, democratic, and optimistic education. We must learn to collect data, disaggregate them, examine them, critique them, and use them, as Cummins (1989) would posit, for advocacy purposes instead of for legitimizing present oppressive and pathologizing educational practices.

Difference is a foundational quality of our society and our education system. If we are to achieve academic excellence and social justice in education, our leaders must be transformative—seeking to transform not only our practices of schooling but our social understandings. We must ensure that educators do not celebrate some differences and pathologize others. Instead, we must open our curriculum, our policies, our hearts, and our minds to challenge inequities, eliminate pathologies, and ensure inclusive and respectful education for all students.

We need to encourage all of our students to tell their stories. But before we do, we must create conditions in which our students will thrive, conditions that nourish their souls, conditions out of which our students will be able to tell stories of acceptance, achievement, and hope. From this soil they will know, to paraphrase Ruth Simmons, that everything belongs to them, that there is nothing that is withheld from them simply because of the conditions of their birth.

NOTES

1. The translation is mine; the published article is in French: "une façon d'être présent aux plus profondes réalités de son propre monde" (p. 12).

2. Yet we both recognize that in a different context, my church or his temple, the discourse is quite different, emphasizing the uniqueness and validity of a particular belief system. While this may have a place in a religious organization, it is not the spiritual discourse that has a place in an educational community of difference.

3. This is one way of identifying the severity of a child's condition: low-incidence conditions appear in very small (low) numbers in the general population and hence demand high levels of accommodation or special care. High-incidence, in contrast, are those whose conditions appear with more frequency, and who require comparatively lower levels of academic accommodation in the typical classroom.

4. Free or reduced lunch programs are funded in the United States by the federal government, which establishes fiscal targets and criteria for eligibility based in large part on family income.

CHAPTER 6

Breaking the Boundaries:
Extending Community

This chapter focuses on ways to transform our thinking about community by disrupting, even breaking, some existing boundaries. In the first part of the chapter, I demonstrate how parents, guardians, and community members might be involved in schools in more meaningful ways. Then I ask educators to transform their thinking about the relationships between students' lives at home and the school curriculum. I reflect on ways we might reconceptualize parental involvement,[1] focusing, in more mutually beneficial ways, on what educators and parents expect of each other. These are ideas we need to explore if we are to tear down some conventional walls and develop the concept of a *community of difference*.

PARENTAL INVOLVEMENT IN A NEW ZEALAND SCHOOL

During my sabbatical in New Zealand, I wanted to visit some multicultural schools that had introduced relevant and successful changes to meet the needs of their heterogeneous student bodies. As I reported in chapter 2, an official from the Regional Office of the Ministry of Education was extremely helpful, identifying programs and personally introducing me to educational leaders. On one occasion, he arranged a visit to Central Elementary School. Central School was particularly interesting, he told me, for its instructional incorporation of cultural content. It would provide an excellent example of how a school could break traditional boundaries and extend its community.

We arrived on one of the designated "culture" afternoons and visited several classrooms in which teachers were engaged in supporting student cultures and providing language instruction through songs, games, and dances. I was introduced, welcomed, and given a tour by the principal and the man from the ministry.

I returned several times to Central School. During my next visit, I went first to a core academic class where my attention was immediately drawn to several boys who were obviously distracted and not paying attention. A little later, I attended a Maori culture class taught by a husband and wife from the community. He is Hawaiian; she is Maori. Three afternoons a week they arrived, with their commitment and cultural knowledge, a guitar, and their eight-month-old son in a stroller. They were given full responsibility for the Maori program. As I watched, I became aware of the same boys I had seen uninvolved and disruptive in the earlier class. They were standing in the front row, muscles taut, gaze alert and intense, swaying and stamping to the traditional rhythms and chanting the words of the Maori songs. I had seen no group of students, anywhere, more completely involved in their classroom activity or better disciplined—and no classroom teachers more actively engaged with their children than these parent-instructors were.

I moved on. So did the man and woman. I caught up with the woman first. She was now surrounded by girls with *poi* balls.[2] Twirling, swinging, slapping, singing, the balls moved to the music. The older girls worked with the younger ones, teaching them and helping them master the intricacies of the patterns and actions of the balls.

I next found her husband, who invited me to move out to the porch because the boys wanted to learn how to welcome me in the official way. A section of the porch was designated as the *marae,* a boy selected to represent the *tangata whenua* (people of the *marae*) and perform the *haka,* a traditional dance punctuated by stamping, fierce gestures, and facial distortions to arouse fear in the heart of the visitor. He learned to issue a *wero,* the traditional challenge to determine whether those who approached (*manuhiri*) came in peace or in combat. Maori language and traditional cultural knowledge were being passed on in the school, even as the children welcomed me and conversed with me. I was struck by the involvement and dedication of these parents, and by the engagement and excitement of the students.

I reflected on what I was seeing—parents in charge of classrooms, children engaged in cultural activities as part of their curriculum, a representative of the Ministry of Education touting the program as exemplary and taking time to accompany me there himself.

COMMUNITY INVOLVEMENT IN A FIJIAN SCHOOL

Some months later, I had another unusual and challenging experience. I visited a four-room Fijian school on a small island an hour and a half by boat off the west coast of Viti Levu, the main island. The smaller island has a population of about four hundred people, three small villages, and one school. In the fifth-grade classroom, a rope strung across the room, corner to corner, held completed pictures from coloring books, attached to the line with clothespins. This was the only artwork visible. The library room was the pride and joy of the principal. Its few shelves held a small set of Bible stories, a modest collection of locally published bilingual books (in Fijian and English), and a motley assortment of other materials, mostly books discarded or donated by tourists and cruise ship passengers.

Most people would describe this school as ill-equipped and very poor—its equipment consisted of a generator that was turned on a few hours a day and a photocopier. It was, however, extremely rich in community involvement. I watched as lunchtime approached. Mothers, chatting and laughing as they walked across the grassy field, carried baskets of cooked lunch. They spread their brightly colored *sulus* to cover the concrete floor of the porch, sat in family groups (with their children and extended family members), and ate lunch together. It was apparent that parents and children were involved together in the daily life of the school.

Perhaps the most striking demonstration of community involvement is student preparation for national exams. Everyone from the island's three villages becomes involved with preparation for the exams held at the end of the sixth and eighth grades. For two months prior to the exams, all children from these grades live with one of the teachers. The children's parents still provide the meals, taking lunch to the school during the day and providing dinner before the extra classes held in the evening hours. If a child comes from a neighboring village, relatives take turns staying in the school village for a week and doing the cooking for all extended family members preparing for exams.

The whole community celebrates exam day. It begins with a large breakfast held in the school. This is followed by speech making, greetings from the chief, good wishes from members of the school committee, and comments from other members of the community. Then all present proudly shake the hands of the children, congratulating them on their achievements thus far and wishing them success. The outcomes of the exam and grades are still to come, but the children know they have the unconditional support and encouragement of the whole community. The principal told me that she could not determine whether the celebration had any impact on student grades (it was held for its own sake); but she could state that knowing they had community support seemed to have encouraged an increased number of students to continue their education at the high school on the main island.

The vision of success as a shared responsibility is consistent with Ogbu's (1992) recommendations that parents and communities need to be empowered to take more responsibility for the academic achievement of their children. He states that it is particularly important for parents from minority communities to become involved, act as role models, and demonstrate the importance of education.

INVOLVING THE COMMUNITY IN
AN EASTERN CANADIAN SCHOOL

Memorable school visits were not limited to faraway and exotic places. I visited a small elementary school in eastern Canada. Fourteen Days in December has become an annual event at Emily Carr School in which the first two weeks of December are set aside to focus on community values. In 1995 the theme of the fourteen-day celebration was "Peace." In 1996 the theme was "Gifts That Can't Be Bought," highlighting values of helpfulness, friendship, caring, and community. At the beginning of each celebration, the youngest member of each family takes home a package containing a schedule of daily events, a candle, and an invitation to the family to create a theme poster (for example, in 1995, a depiction of "what peace means to us"). Throughout the celebration, a series of family activities, conducted both at home and at school, support the chosen theme. At school, a new idea connected to social justice and care issues and related to the annual theme is introduced each morning on school radio PEACE broadcasts and expanded throughout the day in classroom discussions and activities. This example of a school-wide curricular emphasis has its origins, at a profound level, in the concerns of the wider school community. It unites home and school in shared educational experiences and conversations around a common theme.

TOWARD MORE DEMOCRATIC PARENTAL INVOLVEMENT

The three schools—in Fiji, New Zealand, and eastern Canada—lead us to ask a number of questions about the traditional ways in which educators conceptualize things like parental involvement, community participation, and relevant curriculum. What are appropriate roles for parents, guardians, and other caregivers? In what ways can a community show support for its school? How can a school show its support for families and the community? How can we make curriculum more relevant to and more reflective of a given community?

Sadly, in many developed countries parents taking sole responsibility for classes and programs would be frowned on by unions or forbidden by legislation. Likewise, out of a concern for health and safety and a desire to avoid litigation, parents are often forbidden to bring food into the school. Yet there is much we can learn by careful examination of these less traditional ways in which parents provide support for educational endeavors. How can we broaden our interpretation of the regulations that govern us to prevent unnecessary constraints? Can we, for example, comply with the spirit of a law that states that a teacher must be in control of a classroom and, at the same time, encourage parents with special talents to provide leadership for children? How can we think differently about parental and community involvement?

Both experience and research (Coleman et al. 1996; Comer 1988; Epstein et al. 1997) have shown that parental involvement is associated with improved academic performance.[3] Policy makers have become so convinced of the importance of parental involvement that in the United States, funding for some federal programs (Title I and Title VII) and for many state programs is tied to having an acceptable plan for parental participation. In New Zealand, schools are governed by local school boards composed of parents and other community members. In Canada, several provinces have legislative provisions for parent advisory councils, with different levels of decision-making power. The most recent mandate (in 2002) requires parents to have the majority voice in newly mandated councils in British Columbia. Parent advisory boards are also mandatory in Alberta, New Brunswick, Newfoundland, and Quebec, but voluntary in the other five provinces. Among the provinces, the amount of pressure and support offered by the provincial government, as well as the degree of decision-making power held by the council, varies considerably (Plant 1998). Most legislative initiatives are predicated on the assumption that parents should be directly involved in the policies and practices of schools.

Despite many formal mechanisms for parental involvement in school activities and decision making, most opportunities are carefully controlled and orchestrated. Some educators believe that too much parental involvement interferes with the teachers' work; others fear it encourages undue familiarity and increases criticism, confrontation, and conflict. Additionally, many educators report that large numbers of parents, generally those who come from low-income, less-educated, non-English-speaking, or ethnic-minority families are uninvolved in their children's education. Some interpret this as a lack of caring; others assume it is evidence that parents believe that education is best left to the school experts; still others say that parents don't have time for school.

Reconceptualizing parental and community involvement may not help us to attract more parents and community members to the school. It may not result in greater community support for our educational programs. It may not result in improved test scores, but it will likely help educators better meet the needs of children and their families.

Lopez notes that

within education's discourse, parent involvement has typically been an *a priori* given: a universal signifier that refers to specific types of activities. Involvement, for example, evokes images of bake sales, fund-raisers, PTA/PTO, and "back-to-school" nights. It connotes parents serving in the capacity of volunteers in schools, taking time to attend school activ-

ities, as well as participating on parent advisory councils and/or governance boards. (2001, 1)

Most considerations of educational reform have paid little attention to
ways in which parents and the wider community may take more active
and direct roles, as in the examples of parents taking responsibility for
the culture classes at Central Elementary School, community involvement in preparing students for exams in Fiji, or the Fourteen Days in
December initiative based in community social realities and concerns
in Canada. Conversely, there has been little discussion about how the
school may take a larger role in the life of the surrounding community.

I suggest that the answer does not lie in finding strategies that
"work" to bring in "uninvolved parents" to participate in activities in
the school. In many ways, this desire continues to pathologize the lived
experiences of many families. Rather, cross-cultural leaders wanting to
create a community of difference require an approach that is inclusive
and respectful of all students and their families. School communities
need to reflect carefully on what they mean by terms like *parental support, parental involvement,* or *parental partnerships,* and expand their
ideas of how they may be recognized, encouraged, and celebrated. We
need to carefully identify which individuals and groups from the community have little or no contact with the school and then ask questions
about why they are uninvolved, what they could offer the school and,
perhaps most importantly, what the school could offer them. We need
to adopt *transformative* strategies to enlarge the boundaries of our
thinking and action about the role of parents and community members
in developing and maintaining a school community.

Esther's Experience

A popular American program that offers recognition to schools that
enlarge their boundaries, welcoming parents and community members
into the schools and moving their children into various activities in the
wider community, is called Five Star Schools. Esther, whom we met in
chapter 5, identifies John Howard Elementary School as a five-star
school. The award recognizes that the school has achieved excellence
in five designated program areas, including partnerships with business,

an active and representative parent council, representative family and community involvement, a volunteer force that provides the school with a large number of volunteer hours, and payback to the community accomplished by students. Thus the program encourages considerable interaction, in multiple ways, between school and community.

Esther told us that five-star schools are required to have a minimum of 52 percent[4] of parents involved in activities such as active PTO (parent-teacher organization) membership, presence at meetings and parent conferences, and attendance at and support for school programs. They must have a solid cadre of business supporters as well as a strong force of volunteers who help in a variety of ways (for example, tutoring, assisting teachers in the classroom, or helping with field trips). The philosophy is that even in schools with high levels of poverty, children need to learn to give, rather than always be "on the take." Thus five-star schools have to demonstrate that over 50 percent of the children perform some kind of project for the community.

At John Howard School, children participate in two main schoolwide projects as well as others devised by their classroom teachers. One involves bringing in canned food during Thanksgiving for the local care center for needy families; the other is the Make-A-Wish Foundation. Children are directly involved in their communities. The fact that only 10 percent of the county schools have attained a five-star rating is a source of pride for this school and its students, often best known for their problems rather than for their contributions.

I asked Esther whether her previous school, Jerico Elementary, had participated in the Five Star Program. There Esther and her staff had made an attempt to "welcome parents at all hours of the day." A regular newsletter was sent home in English and Spanish. Prekindergarten classes were instituted and non-English-speaking parents were invited to learn common vocabulary words with their children. A high school equivalency (GED) tutoring program for parents was introduced on Monday and Wednesday evenings. On "Wonderful Wednesdays" breakfast was served to both parents and children; on "Drive Through Fridays" parents could drop their children at school and then pick up a cold breakfast and an accompanying sheet of parenting tips. A "Make and Take" room was established to help parents create educational materials to help their children at home. Parents were asked to help students complete practice activities designed to aid their test-taking skills (Shields and Oberg 2000, 37). Despite all these initiatives, Esther did not believe she could document the required parental involvement necessary to become a five-star school.

Esther is an incredible educational leader. She is tireless in her efforts for her students; she rejects a deficit approach and constantly strives to improve their experiences. She pushes, prods, and challenges everyone in her school community to help her students to achieve.

MORE TRANSFORMATIVE APPROACHES

Esther's stories about her present and previous schools raise a number of questions about how best to conceptualize and encourage parental involvement. I am in no way suggesting that programs such as the Five Star Program are not valuable or that they should be stopped. But I believe they sometimes fall into the trap of defining parental involvement too narrowly. We need to be careful not to delineate in middle-class terms the specific practices that may be considered legitimate when there may be more inclusive ways of conceptualizing parental involvement, ways that would be more conducive to the creation of a community of difference.

Sometimes educators expend a great deal of energy doing things *for* children and families rather than *with* them. This may be particularly true in schools with high populations of lower-class or minority children but is not restricted to them. In one school I studied in a middle-class neighborhood in a large city, teachers and staff spent hours making craft items for a Christmas craft sale at which children were able to purchase affordable items for their parents for Christmas. What tremendous dedication on the part of the teachers! What a nice idea! But I still wonder how the experience might have been different had there been an inclusive invitation to all members of the community to participate through making gifts for the children to buy.

Communicating Expectations

Lisa Delpit (1990), as we have seen, asserts the importance of making rules explicit. It is critical to apply this concept to parental involvement in schools. Teachers and principals have described their efforts to do "everything" to encourage parental involvement, phoning them, translating newsletters, and sending invitations. But when I ask if they have helped parents make meaning of the possible experiences, they tend to look at me bewildered and worried. Do they, for example, describe what coming to a "multicultural night" might involve? Would parents be expected to pay? To dress in ethnic costumes? To say anything? Who would be there? Where would they sit? Should they come with their child or not? Making the rules explicit, helping people know what to expect, is one way of alleviating fear and facilitating involvement in activities that may be unfamiliar. Giving adequate information in advance, and then having students or other parents assigned to welcome specific families and walk them through unknown activities, reduces their anxiety and the risk of being embarrassed or humiliated and lays the foundation for new, more inclusive relationships.

I recall the pain in the voice of a colleague in Utah who recounted the experience of his second- and third-grade daughters on the first day of school in their new community. He told me that his daughters had set out happily in the morning, proudly wearing new sundresses tied at the shoulder, made by their mother. He was dismayed by their confusion and hurt when they returned home refusing to wear the dresses again. They eventually told their parents that they had been teased about their new dresses because they did not have sleeves. His children were white, like most of their classmates; but the unwritten rule of the dominant Mormon culture was that bare shoulders were unacceptable. How much pain could have been avoided had the implicit dress code been made explicit and clearly communicated to newcomers and their parents!

My intent here is neither to suggest that the norms were inappropriate nor that the newcomers' practices should automatically be accepted. Rather, the illustration serves to remind educators that as schools become increasingly diverse unquestioned acceptance of the implicit rules of the status quo may have unpleasant, unanticipated consequences that marginalize or exclude some children.

Making rules explicit is a starting point. The activity itself needs to be meaningful and inviting if we are to convince parents that their participation is important. Carl Allison, the principal of a small elementary school on the Navajo reservation, wanted to bring more parents into his school. He used his imagination and raised some funds to support a new kind of experience. Together he and his parent council devised a plan. Carl sent invitations to all parents to a "workshop extravaganza," explaining clearly what they might expect. Parents were first invited to a free dinner, prepared and served in the school cafeteria. After dinner, they were reminded of the rules: each adult was expected to attend a series of four half-hour workshops (helping your child with math, disciplining your child, detecting drug or alcohol abuse, building self-esteem, etc.) offered between 6:00 P.M. and 8:00 P.M. At each workshop, parents were given a token to purchase goods attractively displayed in the school library. Families could pool their tokens to purchase such things as colored pencils, crayons, rulers, picture books, and craft materials. The evening ended with great enthusiasm as families gathered in the library to claim their rewards.

Ensuring that parents knew in advance what was to happen and what would be expected of them helped guarantee the success of the evening. The event proved so popular that parents soon began asking when the next one was to be held. What was particularly interesting was that, despite the initial appeal of free food and tokens, it was the parents' explicitly expressed desire for more information like that presented during the workshops that prompted institution of the evening as a biannual event.

If Carl had believed that these parents were not interested in their children's school success, it is unlikely he would have expended the effort required to organize and host this event. By seeking ways to meet parents' needs and develop better relationships with them, he discovered, as he had suspected, that they were neither uninvolved nor disinterested.

CHANGING NORMS OF INVOLVEMENT: INCLUDING THE WHOLE COMMUNITY

Although making rules explicit may help parents feel more comfortable with school activities, bringing parents into the school is only one of many ways in which they may be involved in the education of their child. Educators need to recognize the importance of parental and community support that goes beyond many of the commonly known typologies.

In his study of migrant workers whose children had experienced outstanding school success and graduated in the top 10 percent of their classes, Lopez (2001) finds that the parents rarely, if ever, interacted with school personnel; neither did they reinforce particular school lessons or help students complete assigned work. They did, however, take their children to work alongside them in the fields or orchards, teaching them the value of hard labor. Parents reported that they explicitly told their children that if they wanted more options and other possible careers, they needed to complete school successfully; otherwise, they would have no option but field work. In that way, an activity that some educators might perceive as detracting from the central work of schools, having children assist with the wage-earning activity of their parents, became a positive orientation of the children toward schooling.

This is an example of what Christenson and colleagues (1997) call home-based rather than school-based involvement. Although most middle-class teachers and parents assume that involvement is based around school activities, the support for schooling and the potential positive influence of these conversations can hardly be disputed.

Ogbu's work (Ogbu 1992; Ogbu and Simons 1998) provides additional insight into ways in which parents may support schooling through home and community activities. Using a broad brush, Ogbu identifies minority students as belonging to one of three categories: refugees, voluntary minority groups, or involuntary minority groups. He says that these distinctions explain (in part) why children from certain groups tend to achieve to high standards in our schools, while children from other groups tend to be overrepresented in statistics of failure and school dropout rates. He indicates that designation as a member of a voluntary or involuntary group often varies with historical and national characteristics. Hence, in North America, Asian immigrant children tend to perform very well in school, while Native American, Latino, and African American children often struggle to achieve academic success. In other countries, the composition of the groups might be different; for example, a Korean child in Japan might be considered a member of an involuntary minority group and find success more elusive than she would in North America. South Asian children often achieve to higher levels in Australia or New Zealand than in many parts of Canada. And so on.

Ogbu describes some pervasive educational characteristics of students from the latter two groups. Voluntary minorities are people who have emigrated, generally because they "desire more economic well-being, better overall opportunities, and/or greater political freedom" (Ogbu 1992, 8). Although they may experience some initial difficulties adapting to a new school system, in general their expectations of a better life help them find ways to respond positively to events, including schooling, in their new culture.

Involuntary minority students come from groups that have been marginalized, conquered, subjugated, perhaps even enslaved, in the historical development of a country. They tend to demonstrate what Ogbu calls "secondary cultural characteristics [they] develop . . . to cope with their subordination" (1992, 8). Secondary characteristics may include differences in style, cultural inversion, and "ambivalent or oppositional social or collective identities vis-à-vis the White American social identity" (p. 9).

In other words, Ogbu (1992) suggests that voluntary minorities tend to accommodate, following the rules and learning new ways, in the belief that they will succeed and prosper. Involuntary minorities are inclined to believe there is nothing they can do to be successful because their subordinate position and repeated experience suggest that the sys tem prevents them from succeeding. Ogbu says that secondary characteristics are likely to be extensive and persistent and hence require extraordinary responses on the part of both educators and minority communities themselves if they are to be overcome.

Ogbu suggests that action needs to occur in a number of ways. He feels strongly that most multicultural education fails because we educators have not really understood minority cultures and also because we have ignored "the minority students' own responsibility for their academic performance" (1992, 6). He is not suggesting another version of deficit thinking or blaming the victim. He is advocating opening up the system to be more inclusive of members of minority communities who have the essential cultural knowledge to support the achievement of their students.

Educators must understand and build on the home cultures of students; we need to develop ways to help students recognize and deal with secondary cultural characteristics, to find ways to overcome the sense that they must become white in order to succeed. Educators should not place the blame on a minority community and tell it to shape up. Rather, we need to work together with the communities from which children come.

Ogbu acknowledges that many of the requisite changes can "most effectively be brought about by community effort" (1992, 12). Again, this does not mean communities are to blame for any current lack of involvement, but we must invite them to take larger roles and create spaces for that to happen. Educators must find ways to persuade communities that some things are best done locally (for example, showing support for education, developing extensive systems of role models). Minority community involvement is particularly critical to enhancing children's sense of belonging, which in turn may have a positive impact on subsequent school achievement.

The following discussion of an innovative program embraced by a minority community demonstrates the possibilities inherent in this approach.

Just Therapy

One example of community involvement strategies may be found in The Academy. In chapter 3, we were introduced to The Academy, a very academic school with an outstanding local reputation located in a predominantly high-socioeconomic area in a large city. The school is adjacent to a First Nations reserve[5] and is the designated high school for the reserve students.

Over the years, the school made various attempts to help its First Nations students stay in school and experience academic success. For example, one ongoing modification was the establishment of an aboriginal support program. Designed to provide First Nations students with a supportive, culturally appropriate environment, the program as initially implemented was another example of extremely good intentions misplaced. Students who were identified as needing extra support were assigned to the program and found an accepting environment in the chosen classroom (a windowless room in the basement near the cafeteria).

When I visited the support program, I found students relaxing, sitting and lounging on desks, eating or chatting if they wanted, all in the name (I was told) of developing a caring and supportive environment within a generally hostile school climate. I do not downplay the importance of creating a supportive environment; indeed a community of difference requires it. But it cannot stand alone. In this program, there was no explicit discussion among educators or between teachers and students of what it might take to help participants succeed at school, why they found the general school environment marginalizing, or how to make school a more accepting and acceptable place. Thus it was not surprising to learn, as one recent analysis showed (Chartrand 2001), that of thirty-nine First Nations students in the school, only five were enrolled in grades 11 or 12, and only one was on the honor roll. Despite the support program, most students who had begun in eighth grade had already dropped out. Moreover, a disproportionate 20 percent of the aboriginal students were enrolled in alternate (not university recognized) courses.

One year, the relationship between the school and the reserve community changed. Members of the council wanted to have a greater influence in how social institutions, including schools, provided support for aboriginal students. They invited some of the teachers and a vice principal from the school to a meeting. In attendance were some New Zealand Maori leaders who had developed an approach called Just Therapy to empower members of marginalized communities and provide more "respectful and effective support to their people" (Chartrand 2001, 31). The reserve made the choice to implement Just Therapy and the school agreed to become a partner.

The vice principal described the process: "The school began by opening a dialogue with the First Nation community in the form of a monthly meeting to discuss the progress of the First Nation children" (Chartrand 2001, 34). He described how representatives from elementary and secondary schools as well as the Band's Education Authority met monthly, alternating the location for the meetings between the school and the community. He portrayed the surprise of the community that teachers would "go to the reserve to discuss their children" (p. 34). He sums up the experience in these words:

> This change of setting permitted increased dialogue, providing an opportunity for the First Nations community to articulate some of its needs, and gave the school the opportunity to respond. The outcome was that members of the reserve community began to feel that they were part of the school. (pp. 36–37)

The new standards of involvement and interaction were quite different from the previous norms. They were now negotiated on terms proposed and understood by members of the reserve community, who demonstrated to educators from the school that the community could be supportive and engaged in education away from the school site. Moreover, they demonstrated that when community members are given the opportunity to solve their own problems, their solutions, although different from the typical script of schooling, could be mutually beneficial. For example, the vice principal explained, without the Just Therapy program the school would never have embarked on an unconventional but successful "horseback riding program as a form of therapy for abused girls." The school also benefited from artists and elders who began to feel comfortable participating in school programs; the community benefited by making explicit its values and sharing them with the school community, beginning the "process of claiming the education of their children" (Chartrand 2001, 61).

When educators begin to open up the school community, boundaries will be broken and expectations about what can or cannot be done and about how we must proceed will change. As we seek to develop shared ownership and collaboratively determine the goals to be achieved, the solutions may be unconventional. But because there is more ownership and wider participation in the process, the solutions also have the potential to be more democratic, just, empathetic, and optimistic, not only for students but for their families as well.

BREAKING THE BOUNDARIES OF FIXED CURRICULUM

Many people have noted that curriculum consists of several explicit and implicit components. English, for example, identifies the formal, informal, and hidden curriculum (1992, 8–9). He suggests that many teachers simply focus on the formal, written, and tested curricula, ignoring the informal and hidden. And yet the informal curriculum often plays a large role in the daily experiences of children. Teachers spend a considerable amount of time each day teaching the implicit values of the informal curriculum by urging children to stay in their seats, work cooperatively, share, put away equipment, and so on. What is missing is a recognition of the hidden curriculum, which requires specific cultural knowledge in order to fully participate in the educational activities of the classroom.

Madeleine Grumet believes that "when we are educating someone, we are introducing that person, young or old, to ways of being and acting in the world that are new to his or her experience" (1995, 17). She defines curriculum as the "conversation that makes sense of things . . . the process of making sense with a group of people of the systems that shape and organize the world we can think about together" (p. 19).

This understanding of curriculum helps us understand the term *hidden curriculum*. If we teach the poem "Mending Wall" with the objective of helping students understand that walls are sometimes unnecessary, that they do not necessarily make good neighbors, we must stop to examine the underlying assumptions. What knowledge do we assume that students bring to make sense of the poem? What metaphors are used? If students do not have experience with farming, cows, orchards, fields, and walls, then how can they be expected to understand the poem? If, for example, we have students who have grown up in the inner city or in refugee camps, how can we engage in conversations that help them make sense of the ideas of the poem? What metaphors and images that we use in our instruction require specific kinds of social, political, and cultural knowledge in order to participate fully in the conversations? These are important questions to answer if we want to ensure that our systems of meaning are just, empathetic, democratic, and optimistic. Freire (1970) puts this well: "To read the word is to read the world."

Using the definition of curriculum as sense-making conversations and relationships, educators will realize the importance of dialogue with parents and other community members in order to find ways to connect the content, knowledge, values, and perspectives of the formal curriculum to the lived experiences of students. Because there will be many perspectives in a community of difference about the systems that shape our lives, educators will strive to create opportunities for multiple voices to be heard.

One example of a school attempting to interact in more inclusive and respectful ways with its community is the elementary school with the Fourteen Days in December program. Emily Carr School is located in a high-poverty, predominantly white community in Atlantic Canada.[6] About 30 percent of the children come from a nearby trailer park and many families live below the poverty level. A colleague who studied Emily Carr School states that much of what is done in the school is "an attempt to recognize and account for social conditions in the community and school. . . . What has developed at the school is not the curriculum of excuses and diminished expectations too common in marginalized community schools" (Vibert, Portelli, and Leighteizer 1998, 136).

During my first visit to the school, I had difficulty determining which adults were parents and which were teachers. Whoever was closest to a ringing phone answered it; whoever saw a child in need of assistance or a hug offered it. Although parent involvement had once been limited to a few volunteers from the richest of the school's catchment areas, this had changed, and the school's very strong teacher-parent co-op was involved in ongoing consultation about many aspects of school policy.

Principal Joey Kyle and her assistant principals had expended considerable effort and many hours of their own time approaching people in their own contexts (meeting parents around a neighbor's kitchen table or holding meetings in community halls) and had gradually developed strong, positive relationships with many parents who had previously been excluded from the life of the school.

School curriculum, although based on the required provincial core, is "rooted in a vision of the school as grounded in and belonging to the community" (Vibert, Portelli, and Leighteizer 1998, 152). One example is the program mentioned earlier, in which families were informed about and invited to participate in the ongoing December celebration. A mathematics unit that was developed in part as a response to a student disciplinary incident is another good illustration. On one occasion, some fifth-grade students were caught shoplifting expensive sunglasses from a neighborhood pharmacy. The owner came to the school and, with the teacher and administrators, developed a strategy. The students would return the sunglasses and apologize to the owner. In addition, the whole class would engage in a study of the economics of shoplifting, its effect on prices and on the store owner's ability to hire help. Because some of the children's parents worked as retail clerks, or were unemployed but actively seeking employment, the graphic lesson relating student behavior to social unemployment and economics helped them to both better understand and begin to take responsibility for the welfare of the wider community.

As one teacher reported, "Whatever the curriculum needs to be at the time" becomes the curriculum. Teachers were not so attached to the prescribed curriculum that they could not take time to explore significant issues from students' daily lives.

Another example from Emily Carr School relates to what became known as "the" poverty discussion. When an article in a local paper described the school population as having many families living in poverty, a number of the more affluent families objected to the characterization and some children expressed a feeling of shame. The sixth-grade class undertook to investigate the social construction of poverty. One student wondered if responding to the article would reinforce the reporter's perspective.

Another responded: "Violence and poverty are things we have to talk about if we want them to go away. The article isn't personal . . . and people taking it that way makes it worse . . . like there's some shame in being poor."

When a different classmate said that the terminology of the article, "many live in poverty," seemed sort of shameful, another reminded him, "But poverty is not poor people's fault. And not having everything you need shouldn't make you feel like less of a person."

Listening to fifth- and sixth-grade students talking about the relationship between shoplifting and employment and grappling with issues related to the social construction of poverty is a sobering experience. Many adults never come to grips with the issue as these children were doing. As a result, many educators feel unprepared to address such topics or help their students explore them. Many believe that young children cannot handle such complex and significant issues. The

Emily Carr experience proves us wrong. Children can, and must, be encouraged to bring the social issues of their daily lives into the curriculum as well as the social life of the classroom.

The inclusive nature of Emily Carr School is not simply demonstrated in the various programs offered for, and by, parent and community volunteers; it pervades every aspect of school life, including the curriculum. The school is characterized by inclusion and a deep respect for the ability of all individuals to think critically about the issues that confront them, find solutions to communal problems, and participate fully in the life of the community. The school staff members do not pathologize the lived experiences of children; they do not pathologize the experiences of the families or community. They build on them.

Parents often attend professional development activities with teachers. They have learned that the school belongs to the community, and hence that they have a right and a responsibility to be involved in decision making. The considerable effort made by administrators and teachers to ensure that everyone feels welcome at the school at any time has paid off.

Extending our understanding of the relationships between school and community is fundamental to broadening the boundaries of our thinking and creating a more inclusive community of difference.

TRANSFORMING SCHOOL-COMMUNITY RELATIONSHIPS

Creating the expectation that the community is a resource for the school but the school is also a community resource is at the heart of transformative cross-cultural leadership.[7] It goes beyond the traditional meanings of parent involvement most frequently characterized by Epstein's typology. She identifies six types of parental involvement: parenting, communicating, volunteering, learning at home, decision making, and collaborating with community (Epstein et al. 1997, 8). Epstein and colleagues explain that help at home means "encouraging, listening, reacting, praising, guiding, monitoring, and discussing—not 'teaching' school subjects" (p. 8). The focus seems broad but remains on school subjects and their meaning, so that the activities and involvement of the migrant parents may be difficult to place under one of these headings and hence may not be recognized as legitimate. Perhaps for this reason, others (see Fine 1993) have critiqued Epstein for continuing to take a modernist approach. They claim that her approach ignores issues of social justice and continues to assume that parents have the opportunity to be equally involved, if they are appropriately trained and supported.

Transforming education to be more just, democratic, empathetic, and optimistic necessitates a reciprocal relationship. It may involve helping parents encourage the activities and understandings that have been initiated at school. It also requires taking the lives of children—their families, communities, social conditions—and building on them, incorporating them into a new vision of schooling and curriculum.

We have seen various representations of parental and community involvement in the schools presented in this and previous chapters. Alicia's Ndahoo'aah is a program that takes seriously the ability of Navajo elders to contribute their wisdom and knowledge to the school programs. Brenda, recognizing the importance placed on education by many of the Maori parents, has given them responsibility for ensuring that children are in class, on time, ready to learn. Central Elementary School in New Zealand has clearly demonstrated that parents can take responsibility, not only for attendance but also for instruction. In Emily Carr School, the core curriculum has been transformed into a *curriculum of life*. And in Fiji, the whole community shows its support for, and pride in, the students and their schools.

To this list, one can undoubtedly add numerous other examples. In each of these schools, we find teachers and administrators exercising leadership to transform parents and community members from shadowy groups of adults standing on the outside of the school community looking in (sometimes lending a hand, sometimes exercising their right to critique) to an empowered constituent group within the school community. But it is equally important for educators to stop being ghostly presences in the lives of children and the community. Hence educators must find ways to become involved in the communities of which the children are a part.

When Epstein talks of school visits, she describes the goal, "to help schools understand families" (Epstein et al. 1997, 8). To her list, a

transformative leader would add empowerment strategies—empowerment of parents by the school in a mutuality of support and interaction
as well as empowerment of children by their parents in ways educators
may find difficult to understand. As Lopez states,

> schools need to make a greater effort to understand how marginalized
> parents are negotiating the concept of involvement for themselves, in or-
> der to effectively "partner" with parents on their own terms, . . . schools
> should begin the process of identifying ways to capitalize on how parents
> are *already* involved in their children's educational lives, . . . to recog-
> nize and validate the culture of the home—including the "funds of
> knowledge" and belief systems of diverse families. (2001, 16)

The need to reconcile conflicting perspectives lies at the heart of the
creation of a community of difference. Emily Carr's principal, Joey
Kyle, underlined this reality; she asked, "How can you have either an
education or a democracy without conflict and struggle?" (Vibert,
Portelli, and Leighteizer 1998, 152). The struggles involve, in part,
finding new ways to think about and enact parental and community involvement as well as figuring out how parents may make their knowledge and abilities central to the life of the school. It requires expanding
our current views of parental support and business partnerships to take
account of the realities of student and community life.

Holding a community celebration on exam day and having the
drugstore owner work with the school to base instruction on the economics of shoplifting are two examples. Another is moving the notion of parental support to the students' community, as in the Just
Therapy initiative. Central School's approach of assigning responsibility to parents for instruction takes this kind of thinking and risk
taking even further.

This is difficult work, not normally undertaken by already stressed
educators in public schools. Joey Kyle, principal of Emily Carr
states:

> We must, firstly, think about who we are in terms of our own class struc-
> ture, where we came from, the kinds of family support we had and the
> opportunities which were available to us before we can possibly begin to
> listen to what children and their parents are saying to us.

Sometimes educators, faced with the enormity of the task of empowering school communities as well as trying to deal with the myriad of academic and social needs within their classes, raise doubts and concerns about what is demanded of them. One educator, in a recent study by Lopez, Scribner, and Mahitivanichcha (2001), states that "my parents know they can call me 24 hours a day, 7 days a week, *para lo que necesiten* [for whatever they need]. They're like *familia* [family] you know? . . . They know I am there for them." Other educators reject this notion as untenable, claiming their right to have some private and family time of their own.

I think it is helpful to recognize that being available by giving people permission to call when they need you is not synonymous with being actively engaged twenty-four hours a day. It is rare that people abuse the invitation. We err in fearing that if we make the offer, others will take advantage of us. Being available is one way of *doing with* others, of building relationships that bring mutual benefits. It is not just educators giving and parents and caregivers taking; doing with others lays the foundation for the deep and lasting reciprocal relationships that are at the heart of a community of difference. It definitely requires a deep personal commitment on the part of educators and a strong sense that accomplishing social justice goals requires more than a clearly defined nine-to-five job.

THE LEADER'S ROLE

It is up to the transformative leader to initiate reflective and critical conversations about these issues. Pervading this discussion of breaking boundaries is the need once again for educational leaders to examine issues of power and our underlying assumptions about education. Do we believe that parents and community members should become part of the school community? Do we think they have anything to teach educators and students? Or do we find the presence of community members in our schools and classrooms disruptive?

Perhaps we even believe, as does one teachers' federation, that parents and volunteers take paid jobs away from certified teacher aides and that their presence should be limited. Some teachers have even suggested that responding to parental concerns is a distraction from which they need to be protected by contract provisions.[8] Each concern is, in fact, a manifestation of power and privilege and how we think about them. Who should be included in educational decision making? Who has the expertise? Who should be permitted to speak with a legitimate and legitimated voice? These and other questions will be explored further in the next chapter. Here it is sufficient to recognize that the exercise of effective leadership will both challenge and change inequitable power relations and break the traditional boundaries of school communities.

Knowing who we are and the resources we bring is a first step. Without this kind of self-knowledge work, we cannot hope to act with understanding, empathy, or justice to educate children whose experiences are significantly different from our own. Transformative cross-cultural leaders will challenge the ways in which curriculum is conceptualized and offered as they move toward the development of more optimistic communities of difference. In order to accomplish this, they will need to tear down the walls that confine us within the boundaries of conventional thinking about parental and community involvement in schools.

NOTES

1. I tend to use the term *parent involvement* because it is commonly used in academic literature; nevertheless, I recognize that many children have other caregivers and that when educators are reaching out to their communities, they must be sensitive to this reality and to the language they use.

2. The Maori *poi* dance is a beguiling traditional dance, performed by women, rhythmically twirling *poi* balls at the ends of long strings, typically about twenty-six inches long. Some report that in the old days only women of high rank knew how to dance the *poi* and jealously guarded this knowledge from the lower classes.

3. We must be careful not to attribute causality to association. Perhaps parents whose children are academically successful find it easier to become involved. Perhaps other factors, such as socioeconomic status or disposable time, underlie both of these findings.

4. Other administrators dispute her number, but all agree that there is a requirement for a high degree of participation that accurately represents all

groups in the school community. Another principal reported, for example, that they needed a number of volunteer hours equal to the number of students in the student body.

5. First Nations is a term widely used in Canada to refer to Canadians of Indian ancestry; recently aboriginal people themselves have tried to distinguish between the term *aboriginal,* which includes Métis and others, and the designation First Nation, which identifies people with specific band and reserve affiliations. (In Canada the term *reserve* is used, while the corresponding term in the United States is *reservation.*)

6. The school was part of a longitudinal national study of student engagement in learning and school life in which I was one of the principal researchers. Three other researchers were primarily responsible for the Nova Scotia portion of the project. See their report in Vibert, Portelli, and Leighteizer (1998).

7. McKnight's (1993) work on community mapping is, in part, based on these premises.

8. The latter two positions were expressed during a labor dispute between a teachers' federation and the legislature that began late in 2001 and continued into 2002.

CHAPTER 7

Critique, Carnival, and Consciousness

In the last chapter, I shared stories of schools that had broken some of the traditional boundaries in order to help us think more broadly about parent and community involvement. As before, this chapter unites theory and practice in order to help educators visualize alternate models and conceptions of schooling. It draws heavily on two different theoretical ideas: the Bakhtinian notion of carnival (Bakhtin 1984) and critical multiculturalism as outlined by McLaren (Estrada and McLaren 1993) and Kincheloe and Steinberg (1997). Examining various approaches to multiculturalism will help us understand several ways in which power operates to perpetuate inequalities in education. Reflecting on carnival will help us find ways to move beyond the status quo to new images of schooling.

These concepts of critique, carnival, and consciousness will push our thinking even further, as we consider, playfully and creatively, additional ways to change inequitable relationships and practices. It is my hope that these concepts will help us live more joyfully together in our school communities.

I start by introducing you to Stephen Lewis Junior Secondary School, a school for students in seventh through ninth grades. From the outside, it looks much like any other junior high school. As you enter, there is a sign asking you to check in at the office. Passing the office, the visitor finds herself standing in an impressive central meeting area/cafeteria, its broad staircase spiraling to the second floor. As you walk through the building and peek into the classrooms, you do not see children in rows with an adult in front of the room. Instead, you see various configurations of young people generally gathered around tables. Classrooms are organized in pods—one large room, often with a sliding divider, with smaller rooms of different sizes attached to it. Teachers use the adjacent spaces for small group work and individual instruction. All spaces are visible from the central classroom. Clusters of pods are arranged into learning communities, each community containing teacher meeting rooms and workrooms as well as numerous student spaces.

The school is described in its handbook as "rich in human resources and ethnocultural groups." Its roughly nine hundred students come from varied socioeconomic and ethnic backgrounds and many other countries including China, India, the Caribbean, South and Central America.

There is no vice principal at Stephen Lewis Junior High School. Principal Naomi St. John, appointed eighteen months before the school opened, fought long and hard to gain permission for each community to have its own learning leader.[1] Although they do not have regularly assigned teaching duties, learning leaders assist with instruction, work with students individually, deal with discipline, and provide key leadership and support. Each learning leader is responsible for the schedule in his or her community.

The curriculum in this junior high school (grades 7–9) is designed to be "responsive to student interests." Students are most frequently organized in multigrade groupings for interdisciplinary instruction. Sometimes teachers divide the students in their learning community relatively equally; sometimes one or two teachers work with larger groups of students to free others to work with small groups or individuals.

Governance, too, is different. A school council, composed of two or three students, two to four staff members, and eight to ten parents,[2] is responsible for dealing with issues brought to it through the parent, student, and teacher/staff assemblies. Weekly staff meetings are held to ensure the development of a sense of "schoolness" and to deal with issues related to curriculum and instruction for which teachers have full responsibility. A further complex system of committees, with representation from each learning community as well as parents and students, recommends policy in areas such as governance, assessment and reporting, professional development, and special events (for example, graduation). There is no elected student council—any student who wants to participate is free to attend meetings.

Stephen Lewis School is planned around a series of innovations in governance as well as in teaching and learning, intended to meet diverse learner needs. In many ways, it represents a sort of educational *carnival*. It is a departure from the typical school organized in hierarchical and uniform lines according to what has become known as the "factory model" of organizational life. As such it provides an appropriate touchstone for a discussion of power relations in schools and suggests ways to both understand and change them.

THINKING ABOUT POWER

When I use the term *power,* I assume that it is neither positive nor negative. Indeed, the etymological roots of the term lie in the old French word *poeir*—a word that (as Mintzberg 1983 pointed out) has become both a noun (*le pouvoir* = power) and a verb (*pouvoir* = to be able). Often we use the word *power* negatively to imply power wielded inappropriately over someone or something, rather than used creatively, *with* others, to create a new order.

Although power may be used in both positive and negative ways, in and of itself power is intrinsically neutral. What we do with power, how we use the power that each of us has, is central to our understanding of schools as communities of difference and our abilities to be transformative leaders.

Unfortunately, schools as traditionally organized implicitly perpetuate forms of power that advantage people from mainstream cultures. Hierarchies, like many traditional structures for decision making, continue to marginalize and exclude many others who have a legitimate right to full participation and membership in the school community. These forms of power are so deeply rooted that we sometimes fail to identify or understand their operation. This was noted, for example, by Gaventa (1980) in his study called *Power and Powerlessness: Quiescence and Rebellion in an Appalachian Valley*. He identified three forms of power that may operate simultaneously in a given situation to marginalize and disenfranchise members of a community.

In the first instance, there is the *assumption* that people have equal access and opportunities to voice their opinions and that those who choose not to exercise that right do so out of informed choice. At this level, one might say that the reason so few parents in multicultural school communities attend meetings of the parent council or become directly involved in their children's education may be that they are, as teachers often suggest, unmotivated or disinterested. But as we have seen in previous chapters, this is clearly not a valid assumption.

At the second level, Gaventa suggests that those in power often *take steps* to organize the existing structures to exclude diverse voices and perspectives. Rather than organize to emphasize and encourage participation, as Stephen Lewis Junior High School did, many schools find ways to discourage discussion of controversial topics. Creating agendas for meetings that relegate the most important issues to the least amount of time at the end of the day or holding school council meetings during the daytime, when few parents are able to attend (even if invited), are common examples.

Gaventa's third level of power operates at an even more insidious level, as the dominant group *shapes the perceptions* of the minority group. This form of power, Gaventa suggests, is so persuasive that ultimately the minority group's perceptions of its needs and wants may conform to the expectations and beliefs of the majority. Bishop notes this phenomenon in discussing the myths perpetuated in New Zealand society about Maori people.[3] He writes: "Sadly many of these myths are believed by Maori and non-Maori alike" (Bishop 2001, 13). An example of one practice leading to such a myth is the enactment at one time or another, in many developed English-speaking nations, of policies that forbade aboriginal and linguistic-minority children to speak their heritage languages at school. Today this English-only practice has become so ingrained that many minority parents hold the mistaken conviction that there is only a binary, forced choice. They believe it is better for their children to speak and learn only English at school than to also learn to speak and thus to retain their own language.[4] One wonders how we have convinced them they need to choose between the two goals.

These are but a few ways in which power operates in inappropriate ways in our educational systems. Macedo, drawing on Foucault's work, emphasizes the role of power in defining what counts as knowledge and, hence, in shaping what we anoint as the official curriculum. He states that power in education needs to be examined though a discussion of the politics of "which content gets taught, to whom, in favor of what, of whom, against what, against whom" (Macedo 1995, 43). Which teachers are invited to be part of curriculum-writing committees and who is not invited? Who makes decisions about class placements for children and who is excluded?

In order to answer these important questions, we need a "critical understanding of the interdependence between schooling and the sociocultural and political reality of the society within which the schools exist" (Macedo 1995, 43). In analyzing the role played by schools of education in preparing teachers to exercise leadership positions in society, Macedo appeals for an understanding that, at present, the dominant curriculum "is designed primarily to reproduce the inequality of social classes, while it mostly benefits the interests of the dominant class" (p. 54).

Understanding how forms of power operate in an organization is a complex task, compounded by issues of class, language, socioeconomic status, levels of education, and historical position. One way of thinking about these interrelationships is to examine various notions of multiculturalism and how they are played out in schools.

FIVE APPROACHES
TO MULTICULTURALISM

Kincheloe and Steinberg, in their 1997 book entitled *Changing Multiculturalism,* suggest that the term *multiculturalism* is used to mean everything and nothing. To help clarify the concept, they explicate five types of multiculturalism. The terms are not particularly important; indeed, others may describe these attitudes differently. What is important is that each type of multiculturalism represents attitudes that need to be recognized and examined. Each has clear implications for transformative leaders wanting to foster the creation of schools as communities of difference. Each is based on good intentions—a desire to ensure that civil society develops in ways that promote democracy and a conception of the good life.

Conservative Multiculturalism or Monoculturalism *overcome differences*

The first type of multiculturalism identified by Kincheloe and Steinberg (1997) has long been recognized in educational institutions. Conservative multiculturalism recognizes the existence of differences but assumes that one function of schooling is to eliminate or overcome differences in order to prevent social divisiveness and conflict. The example of legislation designed to prevent students from speaking their home languages in order to promote fluency in English is a good example. This is the form of multiculturalism that leads to pathologizing the lived experiences of students. It locates educational difficulties or problems in groups of students because of intrinsic cultural differences rather than examining the structures and cultures of schooling that may disadvantage or marginalize them.

A British colleague recently told me a story. Her university operates on a tutorial system and was making an attempt to be responsive to the needs of nonmainstream students. Several male Muslim students were asked if they would be willing to accept a female tutor. All agreed. During the first meeting between a tutor and her student, the tutor reached out her hand, ready to greet the Muslim student with the traditional handshake. He politely declined, indicating that in his tradition, once he was married, it was inappropriate for him to touch another woman. The response of my academic colleagues was that if they were asked to respect the student's beliefs, he should respect their tradition and be willing to shake hands. It seems to me that the effort to be tolerant, respectful, and inclusive broke down at that point, as educators displayed a form of conservative multiculturalism.

The incident raises important questions: Is there a difference between tradition and religious belief? Who should be expected to accommodate? Whose beliefs should take precedence? How should we decide?

Hodgkinson presents a values hierarchy that I find useful in this type of situation (1983, 36–41). He suggests that there are three main types of values. Type 1 values are based on principles; Type 2 deal with consensus and consequences; Type 3 relate to preferences. Decision making around Type 3 values is normally quite easy. I prefer chocolate ice cream while you choose strawberry; and in many instances we can make choices that satisfy both of us. Even if we must decide between them, there is rarely conflict, as one person is normally willing to compromise.

Decision making around Type 1 values, in which principles are involved, is a different matter. When ideology or religious values come into conflict, people tend to dig in, each believing his or her position is right and should therefore be adopted by the other. Resolving the issue of the handshake at the level of principle, therefore, is extremely difficult. If we can move the situation to a level 2 discussion and engage in dialogue that seeks *consensus* around agreed-on *consequences* of an action, the emotional associations may be diffused and a resolution may be found.

If I examine the potential consequence for each party of not shaking hands, I might decide that for the English tutor, not shaking hands would result in a temporary sense of embarrassment or dissonance. For the Muslim student, shaking hands might result in conflict with his wife and ongoing inner turmoil for transgressing against a precept of his religion. This analysis lets me easily decide that the greater good is served by not shaking hands. Of course, another person might analyze the situation differently, and then more extensive dialogue would be necessitated.

To some extent, conservative multiculturalism fans a fear of difference that leads to the perpetuation of present power arrangements. It focuses on principles and draws on arguments such as, "They chose to come to this country, so they should learn our language and our rules—in order to contribute to our democratic society." In the case of my colleagues, it was expressed as, "They came to this country, so they should be willing to shake hands." Educators cannot eliminate difference, nor is it desirable or realistic to try. Hence it is critical to develop some strategies, perhaps by using Hodgkinson's values hierarchy, to help us resolve conflicts as they occur.

Liberal Multiculturalism

Kincheloe and Steinberg state that those who adopt a liberal multicultural stance believe that "individuals from diverse race, class, and gender groups share a natural equality and a common humanity" (1997, 10). The cliché that there is only one race, the human race is a common manifestation of liberal multiculturalism. This is the color-blindness I discussed in chapter 5. It assumes that there are no important differences; if we emphasize commonalities, we will find better ways to live together in society.

Despite its many innovative practices, Stephen Lewis Junior High School exemplified this approach to multiculturalism. Rather than talk about the myriad of cultures and backgrounds represented in the school, the emphasis was on "getting along together." This was explicit in the Student Mission Statement: "everyone is equal and able to discover themselves through trust and respect and voicing their opinions." The research team of which I was a part often wondered how students were taught to develop the trust and respect assumed in this statement without reference to gender, class, or ethnicity. Yet the approach is common in schools.

In a neighboring school, some teachers told us that they did not deal with diversity in their school, either formally or informally. "We don't need to," they said. "We don't have enough diversity." One wonders what constitutes diversity—or multiculturalism—in the minds of these educators. How can students who are different, either visibly or invisibly, find ways to contribute to the school community without denying their own identity? This form of multiculturalism assumes that as members of the human race we are all the same. Thus everyone has the same needs, the same access to education, to social agencies, to decision-making bodies, to life's opportunities. It ignores the reality of discrimination and institutional barriers that still exist for many people—even in so-called democratic societies.

Freire rejects the reality described in the liberal approach to multiculturalism. Because it purports to include everyone, he believes that it actually marginalizes difference: "The truth is . . . that the oppressed are not 'marginals,' are not men living 'outside' society. They have always been 'inside'—inside the structure that made them 'beings for others'" (1970, 55). Freire goes on to state that "the solution is not to 'integrate' them into the structure of oppression but to transform the structure so they can become 'beings for themselves'" (1994, 55). Certainly some transformation of schools is in order to help students develop identities for themselves. The germ of truth in liberal multiculturalism is that there is one human race. It errs by ignoring the richness that comes from acknowledging and understanding, sometimes even celebrating, the diversity that occurs within our common humanity.

Pluralist Multiculturalism

Pluralist multiculturalism represents the other side of the liberal multicultural coin. Where the previous approach minimized differences in order to emphasize common humanity, pluralist approaches focus on difference—and thus celebrate the rich diversity of the human race. Although pluralist multiculturalism recognizes, talks about, and purports to celebrate difference, it does so without disruption to dominant narratives of power and identity. Kincheloe and Steinberg state that advocates of "pluralism argue that democracy involves not merely the concern with rights of all citizens but the history and culture of traditionally marginalized groups as well. . . . Diversity becomes intrinsically valuable" (1997, 15).

Educators operating from this form of multiculturalism often emphasize what has sometimes been called a "3-F" version of multiculturalism—food, fashion, and festivals. Students are often invited to bring ethnic food, dress in a national costume, or perform a song or a dance. Sometimes they are asked to share an item that represents their culture, often with the disturbing effects described by Anish in chapter 5.

Elsewhere, Anish described another multicultural event. When he was in seventh grade, he attended a multicultural evening with his mother. Following the introductions and welcome speeches, his principal encouraged "everyone to savor the variety of ethnic foods to further appreciate the diversity of our school community." Everyone rushed to the tables, while Anish took refuge in the restroom. As the event ended, he suddenly remembered his promise to meet his mother at the front door. He says:

> Since it was my duty to bring back the empty samosa plate, I reluctantly walked over to the food table where the custodians had begun their cleanup. I started to breathe again when I spotted the oval plate which

was pushed to the corner of the back table. The locusts had devoured almost everything. I knew at that moment I had to rush to my locker before anyone saw me. . . . I frantically unsealed the saran wrap of the oval
plate and dumped all sixteen untouched samosas on top of my textbooks.
(Sayani 2001, 10)

Instead of feeling part of the diverse community, Anish continued to
feel marginalized and ashamed, now with the added burden of having
to protect his mother from similar feelings. However well-intentioned
a multicultural fair, evening, or assembly may be, it is not always
the joyful carnival or celebration of diversity that its organizers intend. Yet this is the type of activity most often proposed by pluralist
multiculturalists.

I visited a multicultural day celebration at a small elementary school
on the Navajo reservation. The school's student body was 97 percent
Navajo. The incongruity of seeing Red Rock Elementary School hold
a multicultural day in which students performed Navajo songs and
dances for their parents was so great that I commented on the irony.
"Why would you need a special multicultural day to celebrate and incorporate the culture of 97 percent of the students?" I asked. The principal acknowledged the disjuncture, and the next year when I returned
on Multicultural Day, I found numerous student displays depicting
"Chinese in America," "Irish in America," "Filipinos in America" and
so forth. The pluralist celebration was an improvement but did nothing
to raise issues I still thought were important, such as the lack of Navajo
culture in the state's core curriculum or how a situation could arise
where a group that includes almost the entire student body reacted as if
it were a minority needing to celebrate its culture only one day a year.
How could educators begin to challenge the power structure to ensure
that the curriculum was opened up to make place for cultural perspectives other than the dominant one? Psychological affirmation one day a
year cannot serve a political empowerment function. Yet it is precisely
empowerment that is needed by many minority groups in heterogeneous schools.

My intention is not to suggest eliminating multicultural days. Indeed
they can be useful entry points for exploring important and pervasive
issues. My quarrel is that too often these activities are implemented as

an end in themselves. As we have seen, there is much more to the identity and the cultural reality of a student than being able to play a didgeridoo, perform an aboriginal hoop dance, or conduct an Asian tea ceremony. I could envisage a unit in which students not only heard the music of the Australian instrument but investigated the political repression of those who have preserved the traditions. I might use the hoop dance to introduce a unit about various traditional and spiritual beliefs about the birds and animals depicted in the patterns of the hoops. What if the tea ceremony initiated an inquiry into its origins and the culture out of which it grew? What was life like then? What did the ceremony represent? What were the relationships between male and female in the society? Have they changed, and if so, in what ways and why? Who is advantaged as a result of the changes and who disadvantaged?

Isolated celebrations in the name of multiculturalism tend to relegate multiculturalism to superficial and simplistic interpretations. Using them as starting points for nuanced inquiry, far-ranging discussion, and enhanced understanding is quite different.

Essentialist Multiculturalism

Kincheloe and Steinberg (1997) name left-essentialist multiculturalism as their fourth type, although they recognize that many forms of thought are essentializing. I prefer, for our purposes, to simply use the term *essentialist multiculturalism*. This is the kind of multiculturalism that equates certain characteristics with all members of a given minority culture. It assigns specific characteristics to various constructs of class, ethnicity, or gender without recognizing that culture and cultures are socially constructed and hence dynamic.

Some gender-based approaches to school leadership that claim that women are better administrators than men are essentialist. Fundamentalist religious groups who decry the presence of books on homosexuality in school libraries, as well as those who dismiss their position as simply that of fundamentalist Christians, are both essentializing positions. The principal who wondered if all Navajo think alike was also expressing an essentialist perspective. Teachers who assume that a student of Chinese origin should be placed in an advanced academic math program are engaged in the same type of thinking. Likewise, educators who assume that because children come from poor or migrant families, they will experience difficulty in learning and thus need to be placed in low-level or remedial programs are essentializing them. In other words, generalizing from characteristics sometimes perceived to exist in a specific group and applying them automatically to individuals is an inappropriate but common behavior in schools.

Another aspect of the category of left-essentialist multiculturalism identified by Kincheloe and Steinberg (1997) is the sense that unless one belongs to a particular group, one cannot work with it effectively, understand its situations, or speak about it with any justification or authority. Thus a white English-speaking researcher should confine her research to members of her own class and ethnic group; only Vietnamese workers should visit the homes of Vietnamese students; only African Americans should be considered for principalships in predominantly African American schools, and so on.

A process my friend calls "finish the thought" appropriately demonstrates the faulty logic of this position, especially as it is taken to its extreme. Only teachers from poverty should work with poor kids; only dyslexic teachers should work with kids so identified; only teachers who speak a home language other than English should work with ESL kids and so forth. Who could ever run a school in that way? Moreover, how could we ever create schools as communities of difference if we needed to come from a specific different perspective to relate to it?

Essentialist thinking sometimes goes one step further to suggest that "only authentically oppressed people can possess moral agency" (Kincheloe and Steinberg 1997, 21). The authors continue, "In such an essentialized identity politics one would have to submit proper credentials before offering an opinion on a race or gender issue" (p. 21). Such a view often excludes "morally committed outsiders or nonmembers" (p. 23). Logically, then, I should not talk about the Navajo because I am not one of them; men should not talk about women; and no one could work for social justice across race, class, gender, or religious lines.

It is fortunate indeed that the Tjabukai[5] people from Queensland, Australia, did not subscribe to an essentialist philosophy of multiculturalism. As I visited schools in northern Queensland, around Cairns, I heard the same story in each place I visited. The Tjabukai language had been revived and revitalized single-handedly by an English anthropologist. This particular man, I was told, had come to study the Tjabukai people; he had fallen in love with them and their area, had begun to live among them and to learn their language. He then recognized that only a few elders remained who could speak the language; the young people had lost it. The anthropologist began to volunteer extensively in area schools, teaching the language to various groups of students. Gradually other adults regained their fluency in the language and began to help. By the end of the twentieth century, several bilingual programs existed in area schools.

When I visited the Tjabukai Culture Center in Cairns, at the base of the sky rail that takes the visitor over the Daintree Rainforest to Kuranda, I checked the story with the young Tjabukai guides. They took great pride in sharing their traditional culture, telling about the historical injustices they had overcome, explaining how their ancestors used various plants for food and medicine, demonstrating the making of clothing and household artifacts, and performing their songs and dances. "Where did you learn your language?" I asked. "Did you speak it at home?" Each one told me the same story of having learned it at school thanks to the efforts of the English anthropologist. The story has taken on mythic and apocryphal overtones, yet, if the Tjabukai had not been willing to acknowledge the role of a committed and involved outsider, it might never have been written.

Kincheloe and Steinberg state that "the same is true in other areas of identity, where many racial and ethnic alliances as well as homosexual and disability rights organizations have come to realize that identity alone, especially an essentialized notion of identity, may be insufficient as the grounding for democratic and justice-related movements" (1997, 23). We need to speak out to oppose injustice, advocate for others, and work on their behalf; but we must never forget that we cannot speak *for* another.

Critical Multiculturalism

The proponents of critical multiculturalism claim it is the way forward, a way of thinking that moves us beyond previous approaches, to challenge the inequities of power in the status quo. The other forms may make us feel good about our tolerance and multicultural mind-set but do little to advance the cause of social justice and understanding. Critical multiculturalism is based on a notion of critical theory that promotes individual awareness of, and reflection on, oneself as a social being and how one's beliefs and values have been shaped. It is based on an "emancipatory commitment to social justice and the egalitarian democracy that accompanies it" (Kincheloe and Steinberg 1997, 26). Critical multiculturalists work to understand and make public their values and assumptions; they attempt to understand how issues of race, class, gender, and other axes of power interact to shape both individual consciousness and public practice; they are willing to challenge the status quo.

Transformative cross-cultural educational leaders need to be critical multiculturalists. We need to both understand the world of schooling and attempt to change it to be more inclusive and respectful, more just, democratic, empathetic, and optimistic for all children. We need to get beneath and beyond the day-to-day practices of schooling to begin to understand how they are perceived by, and how they affect, others. For example, although we may hope that there are no powerful dominant forces imposing conformity in our schools, how else might educators explain the pervasiveness of common clichés in various communities? "Acting like a banana," "an apple," "an almond," or "an Oreo cookie" are all phrases that denote being of one color (and ethnicity) on the outside, while acting and thinking "white" on the inside. In each community, the phrase has acquired the negative connotations associated with renouncing one's own identity in order to succeed in a white-dominated institution. Educators must work to ensure that this norm is overturned. Our schools must be places where people may thrive as they are, not as they strive to be someone else.

Powerless people, Kincheloe and Steinberg suggest, have little opportunity to develop their talents throughout their lives, little autonomy to act outside the authority of professionals, and "little hope of being taken seriously, of being listened to with respect, of being treated with dignity" (1997, 96). On the one hand, powerlessness may be a manifestation of learned helplessness in that some people come to believe they have no power within institutions and society. On the other hand, the power structures and inequities in our organizations tend to create and perpetuate the idea that powerlessness is real.

Changing the organizational and leadership structures at Stephen Lewis Junior High School was an attempt to change these realities. Yet as the formal leaders moved on few of the innovations remained. Although the titles changed (from vice principal to learning leader), the underlying assumptions did not. The original model of the school included provisions for inclusion, participation, and flexibility. However, no one engaged in the critical multicultural processes of openly and explicitly challenging inequities and of making beliefs, values, and assumptions public. Instead, there seemed to have been an assumption that increasing the participation of teachers, parents, and students would automatically result in harmonious and democratic practices. Although the structures changed, the underlying assumptions remained implicit rather than explicit. Thus, when principals changed, there was no shared understanding that challenged the reintroduction of more traditional norms of leadership and more common images and forms of schooling.

In the next section, I examine how Bakhtin's concept of carnival may help us institute and institutionalize practices that overturn traditional ways of thinking and acting and offer a glimpse of possibilities for educational renewal.

CARNIVAL AS A RENEWAL AND REFORM

Stephen Lewis Junior High School exemplified many characteristics that, if institutionalized, could empower a greater number of students and their parents and create more inclusive, caring, and academically successful communities of difference. Despite the fact that the changes did not last through three changes of school principal, for at least a while many of the typical structures of schooling were overturned, providing a glimpse of a potentially different (hopefully better) way of being together.

Bakhtin's (1984) use of the term *carnival* provides a new lens through which to view institutional life. In his doctoral dissertation about Rabelais, first submitted in 1940,[6] Bakhtin described an approach to literature and to life that has since become well-known to literary critics and, more recently, to scholars of cultural studies and educators. Bakhtin recognized that the medieval carnival written about so expansively by Rabelais was a literary representation of a social enactment that holds significance for modern times.

Carnival is characterized, according to Bakhtin, by full participation, the use of humor, challenges to existing hierarchical relationships, the use of masks (that enable us to present multiple persona and to overcome fear), new forms of communication, empowerment, and the re-creation of boundaries. New structures, relationships, and patterns of communication rise from the old forms of institutional life, not through punishing individuals who have engaged in what one perceives to be inequitable or uncaring practices, but through new ways of being that help people see alternatives of possibility and justice.

Sometimes people are confused when the concept of carnival is introduced in conversations about schooling. On reflection, educators often find that elements of carnival exist in their schools. Sometimes these are the controversial social activities, disapproved of by those who want schools to be serious places of learning and who conceive of carnival as a waste of time (and money). Bakhtin's work provides a way of grounding the discussions about carnival and offering a theoretical rationale for those who want to both support and expand opportunities for playfulness in education.

Medieval carnival, as Bakhtin interprets it, provides numerous clues about how to change schools to become communities of difference—places in which all children and adults may find new ways of living together in community. In this section, I discuss some of his ideas and demonstrate how they may be helpful in creating new ways of thinking about schooling.

Participating Fully

First, carnival is not a spectator sport. Everyone can be involved; people live in it and participate in it fully. By opening the possibility of participation to everyone, carnival immediately presents a challenge to the common factory model of schooling in which a few people hold power over others. Bakhtin states that carnival celebrated temporary liberation from the prevailing truth and from the established order; it marked the suspension of all hierarchical rank, privileges, norms, and prohibitions. Carnival was the true feast of the time, the feast of becoming, change, and renewal. It was hostile to all that was immortalized and completed. (1984, 10)

While Bakhtin may have exaggerated the effects of carnival in medieval times or the potential of carnival to be totally inclusive, the ideas have merit. We crystallize our structures, programs, cultures, freezing them in our historical realities and considering them immutable. Being critical of beliefs, practices, and traditions that have become immortalized in our institutions is one key to overturning them. Acknowledging the need for continuous, reflective change is a starting point. We assume that our work is done when a new program is introduced or when the school develops and adopts a new mission statement. A new program or concept often becomes enshrined for decades, long past its time of relevance. For example, as a 1960s high school graduate, I know that our new math program is still called new half a century after its introduction.

Breaking out of the hierarchical norms of schooling, opening up access to decision-making forums, and asking questions about what knowledge is legitimate and whose knowledge is represented in the curriculum are the first steps to changing the center of a community to permit greater educational relevance through the fuller participation of all members.

Bakhtin explains that carnival "demanded ever changing, playful, undefined forms" (1986, 11). What would it mean to create a school based on ever-changing, playful, undefined forms? At Stephen Lewis Junior High School, learning communities were playful, undefined, and dynamic ways of organizing and reorganizing students for instruction, in that groupings were constantly being configured and reconfigured to meet student needs. Involving parents to teach elements of Maori culture at Central School in New Zealand, displaying student art throughout Regal High school, celebrating exam day in the Fijian school—all provided aspects of a carnivalesque atmosphere. How can we find other, more flexible ways for more people to participate in the educational endeavor?

Using Humor

Another important element of carnival is laughter and fun—frequently missing in schooling. When we asked students in schools across Canada, as part of a national student engagement study, what constituted good teaching, they frequently indicated that making instruction fun was a key component. Sadly, they commented, fun was often absent from classroom life. When it is present, they recognize and celebrate it.

The union of laughter and learning is clearly presented by this ninth-grade student (from another study) describing her favorite teacher:

> I think the best teacher I have ever had [and still have], is Mr. B. Mr. B. . . . is my band teacher. He is about five feet, seven inches tall, has grey hair (well, what's left of it, anyway), and looks to be about 45 years old. He conducts our band very vigorously, and sometimes loses his baton in doing so. When this happens, he just laughs, and picks it up and starts conducting again. He is a very good-natured teacher, and jokes a lot. When he does get mad, he manages to joke and chew us out at the same time. He always includes everyone, and makes them feel welcome. *It's as if he can see right into our hearts, and knows what's there, and exactly how to bring the best that is inside us out into the open.* When he scolds, he does it so that you know exactly what you are doing wrong and how to do it right, and he does it in a way that you have confidence that you can be the best. He is just the greatest teacher I have had, and anyone who has not had him for a teacher is missing out on one of the greatest things that could happen! (emphasis added)

Joking and chewing them out at the same time! Scolding them and giving them confidence that they can be the best! Including everyone and seeing into their hearts—Mr. B. is obviously a master at inverting the typical classroom structures.

Bakhtin talks about how, as time progressed, the "joyful and triumphant hilarity" of medieval and Renaissance grotesque was replaced in subsequent centuries by a seriousness that was antithetical to the original spirit of carnival. In schools, we have to guard against excessive seriousness as well as cold humor, irony, and sarcasm that are anti-thetical to the good-natured fun and frivolity that have positive effects on behavior, relationships, and learning. Teachers and students sometimes laugh at or ridicule each other, but this is far from the spirit of carnival. To be effective, laughter needs to belong to the people. In education, this means that laughter must belong to both teachers and students if it is to have the power of regeneration and re-creation.

At Emily Carr Elementary School, a series of town-hall meetings was instituted to help create a participatory democratic forum for discussion and communication. A surprise tribute to the departing principal took, in part, the form of a parody of her common behaviors and sayings. Another teacher,

> in apt mimicry, brushed his mop hair out of his eyes, kicked off his shoes to dance a few jig steps, and, glasses perched on top of his head, called out in a perfect imitation of the principal's tremulous soprano, "Good morning, . . . now I have a few announcements to read, but I can't seem to find my glasses!" (Vibert, Portelli, and Leighteizer 1998, 140)

The authors of this report commented, "Humor, often in the form of a gentle self-parody, appears to be more than casual here. It seems to operate as one way of subverting the normal institutional culture, and hence becomes important to the quite serious humanity of the place" (Vibert, Portelli, and Leighteizer 1998, 140). Humor is not antithetical to serious work but is integral to it. Carnival has become part of the institutional life in this school.

Challenging Hierarchical Relations

The temporary suspension of hierarchic distinctions and barriers among people present in carnival is based on what Bakhtin calls "an ideal and at the same time real type of communication, impossible in ordinary life" (1984, 16). This communication knows no barriers about who should talk to whom about what. Indeed, even the commonplace, the bawdy (and body), the sacred traditions, and the profane may be disrupted through the use of folk humor that "denies, revives, and renews at the same time" (p. 11). Once a relationship, belief, or practice has been challenged through humor, it is difficult for the previous norms of behavior to remain unchanged.

In schools, one way we introduce behaviors that challenge the existing hierarchy is by holding competitive activities between staff and students.

Once a student has defeated the principal in a wrestling match or has had a teacher score a goal against him in a hockey match, the relationships are subtly changed. Other noncompetitive activities may serve the same function. Consider the student who participates in a music festival, playing a duet with her teacher. Recall the atmosphere created by dress-up days in which students and teachers alike wear pajamas or beach clothes, or when teachers present a play or skit parodying students. These activities may provide more than just a welcome break in routine. They can be celebrations of togetherness. They are carnival.

Changing patterns of relationships disrupts our underlying assumptions and behaviors. It is much more difficult for a teacher to retain an authoritarian posture when, only a few hours (or days) before, teacher and student were competing as equals. It is unlikely that the music teacher would harshly rebuke a student for a false note if they had practiced together for many hours for a festival competition, seeing each other make and correct mistakes. How could a teacher punish a student for poking fun at her, when the day before, during a staged staff play, the teacher impersonated the impudent student, to the delight of the whole student body?

I am not suggesting that there should be no hierarchical relationships, that we do not, for example, need leaders, or that we should create chaotic organizations with no clear lines of communication and no accountability. Indeed, Weber's concept of bureaucracy was developed to counteract the types of capricious and unjust behavior that may occur in chaotic situations. I am suggesting that even as we engage in brief activities that disrupt normal power relationships, we can create more permeable borders and less fixed boundaries of rules and roles that may have lasting implications.

Some years ago, I wrote an article with a colleague (see Pillsbury and Shields 1999), "Shared Journeys and Border Crossings: When 'They' Becomes 'We.'" In it, Jerry and I examined some interactions in which boundaries seemed fixed and others in which they seemed permeable. We concluded, in part, that one way to overcome fixed boundaries of racism and exclusion and permit identification with the "other" may be to enhance the possibility of unimpeded movement across borders.

We shared the graphic example of a teacher in a small school serving predominantly Navajo students, whose inflexible attitudes created barriers that could not be penetrated. I had engaged the staff in an afternoon workshop trying to discover why students, despite several years of concerted effort on the part of teachers to help them be successful, were still achieving below the tenth percentile on a nationally normed standardized achievement test. Following the workshop, one teacher commented, "These students are just not hungry enough. We prepare a smorgasbord for them but *they* just don't eat."

I suggested that perhaps the food was not appetizing or that it might not be what these patrons wanted to order, but he persisted, "No, the food is fine; *they* are just not hungry."

I tried to personalize the situation by explaining that even after many years of teaching experience, I always reflect on how I might make lessons relevant for particular students. Although that was fine for me, he replied, "*I* don't need to change. What *I* do is fine; *they* just do not want to learn."

When Jerry and I reflected on the incident, the teacher's use of the pronouns "we" and "they" appeared to be a way of erecting an impermeable or unalterable border, one that denied all teacher responsibility for student learning and relegated blame totally to the students he perceived as recalcitrant and unmotivated.

In contrast, we presented another incident, drawn from an interview Jerry had conducted with a college basketball player, which we interpreted as illustrative of an occasion when "we" became broad enough to include "they." Julia, a co-captain, was asked about her reactions immediately following her team's loss to its arch rival. She stated,

I know Coach Wilson pretty well and a couple of players who graduated and so I . . . went in and had a chat with Coach Wilson and talked to her for a while. It's kind of interesting when they come. I think, "Well, what if it had been the other way around. What if I had been playing for them and we had been playing Huntington?"

We believe that what happened in the brevity of these words was significant. Julia tentatively tried on membership in the rival group, making them into her hypothetical "we," thus converting her present team to a hypothetical "they." This imaginary reversal of the situation provided the impetus for her to wonder how she would have responded had the roles been reversed.

It is the possibility of at least a temporary identification with others that comes from reconceptualizing present relationships which makes this illustration so intriguing. Others lose some of their threat and the barriers that divide are lowered when we place ourselves in a temporary empathetic position of identification with them.

The Role of Masks

Throughout history, masks have been used for ritual, spiritual, and decorative purposes. One explanation for the enduring appeal of masks is the vividness of their folk art characteristics (directness and freshness of vision, outrageous humor, simple, bright colors, intricate and expressive carving or modeling) as well as the complex and intriguing beliefs they often exemplify. Masks, as the typical depiction of the twin Greek masks of tragedy and comedy demonstrate, portray a wide range of human emotions.

Perhaps the most universal appeal of masks is their ability to provide the wearer with a temporary, alternate identity. Made from various materials, in innumerable designs, masks universally represent *transformation*. By simply putting on another face, the mask wearer takes on an alternative role and magically enters an altered state.

In carnival, one not only chooses to play the part of another; one chooses to wear the mask. There is no shame, no forced hiding, no fear—everyone is equally "other" and for a brief moment, power structures are leveled. The masks of carnival, then, are quite different from the masks we sometimes feel forced to wear in order to protect ourselves. In carnival, there is agency. And there is safety. Too often in schools, masks are forced and enforced by a sense that we cannot permit people to see us as we are. In carnival, it is exactly the opposite. We select a mask to let people see us as we choose to be—for a time.

Bakhtin (1986) uses the theme of masks to exemplify how carnival embodies some characteristics of a community of difference—a community in which people experience a sense of agency and choose to contribute, as well as when and how to participate. How can we give students permission to remove masks that are not of their choosing? How can we create the conditions under which masks become voluntary and temporarily liberating, and not increasingly layered representations of marginalization and oppression?

The theme of masks is a complex and intrinsic component of carnival and folk culture. In general, however, school activities are more like staid rituals than celebratory carnivals. Students too often wear frozen masks of conformity (apple, banana, Oreo cookie), or masks of classroom clown, detached observer, high-achieving math student. Each hides private feelings of discomfort, insecurity, inadequacy, or pride. In carnival, masks permit people to become other—to interact in new ways, with new freedom and a new sense of empowerment. A mask hides something, but it represents something else.

In talking about masks, a friend spoke about his desire to explore the notion of masks with respect to his own situation—black and white, American and Canadian, marginalized and included. For him and many other students, various instructional techniques akin to carnival, such as reader's theater, role playing, and improvisational drama, may permit students to be other, to take on roles through which they can portray dangerous emotions (hurt or confusion, for example) in relative safety.

One diverse inner-city high school was described by an educator colleague, who was familiar with many schools in the area, as "having a much greater acceptance of diversity in comparison to other schools." In that school, an extensive drama program provided the way for students to both mask and unmask. Of the thousand-member student body, almost half of the students participated in elective drama classes offered by the school's two full-time drama teachers. Architecturally, the theater, a tall black cube in the middle of the building, provided a focal point for activities that involved and invited the whole school community.

Some activities were large-scale productions that involved many students, their families, and the wider community. Other smaller-scale activities occurred throughout the year. Each twelfth-grade student who enrolled in a directing class held auditions, worked with stage crew, set and costume designers, and selected a cast to stage his or her chosen play. Eighth-grade students performed for their own classes in air bands

selecting music from the 1960s or 1970s; they made papier-mâché gar-
goyle masks to wear in other in-class productions.

Through drama, students learned that there is plasticity and elastic-
ity in identities. Some were able to step outside harmful representations
and re-create themselves in different ways. One young man, a "social
misfit" bounced from his father to a mental health clinic to a group
home, was taken under the wing of a drama teacher, began hanging out
with a drama group, and developed a new persona—the resident lighting expert. Another boy, who had been cast out of one school after another because of his violent behavior, was able to achieve a level of acceptance and gain a sense of self-worth through various acting parts.

Many educators are familiar with the example of a school drama
program having a positive carnivalesque impact on students. Here a
large drama program helped create a new sense of community within
the school, providing students with the opportunity to try on different
roles and to escape roles others had assigned to them. As roles and responsibilities changed with each presentation, students began to understand the complexity and the fluidity of identity and community.

Experimenting with various roles and masks may help students understand the socially constructed nature of their own identities, think
about how they want to be represented, and find acceptable ways to
represent themselves to others in their community. Identifying some of
the masks we wear and then, perhaps, using Taubman's (1993) registers (the fictional, communal, and autobiographical—discussed in
chapter 5) to explore them, may help students experience greater
agency as they become more aware of how we present ourselves to others and why we choose particular masks and roles to represent us.

Developing New Forms of Communication

Carnival permits us to explore some of the barriers to communication imposed by labels and the creation of impermeable rules and roles
for interaction. In one high school, Sonia gave a graphic illustration of
how we tend to impose, rather than facilitate, the removal of masks.
She described her frustration with a particular teacher and the ways in
which she tried to communicate with him. She could not think of a time
he had listened to her when she made a suggestion. She explained,

"I've even taken the counselor's approach: I feel—because—I want. . . . I wrote out a huge protest paper so he could read it over. He tore it up in front of my face and said, 'I don't need this from a student.'"

It does not take a great deal of imagination to imagine the mask this student put on as she heard his words, or what mask she would wear for the rest of the year, not only in his class but in her other classes as well. Although this particular teacher may need more help than simply finding a new way of communicating, carnivalesque approaches may offer tools not only to students such as this girl but also to teachers who want to transform untenable situations into possibilities.

A more successful example of experimenting with new forms of communication comes from the research conducted by Pillsbury (see Pillsbury and Shields 1999) in a first-grade class. Wanting to determine whether first graders could actually be involved in a meaningful conversation about self and others, Jerry asked them,

Is it wrong to call a bunch of people "they"?

During the conversation, one student asked, "What if someone said, We're playing by ourselves?"

After two intervening statements, a little girl reflected, "Umm, like, we're playing by ourselves so you can't play."

As they explored this issue, a boy said softly, almost to himself, "Oh no, don't say that you can't play."

Shortly thereafter, another boy, recognizing the potential for hurt, asked, "But how are you going to describe someone else without saying 'they'?"

Therein lies the problem, clearly delineated by first-graders.

A girl continued, "When you say 'they,' it's like . . . 'they' is different and whenever we say 'we' it's not different." (Pillsbury and Shields 1999, 426)

This example of a conversation between a researcher and a first-grade class shows clearly the power of attempting new forms of communication—even with very young children. As these children began to recognize, it is not that the use of "we" or "they" is inherently right or wrong; rather, it is how a comment is framed and what sense of self or other is being represented that is important.

Unless we engage members of the community in explicit conversation about the meaning of the norms that exist and of ways in which we want to behave together in community, the status quo remains unchallenged and few changes occur. On the other hand, when a leader takes the initiative and engages the community in dialogue, empowerment may transpire and boundaries may be reconstructed.

Empowering Self and Others

We often talk about the need to empower others as if saying the word or waving a magic wand would make empowerment happen. I have a friend who used to say, "Empower is not a transitive verb." It is not something we can do to others. But we can, and must, create the conditions under which empowerment may occur. The following illustration shows that even young children can be taught that they have the power to solve problems and shape their educational experiences for themselves and their friends.

At Emily Carr Elementary School, weekly town-hall meetings helped students exercise their power to deal with problems without adult intervention. Vibert and colleagues describe one town hall meeting:

> A first-grade student addressed the assembly on the issue of sharing access to playground equipment. He was raising a community problem, one of the purposes for which the Town Hall forum was intended. Not everyone, he pointed out, had equal access to swings; sometimes the smaller children in particular could wait all recess without ever getting an opportunity to swing. He called for suggestions from the assembly, and after a sometimes tangential discussion, the children agreed to set a time limit on the use of play ground equipment when there is a waiting line. It was a striking example of children engaging in, identifying, and negotiating their own communal concerns. (1998, 139)

The meetings permitted children to become problem solvers, resolve conflicts, and participate more fully in the creation of their school community.

The words of Bakhtin seem to sum up this incident: a "new concept of realism has a different way of drawing boundaries between bodies and objects" (1984, 53). At Emily Carr School, empowering students though activities such as town-hall meetings did in fact redraw boundaries. It overcame the traditional structures of teachers as rule makers and students as rule followers and led to new processes and new solutions to problems.

Recreating Boundaries

Once we choose to overthrow hierarchy, hegemony, and power, there is no turning back. We cannot disrupt our assumptions and then simplistically return to them. We cannot simultaneously have a community of difference with democratic participation and retain traditional, hierarchical decision-making structures and processes.

When Stephen Lewis School was opened, having learning leaders instead of vice principals created anxiety among those who saw varied practices developing in each learning community—different celebrations and daily schedules and alternative ways of dealing with problem situations or with students who were struggling in various ways to make sense of their learning. But it also taught educators, parents, and students that there were different ways of thinking about schooling. What a departure to empower and include students to the extent that they complained about too many parents on the School Council! While many educators struggle with the notion of having parents on a school advisory council, here was a school in which students were concerned that parents, who did not know the situation firsthand, might prevent student voices from being fully heard.

The Spirit of Carnival

The spirit of carnival, Bakhtin says, "liberates the world from all that is dark and terrifying; it takes away all fears and is therefore gay and bright. All that was frightening in ordinary life is turned into amusing or ludicrous monstrosities" (1984, 47). Carnival may not be the panacea suggested in this quotation, since even in the gay and bright atmosphere there are still shadows. Perhaps our fears seem more amusing and less threatening during carnival, but we do not leave a carnival with all our problems solved. Carnival may show us what we need to change; it may offer a glimpse of a different order and new relationships; but more is needed.

According to Bakhtin, carnival

> seeks to grasp in its imagery the very act of becoming and growth, the eternal incomplete unfinished nature of being. Its images present simultaneously the two poles of becoming: that which is receding and dying, and that which is being born; they show two bodies in one, the budding and the division of the living cell. At the summit of grotesque and folklore realism, as in the death of one-cell organisms, no dead body remains. (That is, when the single cell divides into two other organisms, it dies in a sense but also reproduces; there is no departure from life into death.) (1984, 52)

The notion of birth from existing forms is critical to thinking about new models of schooling, new ways of being together in the world. It may be uncomfortable, but it is not a killer. Change theorists sometimes remind us that change is always accompanied by anxiety. Even if the change is one we desire fervently, one whose benefits we anticipate, such as marriage, the birth of a child, starting a new job, there is always a sense of tense anticipation.

Effecting change through the principles of carnival (inviting full participation, using humor, challenging hierarchical relationships, using masks, developing new forms of communication, drawing new boundaries, and empowering participants) may make it easier. There will still be apprehension, but there will be, as Bakhtin puts it, "no dead bodies remaining." For, like the phoenix, a new school community will surely rise from the ashes of the old.

CHANGING BELIEFS, BREAKING BONDS

Carnival emphasizes changes in action—acting joyously, fearlessly, a little irreverently—in order to overthrow the bonds that hold us hostage to tradition or to dominant patterns of power and privilege. In change theory there is another adage that says, "Belief follows action." Until more members of the school community—teachers, students, parents, and community leaders—feel welcome to participate in school activities and unless they may speak openly and freely without fear of reprisal, the current norms of power and influence will continue to advantage some at the expense of others. Carnivalesque behaviors provide a way for new norms to gain a toehold.

Emily Carr has done it through town-hall meetings; Regal High School in New Zealand instituted a form of carnival through the use of art. Canyon Collegiate offers the Ndahoo'aah program (Navajo weaving, bead work, and basketry bringing elders and students together, uniting computers and vertical looms). To some extent all are unusual combinations for new learning. Central Elementary School, New Zealand language nests (Kaura Kaupapa Maori), and the small Fijian school have introduced forms of carnival by integrating parents more fully into the life of the school. Stephen Lewis changed the institutional norms and introduced new patterns for governance and for teaching and learning. Others have done it by developing an extensive drama program, while still others have instituted new forms of dialogue with community members.

The key for us is to learn from the daily lived experiences of others—to personalize their experiences of schooling and our roles in it—to understand not just the abstract notion of racism or prejudice, but the concreteness and sharp pain of Sonia's failure to communicate with her teacher or the shame felt by Anish when he dumped the *samosas* on top of his books. It requires us to celebrate specifics—to rejoice at the first-grader's success in finding a solution to the problem of access to the swings, not simply to delight in vague notions of liberty or empowerment.

Developing a critical consciousness about the various forms of multiculturalism and their potential for challenging and changing (or reinforcing) the inequities in the status quo is one aspect of becoming a transformative educational leader. Using our new consciousness to introduce elements of carnival into the fabric of school life is one way to disrupt the present boundaries between the powerful and the powerless, between those who hold power in the current hierarchical structure and those who do not, between those whose voices are heard and those who are silenced.

Bishop and Glynn assert that among colonized peoples, such as the New Zealand Maori population, colonization has created a series of problems that need to be overcome "before addressing cultural diversity

from within the dominant discourse. These are problems of power im-
balance; the development of a relationship of dominance and subordination as the result of colonialism" (1999, 52). Unless the primary imbalanced relationship is rectified, they claim, "The pattern will
dominate the way in which cultural diversity is understood and discussed" (p. 52). They argue that if educational leaders and others in
power continue to make decisions about what is best for others without
the full participation of members of traditionally disenfranchised
groups, no meaningful change can occur.

The possibilities are endless. What is critical is that we change the
dominant power relations in schools and begin to engage in a form of
power exercised *with,* not *over,* others. Dewey, in *Liberalism and Social Action,* decries notions of liberty and expression that are not, at the
same time, modes of action:

> It is false that freedom of inquiry and modes of expression are not modes
> of action. They are exceedingly potent modes of action. The reactionary
> grasps this fact, in practice if not in express idea, more quickly than the
> liberal, who is too much given to holding that freedom is innocent of
> consequences, as well as being a merely individual right. The result is
> that this liberty is tolerated as long as it does not seem to menace in any
> way the *status quo* of society. When it does, every effort is put forth to
> identify the established order with the public good. (1989, 45)

Some may argue that schools, as they are currently conceived, are instruments of the public good and do not need radical transformation. I
contend, with Dewey, that it is not enough to use the words *public good*
or *freedom* without making the image concrete. We must specify for
whom, in what way, at what cost freedom is to be found. What will
need to change?

It is not adequate to act with good intentions if we lack a vision of
the desired end. It is not enough to talk about social justice but fail to
identify changes that we must initiate in our own practice. Transformative and critical educational leaders must be willing to take a stand, to
create schools that are just, empathetic, democratic, and optimistic. We
must, as Bakhtin prompts us, use carnival as an instrument of educational change to build new forms of schooling in opposition to tradi-

tional ones—modes that offer caring, respectful, inclusive, critical, joyful, and educative learning opportunities.

A TIME FOR PLAY

Combining Bakhtin's vision of carnival and the focus of critical multiculturalism permits us to dream about a different educational reality for our children and their children. They offer new ways for the transformative leader to begin to effect cultural change in his or her community.

Leading from a critical multicultural perspective requires the leader to adopt a commitment to social justice, to understand the instruments of exclusion and marginalization that operate in our school communities to disempower some students. It requires acknowledging the mechanisms of power and privilege that continue to empower other students. The transformative leader will engage individuals and groups in a school in a continuous exploration of ways in which we can ensure that all are being taken seriously, treated with dignity, and afforded the opportunity to tell their stories and to have them heard in a spirit of respect.

Leading an organization from a carnivalesque approach requires simultaneously taking self and others seriously, and not taking self and others too seriously. It requires us to challenge and critique the very things we earnestly believe and to use playfulness to overthrow rules, hierarchy, and roles that have become fixed and sacrosanct.

At the core of developing new norms for a community of difference are carnival and multiculturalism. They remind us that as members of our school communities become comfortable with ambiguity, engage in playfulness, and challenge inequitable practices and power structures, change can occur. The transformative educational leader will demonstrate to parents, teachers, and students, by example as well as by precept, that everything is open to challenge, discussion, and renegotiation.

NOTES

1. The school was designed and opened in 1994 as a multitrack year-round school with numerous pedagogical and organizational innovations that are the

focus of the discussion in this chapter. The calendar change and related structural issues will be discussed in the next chapter. Although the depiction of this school reflects its first three years in operation, little of the original innovative character remains, seven years and three principals later. This begs the question of sustainability discussed in chapters 9–10.

2. By legislation, parents in this jurisdiction needed to constitute the majority membership on school councils—a bone of contention for students who worried that their voices might be overshadowed.

3. For example, Bishop describes recent studies of professionals who believe that Maori are genetically predisposed to mental illness and that children's cultural deprivation accounts for school failure (Bishop 2001, citing Nicholson 2000 and Read and Johnstone 2000).

4. The practice was widespread: Australia, Canada, New Zealand, and the United States (Hawaii) had well-intentioned official policies with respect to suppressing the heritage language of aboriginal people as well as unofficial practices of discouraging and forbidding immigrant students from communicating in their home languages. Discredited now as having neither social nor educational benefits, the practices, which caused irreparable damage to some language groups, are still supported by some minority-language parents.

5. Sometimes also spelled Djabukai.

6. The thesis could not be defended until after the war, but in 1946 and 1949 his defense "split the Moscow scholarly world into two camps; his doctorate was finally awarded when the government stepped in. It took until 1965 before the thesis could be published" (Holquist 2000, xxv).

CHAPTER 8

Walls, Fences, and Other Structural Changes

The concept of carnival elaborated in the previous chapter provides educational leaders with some tools for thinking about effecting cultural change—changes in the way things are done in a particular school community. Introducing moments of carnival and new forms of thinking about multiculturalism can address both cultural and structural components in schools. Despite the common aphorism that we need to reculture, not restructure, it seems clear that changing educational communities involves both. Neither structure nor culture exists in a vacuum and, regardless of one's starting point, it is important for the transformative leader to understand and facilitate both types of change. In this chapter, we examine the notion of structure, exemplified by Frost's wall metaphor.

AN ILLUSTRATION: MARTIN POPPER ELEMENTARY SCHOOL

I want to begin by telling you the story of a school that instituted widespread changes—structural and cultural changes for the benefit of its student body. Martin Popper Elementary School is located in one of the poorest areas I have visited in the United States. Small camper-trailers sit on concrete pads, single-wide trailers with broken doors and windows line the streets, tiny shacks that have seen better days are scattered here and there. The better housing in the immediate vicinity of the school consists of trailers parked behind fences or in walled compounds—looking more like internment camps than places for families and children.

Jane, the school's principal, has been there over twenty-four years (her first sixteen as a teacher and assistant principal), building relationships with the community, leading her staff, and working to change attitudes and expectations. She summed up her teachers' commitment to going beyond the typical school day and exerting unusual effort on behalf of their students with the comment (reminiscent of Esther's words in chapter 5) "My teachers know they are on a mission field." She explained further:

> When I interview teachers I always say that if you don't feel called to the mission field, then this is not the school for you because you're going to do more when you come here than just teach academics. You need to do a lot of wrap around-type service. . . . So, don't be here if you're not a flexible person.

Jane recognizes that there are a lot of dynamic teachers who are not cut out for Martin Popper School.

Recently, in a one-year period, Jane's school moved from Florida's D-list of poorly performing schools to its A-list of high-achieving schools. With a high migrant population and a free and reduced lunch rate of 87 percent, Martin Popper receives some additional resources to address the needs of its student population. Jane has used them with determination in an innovative approach to developing a school-wide program of high expectations and sound pedagogy. She says she began with a focus on school-wide approaches: "I feel that we have to do things school-wide. I'm a real believer in that in all the years I've been in education, I've learned that what you do school-wide is going to be effective." Title I funds have been used to hire master teachers in reading, writing, and math. Each master teacher works with the grade-level teachers to develop a consistent program, implement interactive strategies, and utilize solid assessment processes.

In addition, Jane set out to change the school calendar to make it more conducive to student learning. After listening to pressure from several enthusiastic teachers, Jane conducted her own research into the possibility of a more balanced calendar. After reflecting on the needs of her students and examining the research, she became convinced that instituting a calendar in which students attended school for ten weeks at a time and then had a three-week vacation, followed by similar in-school and vacation time, would facilitate the learning (including remediation and enrichment) of her students.

Once convinced, she pursued the possibility relentlessly. Although twenty-one principals requested permission from the district to change their school calendar to a single-track year-round school[1] calendar, only five actually received permission before a district-imposed freeze. Jane was one of them.

She firmly believes that although the socioeconomic situation of her students presents challenges to her teachers, they must not relax their expectations. She elaborates:

> We know that the home situations sometimes can affect the way a child comes to school, how he feels that day—you know, mother is in jail, or . . . Everyday you know stories that could just make you sit down and cry, but we always have to focus. We have to remind ourselves that everyday. We have to focus on our job. That is just to give them the best that we can give them—in academics, in love, (emotional strength while they are with us). We just do the best we can and it's like being on a mission field.

Jane hoped that changing the calendar would provide alternate structures for meeting students' needs and for responding to some of their educational challenges. Thus she devised an elaborate intersession program. During the three-week breaks, Jane and her master teachers provided enrichment for those students deemed most in need of additional learning experiences and instruction in order to succeed. Together teachers determined which students might profit most from extra instructional time and issued invitations. Over 65 percent of those invited attended the sessions in which teachers presented material in innovative ways so students would want to be there. "They do not need 'fiction,'" Jane told us, thinking about the type of small picture books that are sometimes produced to interest low-achieving students. "They need life experiences and we try to give them enrichment."

Using this school-wide approach, both teachers and students have blossomed. The vice principal, newly arrived at the school, after serving as both a teacher and an administrator at several other schools, says he has never seen such a school-wide initiative:

> When I came to this school, I knew it was a year-round school but as I saw things happen, it was just amazing! Intersession and the things that went on in classrooms, and this school-wide thing, teachers doing the same thing from one classroom to the next!

The new balanced calendar and voluntary intersession activities seemed to pay off. Jane describes the scene as she returned from a vacation to find her daughter at the airport, waving the school's test results from the statewide program in hand. Her daughter's greeting was, "I think you're going to want to see this!" Jane described her initial reaction:

> I was praying for a C because we're a D right? She hands it to me and I'm looking at a B. I went ballistic right there. We're just coming off the gate—people all around I didn't even know—I'm screaming and hollering hallelujah. You know, we were thrilled that we were a B and we held a big celebration breakfast at the school.

But then the story took an unusual twist. Jane and the teachers began to examine the data, looking at the criteria for being an A school. And they found they had actually met the A criteria. After a lengthy period of gathering and compiling additional data, they submitted their appeal through the district office. To Jane's surprise, she received a phone call from someone at the district:

> Do you really want to go through with this? Isn't a move from a D to a B good enough? We might want to go slowly. . . . You know once you get to an A it's hard to maintain. You might want to wait and see if you become an A next year.

Jane says that it did not take long for her to respond. "We were a D and now we're an A. We may never again be an A school.[2] Right now our parents think we're the best school in the world. So the decision was easy." Rejecting a deficit perspective and overcoming a reputation for poor performance required Jane to take a courageous stand, even against the recommendation of the district. By fighting for an A, she sent a clear message that she believed in the potential of the students in her school. Thinking about the future, Jane mused:

> I would like to see our achievement continue to go up and to improve. I would like to see our children leave Martin Popper and do well socially in their lives because that's why we work so hard on our social skills. I would like to see them rise above their circumstances to maybe go out in the workplace and get some really decent jobs as a result of the confidence they have gained from learning so much more here. . . . I'd like to have Martin Popper be a school where people say, "Even though you have at-risk children, there's learning going on, good teaching going on, and they are making a difference."

Taken together, the changes at Martin Popper School have worked wonders! Here is a school with high poverty, a high visible minority population, high expectations and a no-excuse philosophy, a schoolwide curricular emphasis, thematic interdisciplinary instruction, and a focus on learning. All these, combined with love and respect for each other, and excellent results—how could we clone the approach?

Of course, we cannot clone Jane, nor would we want to. Each school is unique; each community of teachers and students needs to identify its own goals and strategies because the impetus comes from within—it cannot be imposed.

The story of Martin Popper, however, raises new questions. Until now I have focused on issues such as culture, identity, and power. Here I want to focus on school structures and how changing structural arrangements may be a catalyst for other types of change, in particular, more equitable student learning.

In the first half of this chapter, I examine structural changes in general and show that they are inseparably linked to how we think about and practice equity and social justice in schools. In the second half, I elaborate the discussion of the structural change chosen by Jane at Martin Popper Elementary School to demonstrate how a change of school calendar may promote equity and equality as well as excellence for all students.

AND THE WALLS COME TUMBLING DOWN

In Frost's poem, the wall tumbles each year and is as quickly rebuilt. In schools, walls that have been constructed over years of tradition or mistrust of difference are often maintained as carefully. Whenever a stone falls, it is quickly replaced—keeping some people, ideas, and cultures in, and others out.

Structures, some researchers would have us believe (Hargreaves and Fullan 1998; Levin 2001), have little to do with student learning. They claim their research shows that changing structures does not positively affect the achievement of students. I would suggest that while changing some structures may not affect student learning, changing others may have a significant impact. Moreover, unless educational change is somehow institutionalized through its structures as well as kept alive and vibrant through its people, it may not be sustainable.

If two teachers, for example, believe that thematic and interdisciplinary instruction is useful, they may decide to collaborate to provide such instruction. However, if the teachers leave the school, the initiative is unlikely to persist. On the other hand, if the schedule has been modified to facilitate the change and a written curriculum is in place, the momentum is more likely to be maintained.

If a teacher is particularly interested in new approaches to helping her class engage in dialogue about social issues or in encouraging parents to volunteer in her classroom, the impact on her students each year may be profound. However, unless, as Jane insisted, the initiative becomes school-wide, it remains an isolated good idea that may not affect the core of the school community.

In some countries during the past two decades, considerable attention has been paid to changing educational structures. In New Zealand, a separate branch of the Ministry of Education has been established to ensure that Maori language and culture receive appropriate attention in schools and regional education offices. In England, a now almost defunct experiment with Grant Maintained Schools and new accountability structures received international attention. Many other jurisdictions introduced extensive structural change.

Some believe (and I concur) that in North America, too little attention has been paid to the ways in which educational structures inhibit just, empathetic, democratic, and optimistic education—or facilitate it. Without legislation, for example, how long might it have taken for school integration to transpire in the southern United States? Even after the initial court decision, subsequent structures had to be monitored to ensure that integration actually occurred. Without the legislative establishment and protection of parent advisory councils, how many schools and educational leaders would automatically have developed processes for the direct input of parents into decision making? Indeed, structures, both physical and organizational, are symbolic of our core beliefs and deserve to be taken much more seriously than they frequently are.

In many parts of the world, separate structures are provided as a way of addressing difference. In Fiji, for example, walls exist both physically and psychologically between native Fijians and Indian Fijians: students from each group attend separate schools. In Canada many Indian bands and in the United States, the Bureau of Indian Affairs, in the name of local control and empowerment, often create separate schools for aboriginal students. These schools may enhance opportunities for parental involvement, for children to receive education in their home communities, and for indigenous languages to be taught. Likewise, in many other places, such as Hawaii, New Zealand, and Australia, there are strong advocates for separate schools to promote the language and culture of minority groups. In some American states, separate schools have been established for black male students. In still other places, charter schools are permitted and independent religious schools are funded.

Although separate structures may help previously marginalized groups develop a needed sense of competence, I believe they should be seen as temporary measures. Separate structures may be a necessary intermediate step to assist formerly powerless and marginalized groups to find their voices, explore their power, and develop the confidence and competence to participate on an equal footing. Nevertheless, if separate structures persist over a long period of time, I am convinced that they inhibit the possibility of learning together, from one another, in a community of difference.

Examining Physical Barriers

Sometimes school buildings themselves represent walls that need to be torn down—barriers to respectful, inclusive education for all community members. Kozol, in *Savage Inequalities* (1992), demonstrates graphically some of the inequities present in American schooling, as evidenced by the abominable and abysmal physical conditions and limited resource availability in some public schools and the extravagant abundance in others. The situation is, of course, not confined to the United States.

Many of the strategies available to schools to enhance playgrounds, acquire high-tech equipment, or in some cases even purchase new textbooks, depend on the wealth of a school's population and community. Frequently decisions about how to spend money in a school are highly contentious. We saw in chapter 3, for example, that many teachers at Marco Polo Elementary School resented spending money for new couches to improve the foyer because they felt they would not be appreciated either by the students or by the parent community.

Sandra Dean, in *Hearts and Minds: A Public School Miracle* (2000), describes how changing the physical appearance of a school was the first step in tearing down perceptions of disadvantage and worthlessness. After becoming principal of a run-down, demoralized, inner-city elementary school, she spent her first summer painting the walls, cleaning up the yard, repairing basketball hoops, installing motion-sensor lights, and throwing out "any article that could not be restored to its original condition" (Dean 2000, 34). There would be no makeshift furniture in her building, for she intended to show her students that they deserved the very best. Dean describes the effects: "Over time, the broken bottles and graffiti decreased, and one morning we arrived to discover the basketball court festooned with a hundred colourful balloons. 'It's a thank you note,' someone said, and I agreed with her totally" (p. 37).

Dean's efforts to improve both the physical and emotional climate of the school quickly garnered support from the custodial staff. Soon offers of help came from local service clubs; believing she was on the right track, they offered to become partners to help in any way they could (p. 43).

In chapter 4, we saw that changing the appearance of a school could be a useful first step in making people feel welcome and in making cultures more relevant and meaningful. Yet physical barriers are not the only structural ways in which we exclude people from full participation in our school communities.

Examining Policy Barriers

Our educational policies themselves often constitute barriers to just, democratic, empathetic, and optimistic education. Examining how parent councils are structured and governed is illustrative. Parent councils can often raise money and determine how it is to be spent. Parents of the graduating class from the upper-middle-class school called the Academy are able to raise approximately $8,000 each Christmas season by selling poinsettias, while the parents from a neighboring school in a less affluent area struggle to find money to send children to an annual eighth-grade camp. Parents want to raise money for their children, but not all parents have the same time and resources to do so. Can we expect affluent parents to fund-raise for students in other schools? This is a tricky ethical issue. Rather than permit school parent councils to have sole responsibility for funds raised, could we change the policy structures, entitling a district to retain a certain percentage of funds raised, perhaps 15 percent, for allocation to other schools according to need?

Sometimes, even when school councils acknowledge their advantage, well-intentioned efforts may not bring about the desired results. For example, parents from one middle class community school resolved to partner with a neighboring school in an inner city. They would raise funds for the diverse inner-city school, while students from the latter would perform multicultural dances at their school's assembly. The initiative was definitely well-intentioned. Yet a one-sided partnership decision tends to perpetuate a deficit mentality, in which some parents and children are seen as donors and others as recipients of their generosity. What kind of policies and procedures might a transformative educational leader introduce that could bring parent councils from the two groups together in a full partnership, working together on both fund-raising and performing?

Even if the intention is to tear down walls, there are sometimes structures that inhibit change. In one district, a wealthy citizen wanted to donate a piano to a school on an Indian reservation that was attempting to enhance its music program. Unfortunately, the district policy did not permit one school to have a grand piano unless every school had one. The options were limited. The intended recipient could refuse to accept the gift, the donor could provide fourteen pianos, or the district could allocate funds (already designated to other uses) to provide a similar instrument for every school. In this case, the structure implied that equity required treating every school in exactly the same way and prevented a needy school from accepting a generous gift. In what ways could the policy be changed to ensure that no single school was unduly privileged by generous donations while permitting the individual needs of schools to be addressed?

Educational policy provides a structural framework for what happens in schools. Policy makers, therefore, need to find ways to promote equity and be flexible enough to encourage initiative.

Examining Organizational Barriers

In addition to physical impediments and policy barriers, organizational barriers to equity and excellence often exist. Walls of tradition often structure the ways in which teachers and children are assigned to classes and classes are organized for instruction.

In Red Rock Elementary School, Carl learned in his first year as principal that some teachers had taught at the same grade level for more than fifteen years, without any upgrading or professional development activities to foster renewal. Moreover, at the intermediate level (grades 4–6), there were some very weak teachers. He decided to change the organizational structures. Carl first asked all teachers at the primary level who had been assigned to the same grade level for more than three years to give him their top two choices of alternative grades they were willing to teach. Each was given a new assignment. At the intermediate level, he knew he could not help each teacher improve instruction in every required curricular area all at once, and so he reorganized the instruction. He created a team approach so that each teacher could focus on his or her areas of strength, teaching one or two subjects at three grade levels. A fifth-grade teacher who previously had sole charge of her class took responsibility for teaching reading to all classes in the fourth, fifth, and sixth grades. Likewise, the former sixth-grade teacher began to teach math at all three grade levels and focus his professional development activities on learning new mathematics strategies.

At first, as might be expected, the teachers complained bitterly. However, when I interviewed the teachers later in the school year, they unanimously agreed that the changes had been the best thing that had happened to the school in some time. Changing the structures had changed the climate, the patterns of interaction, and the motivation of the teachers to improve their instructional practice.

EXAMINING THE REALITY OF STRUCTURAL BARRIERS

There is no doubt that schools have historically disadvantaged some students and privileged others. Walls do not have to be physical to be real. Many of the structures we create—separate schools, programs for gifted students, English as a second language programs, International Baccalaureate programs—tend to separate rather than unite. I often wonder how we can find ways of living together in community if we balkanize schools, claiming that the only way to preserve and protect heritage and culture is separation. The questions need to be asked and answered carefully. Do good fences make good neighbors? Do strong walls create communities? Does this structure enhance our civil society?

Many educators are suspicious of structural change, believing it is a form of tinkering with the organization and leaving the central core of teaching and learning intact. Structural change, they claim, does not really reach areas where the major changes need to occur. Hargreaves and Fullan, for example, state that restructuring which refers to "changes in the formal structure of schooling in terms of organization, timetables, roles and the like [has a] terrible track record" (1998, 118).

Levin, in his analysis of reform in five jurisdictions, supports this perspective. He studied structural reforms related to school choice, charter schools, increased testing, stricter curriculum guides, and changes in governance in England, New Zealand, Canada (Manitoba and Alberta), and the United States (Minnesota). Overall, he found that the changes had little significant impact on student achievement. Levin supports his argument by citing Elmore who wrote: "Changes in structure are weakly related to changes in teaching practice, and therefore structural change does not necessarily lead to changes in teaching, learning, and student performance" (as cited in Levin 2001, 27).

The claim that restructuring has no impact on student learning is much too strong a response; I believe that a more prudent approach would be Margaret Wheatley's (1993) simple: "It depends." If restructuring is confined to moving pieces around within existing boxes, an assessment of "no impact" may well be true. There is, for example, little convincing evidence that a change on the part of a high school to or from block scheduling or semestering without any concomitant changes in pedagogical strategies has any significant or lasting effect on student learning (Brake 2000; Pisapia and Westfall 1997). Likewise, if we change the levels of responsibility or the lines of communication in a district office, there is little reason to think the new organization will have a more direct impact on student learning than the previous one. If we move the site of funding decisions from a district committee to a school committee, there may be a better chance that local conditions and needs will be considered. But unless the decision relates to classroom equipment or learning materials, it is unlikely to be noticed by the students or to have any identifiable impact on their learning environment.

Changes that have a direct effect on the lives of teachers and students are much more likely to affect classroom practice and hence the core functions of learning and teaching. Yet even here we need to be cautious. Despite considerable research into class size, an aspect of schooling that definitely pertains to the classroom, more than 50 percent of all studies have found an inconclusive impact on student performance (Hanushek 1998). Nevertheless, a new math curriculum, for example, is more likely to change the way in which math is both taught and understood than increasing the number of parents on a committee. A change from segregated programming for ESL or learning-disabled students will change the classroom relationships and the norms of instruction. Hargreaves and Fullan acknowledge that restructuring is "part of the picture of successful reform" (1998, 119) but assert that it only comes into play after "people have invested emotionally in transforming the culture and relationships in a school over many years" (p. 119).

One might claim that the changes which Jane instituted at Martin Popper School began with attitudinal and cultural change and culminated in calendar change after many years. Yet my empirical studies of school-calendar change[3] provide no evidence that one necessarily precedes the other; rather, both structural and cultural change may effect changes in norms and relationships and prompt people to begin to think and work differently. Interestingly, just as cultural changes may work to support structural change, so I have often found that structural change may act as a catalyst for alterations that result in more equitable opportunities and outcomes for all students.

In the next section, to illustrate a structural reform with the potential to increase equity and enhance student learning, I examine in more detail the concept of year round schooling chosen by Jane and the staff of Martin Popper Elementary School.

STRUCTURES MATTER: EXAMINING THE SCHOOL CALENDAR

One of the most traditional structures in Western education is the school calendar. Developed in North America around the turn of the last century, the nine- to ten-month school year with a long summer break (often mistakenly called the agrarian calendar) has become the norm. What many believe is a vestige of an earlier, more agrarian society actually resulted from a compromise. At the turn of the nineteenth century, rural schools were in operation for roughly six months a year and urban schools tended to be open for eleven or twelve months. When Horace Mann (in the United States) and Edgar Ryerson (in Canada) wanted to introduce a common curriculum, a compromise was needed and the current school year was born.

What would our calendar look like if we were to start from scratch and develop a new structure that takes into account life in our twenty-first-century world? Despite the fact that the present calendar may have outlived its usefulness, attempts to modify the school year are frequently met with considerable distrust and strong opposition.

In North America, a calendar change to year-round schooling (YRS) is often met with suspicion and confusion, in part because the term is a misnomer, suggesting that students will be forced to spend all year in school. In general, the term YRS simply refers to a reallocation of in-class and vacation time, reducing the length of the summer vacation and introducing longer and more evenly spaced breaks throughout the school year. Although the school year is sometimes extended through voluntary attendance at intersession, YRS is rarely accompanied by a mandate for a longer school year.

The concept of balanced or modified calendars or year-round schooling is definitely not new, with the first year-round calendars having been introduced in the United States in 1905. More recently, the continued appeal of calendar change has resulted in three modern phases of year-round schooling that span approximately thirty years.

A First Wave: Cost Savings through Multitrack Calendars

During the 1970s, the first modern wave of year-round schooling was instituted to respond to periods of rapid growth during which districts needed (or wanted) to place more children in existing school buildings by using a multitrack (MT) calendar.[4] This approach was effective when districts were having difficulty keeping up with rapidly increasing enrollment, when there were inadequate available funds to build new buildings, or when the projected enrollment increase seemed to be a temporary bubble. In a multitrack calendar, children are assigned to overlapping schedules so that while some are on vacation, others are in class. Thus a school that could normally house six hundred students on a traditional or single-track schedule could serve eight hundred (an increase of 33 percent) on a four-track schedule by rotating groups of two hundred students and their teachers throughout the year. The cost-effectiveness of this calendar when per pupil costs are calculated on a per district and not a per school basis continues to make it an attractive option for fiscal efficiency. The multitrack calendar is generally not a calendar of choice, but one mandated to address fiscal and capital challenges. Where this has happened, people are sometimes concerned that the impetus has been economic rather than educational. Nevertheless, student learning has often been positively affected by the change (Shields and Oberg 1999).

A Second Wave: Confusion about Goals

In the second wave that occurred roughly from the mid-1980s to the mid-1990s (depending on venue), many schools and districts in North America toyed with structural change in the form of modified calendars, but with a disconcerting lack of clarity about the goals of the proposed innovation. The timing coincided with a frenzy of school-reform initiatives, attempts to introduce elements of decentralized decision making, and a desire to provide parental choice. People who had experienced multitrack calendars reported benefits associated with the more relaxed rhythm of schooling; hence, some educators anticipated that better attendance, higher levels of motivation (for teachers and students), and perhaps better academic achievement could be captured in single-track[5] or even dual-track[6] models. This exploratory period was marked by various examinations and interpretations of what was, for the most part, a very uneven and problematic literature related to year-round schooling—a literature dominated by adversarial and advocacy perspectives that are still cited by those ideologically opposed to a calendar change.

A Third Wave: A Clear Focus on Learning

The third wave of calendar reform has a clear focus—on reducing the achievement gap between students who are successful and those who are not, enhancing the possibility that all students can achieve to a high level. This focus on finding a calendar that more adequately addresses the needs of modern students has occurred not only in North America but in other countries as well. In 1996 the government of New Zealand, recognizing the ways in which traditional structures of education inhibited student learning, introduced a new national calendar consisting of four ten-week terms interspersed with three two-week holidays and one six-week vacation period. In December 2001, the Independent Commission on the School Year in Britain recommended that Britain move to a six-term year consisting of two seven-week and four six-week terms, interspersed with five two-week breaks and one four-week holiday period.

As the research has become more sophisticated and clearer about what is and is not being studied, there is convincing evidence that a calendar change holds the potential to improve the learning environment and the achievement of children (Kneese 1996; Shields and Oberg 2000). Thus educators in many schools and districts in North America have begun to introduce balanced calendars (previously called single-track year-round schooling).

By the beginning of the twenty-first century in North America, more than two million children in over three thousand schools and six hundred districts were being educated on a form of year-round school calendar, sometimes called a modified or alternative calendar. Personally, I think the term used by Martin Popper School, *balanced calendar*, is a much better way of thinking about the calendar change in which the school year is reorganized, the long summer vacation period is reduced somewhat, and students and teachers attend classes on a more regular rhythm of roughly forty-five days in class followed by fifteen-day vacation periods.[7]

Thinking about how to improve student achievement is central to the role of any transformative school administrator, especially if she is in a school with a very diverse population where achievement has traditionally been low and morale is depressed. If, as in Jane's case, she can find a structural change that garners parental and community support and increases attendance and decreases transience (from 74 percent to 61 percent in one year), it is an added bonus and warrants further consideration. Based on my research and that of others, there are three main ways in which changing to a more regular, or balanced, calendar may have a positive impact on student learning.

A More Regular Rhythm Facilitates Learning

In 1994 we[8] began to study the effects of a calendar change on a school district in Utah that had introduced a multitrack YRS calendar primarily to accommodate increasing numbers of children in existing buildings. The research team compared the achievement of eleven thousand elementary students in multitrack schools to the achievement of nineteen thousand students in traditional calendar schools relative to their school-wide achievement over six years on a statewide achievement test. Our comparison was based not on raw scores, but on an examination of how students performed vis-à-vis their expected performance as designated by a state-determined "predicted range of achievement" for every school. This was an important indicator because it took into consideration home and at-risk factors of students, including their socioeconomic status and recognized between-school differences in student populations.

Overall, we found that 21 percent of the mean fifth-grade scores from the district's traditional calendar schools fell below their school's predicted range of achievement, while only 4 percent of the scores from students in MT-YRS fell below the predicted range (Shields and Oberg 1999). This substantive change was of particular importance in that the district had selected a MT calendar to avoid the cost of building new schools and had not made any other changes related to instruction or curriculum.

Upon further inquiry, based on a survey of fifth-grade students and their parents, as well as interviews of principals and fifth-grade teachers, we found that the more regular rhythm of schooling and vacation time facilitated better attendance, greater motivation, and less burnout on the part of teachers and students. Teachers reported spending less time re viewing material after shorter breaks, expending less time and energy on discipline, and maintaining a more consistent focus on instruction.

The new calendar also seemed conducive to more professional school-wide conversation about teaching and learning due to the more relaxed rhythm of schooling. Teachers reported that they planned differently, in three-, six-, or nine-week blocks (depending on whether or not they wanted to team teach with a colleague on a different rotation) and that they focused more on instructional goals and how to achieve them through supporting materials and activities than on the A–Z coverage of the textbook. Planning in this way, focusing on the curricular goal and then gathering materials to help teach it, permitted teachers to select more responsive curricular materials and to be more inclusive in their instructional practices.

There is evidence that a balanced calendar is accompanied by higher test scores, better attendance, and less burnout for students and teachers.

But perhaps equally compelling is the fact that the vast majority of people who have experienced a modified calendar are enthusiastic supporters. Overall, in ten years of studies and examination of the literature, we have found that the support is overwhelming, with 98 percent of administrators, 94 percent of teachers, and 86 percent of parents stating that they strongly prefer a balanced calendar to the traditional one (Shields and Oberg 2000). Despite these strong personal preferences, the most convincing argument for the introduction of a more balanced calendar comes from the research on summer learning loss.

Reducing Summer Learning Loss

Over twenty-five years, the research is conclusive: in the traditional organization of schools, students from the least advantaged families are most disadvantaged by the long vacation periods and increasingly fall farther behind their more advantaged peers.[9] The finding that a balanced calendar may be more conducive to teaching and learning is particularly important for these children, who are already among the most marginalized in our present systems.

In 1978 a study conducted for the New York Board of Regents (*Learning, Retention, and Forgetting*) concluded, as educators know only too well, that in most school organizations, the gap between advantaged and disadvantaged students increases dramatically from year to year. Their data demonstrate that advantaged students typically make thirteen months of academic progress during the school year and gain an additional three to four months during the summer, perhaps because they enroll in enrichment activities, camps, and sports programs, or travel with their families. Their overall gain was approximately fifteen to sixteen months learning per academic year. Disadvantaged students, on the other hand, gain eleven or twelve months during the school year and lose three to four months during the summer, when they are often left on their own, separated from the routines of learning. Their net gain is seven to nine months per year. Imagine the cumulative effects of this difference over ten years of formal schooling!

Most recently, Alexander, Entwisle, and Olsen (2001) followed a cohort of students from traditional-calendar schools in one district for five years, from the beginning of first grade to the end of fifth grade, testing the students each fall and each spring. The good news was that during the academic terms, schools and teachers mitigated the effects of poverty and difficult home situations and helped students from disadvantaged homes to keep up. The bad news was that, during the summer, children from poor families lost considerable ground, which negatively affected their ability to continue to achieve on a level similar to their more economically advantaged peers. Moreover, they found the greatest differences for achievement in mathematics and among children in the early years. Thus, although poorer children learn as well as their more advantaged peers, their annual starting point falls farther and farther behind.

This is not an indictment of the home situation, but a description of how schools fail to address the needs of children from lower socioeconomic status homes. Taken to its logical conclusion, unless we change the ways schools respond to these children, by the end of elementary school, some of them will be roughly four years behind their peers. This finding does not present an optimistic outlook and hence does not respond to the criteria I have used for a socially just and academically excellent community of difference. We must introduce structures that have the potential to equalize the educational achievement and the life chances of our more educationally disadvantaged children.

Intersession: Continuous Learning Opportunities

Offering remediation through summer school is a typical educational intervention, but most educators recognize that it does little to address student failure on a long-term basis. For one thing, summer school generally has a stigma attached to it. You fail during the year; your "reward" is to attend school during the holiday period when your more successful peers are free from the constraints of schooling. And by the time school starts again in the fall, you will have forgotten most of what you were supposed to have learned in summer school. Again, you start behind many of your peers.

Many schools that have moved to a more balanced year-round calendar are able to offer remediation as well as enrichment during part of the vacation breaks or intersession periods that are dispersed throughout the regular school year. Intersession instruction permits those who are falling behind to receive remediation as they require it, and then to continue the school year without the common feeling of being so far behind there is no point in exerting any effort to succeed. It permits teachers to prepare students who need to learn about a specific aspect of the world prior to the next instructional unit. Children whose home languages are not English do not experience several months of vacation time during which they predominantly speak their home language, losing some of their newly acquired proficiency in English; intersession allows them to continue speaking English during their breaks and perhaps to benefit from intensive language instruction. The stigma attached to attending summer school during vacation periods may also be reduced if schools offer both remedial and enrichment activities and invite all students to participate.

Sometimes all students are offered enrichment opportunities. Sometimes enrichment is combined with remediation for those who need it most. Many schools have found it helpful to invite specific children to spend part of their vacation time (generally one of the three weeks) in intensive, small group instruction, often with an emphasis on experiential learning. Using this approach, a school might invite three groups of twenty children for a one-week session during which they may be given background material, taken on a field trip, or provided with an emphasis on the specific skills required for success in the next term. No student is forced to attend, but many educators have found that parents and children enthusiastically take advantage of extended learning opportunities.

Intersession is offered by schools in various ways. Sometimes it is funded by a reallocation of district summer school funding; at other times, more creativity is needed. On occasion some specialist teachers may elect to work for a four-day week during the regular term and teach during the intersession. Sometimes student teachers or interns provide support; at other times, members of the wider community and volunteers from service clubs become involved. All of these interventions reduce learning loss and enhance achievement.

A Catalytic Effect

Secondary schools that have instituted balanced calendars have identified similar outcomes. Where students have been given the opportunity between terms to complete work that was incomplete, retake a failed course in an intensive session, or enroll in a new course offered in an alternative format for credit, the results are positive. Statistics show these schools document lower dropout rates and higher graduation rates, with graduates also accumulating more credits, than high schools with a traditional calendar.

Overall, changing the school calendar may be one way of helping educators rethink how and what they teach. This is certainly one of the strategies used profitably by Esther to move Jerico Elementary School off Florida's "critically low" list. It is also one of the strengths of Jane's restructured program at Martin Popper Elementary School. One Arizona school with a high-needs, largely Hispanic population moved from being one of the lowest-performing schools in its district to being an A+ (blue ribbon) school by instituting a year-round schedule with intersession. In four years, a school in Washington state improved its achievement from well below the district's average, with only 12 percent of its students meeting the state standards in math and 33 percent in reading, to a position well above the average, with 53 percent meeting the math standards and 66 percent achieving the required reading levels. A balanced calendar offers possibilities for enrichment, acceleration, and remediation that the traditional calendar, at least in North America, does not offer.

Considering Contextual Factors

Jane, like Esther and many other educators, is working in a high-stakes testing environment in which schools are ranked and financially rewarded or punished according to student performance on state-mandated tests. Many people are concerned that in such an environment, efforts to raise test scores may unduly narrow the curriculum, restricting children's future opportunities for success. Others, like Jane and Esther, see in the testing movement a way of identifying which children are not being successful and finding ways to facilitate their success.

It is useful here to remember the criteria we have been using; we are working to create schools that are just, democratic, empathetic, and optimistic. As we have seen, this cannot be accomplished without reducing the achievement gap. But neither can we consider ourselves successful if we have restricted the future opportunities and life choices of our students. A structural change must be implemented with clear criteria and goals of excellence and equity in mind so that, to reiterate Jane's goal, the students will do "well with the rest of their lives."

Some of the inequities perpetuated by present school organizations are symbolized by this discussion about school calendars. Changing the calendar and making use of intersession periods for voluntary and targeted enrichment and remediation are ways to achieve greater equity in our educational system. Moreover, as achievement and self-confidence increase, so does the sense of community within a school. Whenever certain groups of students are stigmatized, relegated to remedial programs or summer school, and singled out as low-achieving and unsuccessful, it is difficult for them to feel they are an integral part of the school community. In Martin Popper, a new calendar structure helped change the norms of student achievement, reduced transiency, and led, almost immediately, to a greater sense of school community.

Responsiveness to Communities

In other instances, changing the calendar provided the impetus for thinking about how to be more responsive to the specific needs of individual school communities. In one remote northern community, where declining enrollment threatened the continued existence of the school, the school board decided to implement a calendar that was more consistent with the life and economic base of the community. Because loggers could not get into the woods during the periods of fall freeze-up or spring breakup, school vacations were set to coincide with these down times in the community and permit families to take vacations together without having children lose school time. Because of this more responsive structure, the school has remained open, has subsequently experienced an influx of children from other schools, and now maintains a waiting list.

Implementing responsive calendars is also one way schools can work together in respectful and caring ways with communities, honoring and supporting their traditional ways of learning. In aboriginal communities in Canada, for example, some schools have set vacation periods to coincide with the beginning of hunting and fishing periods, thus enabling traditional learning with elders to extend, rather than conflict with, the program of the school. The converse is also the case: the school program is seen as supplementing the teaching of the elders. Likewise, schools in agricultural areas may find it useful to reconsider vacation times to permit students to join their families in the harvest, since our current "agrarian calendar" (despite its name) does not coincide with growing seasons in most of North America.

EMPOWERMENT THROUGH RESTRUCTURING

In 1992, after reviewing the current literature on restructuring, Murphy found that initiatives generally fell into four categories: organization and governance, voice and choice, teacher empowerment and professionalism, and teaching for meaningful understanding (what I call pedagogical reform). Although he discusses them as discrete topics, as the example of Stephen Lewis shows, it is almost impossible to introduce one structural change without additional complementary changes occurring as a result.

We noted in the last chapter that Stephen Lewis Junior High School used changes in organization and governance structure to promote more inclusive and democratic practice. When it opened, the school opted for a five-track year-round school calendar. Because the chosen structures both required and facilitated the participation of parents and students, they enhanced the opportunities for voice in school decision making. The introduction of learning communities with learning leaders rather than formal administrators enhanced the professionalism of teachers and resulted in new approaches to organizing for instruction as well as in a curriculum that was interdisciplinary and multigraded. An element of choice was provided as parents and children were permitted to choose which of the five tracks most closely suited their preferences and lifestyle.

Sometimes a structural change results in unexpected benefits for the wider community. In the case of a change to year-round schooling, the calendar change is generally preceded by extensive discussion and community consultation. There is a tendency for the consultative process itself to garner support in the school community. People are appreciative of the opportunity for input, feeling they have been provided with important information and an opportunity to be heard. Sometimes a community organization, such as a YWCA, offers supplemental programs such as swimming lessons during a school's three-week breaks. Additional opportunities for voice may be provided as various enrichment opportunities are offered by community members as part of an extended intersession program.

Teachers often find that the calendar change empowers them in unanticipated ways. Those who are taking university courses appreciate the time during term to complete academic papers. Some use the school breaks for finding additional resources, planning new units, attending a conference, or even visiting and observing colleagues in traditional calendar schools. School bands and other music groups may use the breaks to give concerts in traditional calendar schools and throughout the community. Yearbook staffs may use the time for training or to complete layouts, eliminating some of the lost class time that often occurs when students on a traditional calendar are trying to meet deadlines, when there is no possibility of working through a designated break. In short, when one structure changes, there may be a domino effect.

The structural change does not need to be a calendar change. Depending on the desired effects and identified goals, selecting and implementing other structural changes may also produce the desired effect. The town-hall meetings instituted by Emily Carr School changed the fundamental power relationships between students and teachers, as children learned to solve their own problems. Following the lead of Central Elementary School and inviting parents to become teachers, allocating them full responsibility for specific instructional areas, might change governance structures as it empowers parents to become more fully involved in the life of the school. In Canyon Collegiate, as elders became more comfortable entering the school as part of the Ndahoo'aah program, other community members also became more visible; soon Alicia allocated a room to be the parent center in the school.

A CAUTION

Structural changes do not automatically produce increased equity, more democracy, or more empathetic attitudes in a school. They are neither panaceas nor silver bullets. Indeed, the caution proffered by Hargreaves and Fullan (1998) and Levin (2001) that restructuring often results in minimal change is still too true. Where those in charge introduce structural changes without examining how they relate to beliefs, values, and assumptions or how they may act as a catalyst for pedagogical or cultural changes, they may simply perpetuate the status quo Wrapped in recycled paper and tied with an old ribbon, some structural changes offer few opportunities for renewed school communities.

Where educators instigate changes to improve student learning, provide opportunities for those most commonly disadvantaged by our present system, and redress power imbalances, they are most likely to promote more inclusive, respectful, and optimistic communities of difference.

NOTES

1. The term *year-round school* will be more fully explained later. It refers to a calendar in which the summer vacation period is shortened and vacation time redistributed to provide additional breaks throughout the year. These intersession periods are not used for vacation time only, but also for remediation and enrichment.

2. In the following year, in part because the bar is raised annually for schools that want to remain A schools, Martin Popper missed it by a single percent in one area. No one was sorry they had chosen to be an A school for a year, and all look forward to a time when they will regain that status.

3. In addition to studies in cross-cultural leadership, I have been conducting research for the past ten years into the role of school-calendar change, most commonly known as year-round schooling. This research is most fully reported in Shields and Oberg (2000) as well as several other articles and reports and my website: www.educationalresearch.com. For the purposes of this chapter, I focus on how changing school calendars may have an impact on student learning.

4. For an example of this calendar, see appendix B.

5. In the single-track calendar, the whole school operates on a modified calendar with in-class and vacation periods often chosen to suit community needs.

6. A dual-track model offers parents, students, and teachers the choice of remaining on the traditional calendar or opting for a single-track modified calendar, both of which are offered in the same building.

7. Other popular forms include 45-10, 60-15, 60-10, and 60-20 calendars with various rotations of in-class and vacation period. Local conditions usually result in modifying one of these forms slightly and in the adoption of a somewhat less regular calendar.

8. Generally, I make use of a research team approach that combines practitioners in schools, doctoral assistants, and university colleagues in the data collection, analysis, and interpretation.

9. For some of the research, see also Alexander, Entwisle, and Olsen 2001; Cooper et al. 1996; Entwisle and Alexander 1992; *Learning, Retention, and Forgetting* 1978.

PART 3

Understanding Deeply, Making New Meaning

The work of hunters is another thing.
I have come after them and made repair
Where they have left not one stone on a stone,
But they would have the rabbit out of hiding,
To please the yelping dogs. The gaps I mean,
No one has seen them made or heard them made,
But at spring mending-time we find them there.
I let my neighbor know beyond the hill;
And on a day we meet to walk the line
And set the wall between us once again.

Part 1 consisted of three chapters that provided the theoretical under-pinnings for this book. I built up a picture of transformative cross-cultural leadership, clarified the concept of schools as communities of difference, and identified social justice criteria (justice, empathy, de-mocracy, and optimism) as benchmarks for educators wanting to intro-duce meaningful reform.

Part 2 described how school leaders have worked in various settings to move their schools toward becoming communities of difference, inclu-sive and caring organizations in which all students are expected to suc-ceed to high standards. Visiting these schools in several countries, in ur-ban and rural settings, schools of wealth and of poverty, small structures and large, sprawling campuses, demonstrated that with well-intentioned and knowledgeable leadership, just and optimistic changes may be made. I began in chapter 4 with an examination of some elements of culture(s) and ended in chapter 8 with structure, two cornerstones of organizational life and educational reform. The in-between chapters raised our consciousness and asked questions about issues like identity (chapter 5), parental and community involvement (chapter 6), and power, carnival, and critique (chapter 7).

I could, of course, have chosen different topics as organizers for the book, ideas like governance, pedagogy, curriculum, testing, or accountability. Interestingly, given the thesis of the book, that transformative cross-cultural leaders need to move schools toward being communities of difference, that schools should exhibit the characteristics of justice, democracy, empathy, and optimism, we would likely have talked about similar underlying issues. Overall, regardless of the starting point, transformative leaders need to ensure that people's beliefs and assumptions are made explicit and their underlying values clearly understood. When we ask questions about who is excluded and included, who is privileged or marginalized, advantaged or disadvantaged by specific decisions, we are led back to the underlying issues of power, equity, and excellence.

We may be marginalizing people when we exclude them from decision-making structures. We are proceeding unjustly if full access to the available range of programs is denied some students. We are acting disrespectfully if we are not caring and empathetic, if we essentialize groups of people or represent them inaccurately. And we are not providing an optimistic education if we limit the opportunities of any groups of children by pathologizing their lived experiences. If we are using power to perpetuate the privilege of groups who traditionally have power, rather than change the center of the community, to open it to possibilities of negotiating new norms, we may be guilty of hegemony. These principles hold true whether we are talking about curriculum, governance, or accountability measures.

It is often easy to criticize, as I have done where I have identified educational practices that have marginalized or excluded legitimate members of school communities. It is also relatively effortless to identify exceptions, schools that because of a particular convergence of people and circumstances seem to have introduced changes that make them different, "not just like any other schools," to paraphrase Alicia from Canyon Collegiate. It is quite another thing to work where we are to implement changes that will be meaningful, just, and sustainable; even some of the illustrations provided earlier were not sustained once the school principal and a core of committed staff moved on.

We have been hunters—have taken the rabbit out of hiding and begun to knock down some walls. But unlike the neighbors in Frost's poem, it is my hope that we will identify with neither the yelping dogs nor the neighbors who rebuild. In this section, I want to do three things: revisit the criteria in a holistic way, consider some steps an administrator might take to "make it happen," and then, using a case study as a starting point, reflect on how to overcome some of the barriers to meaningful change in schools.

In chapter 9, I try to put it all together—what have we learned about creating a school that is a community of difference? What would it look like? How might it be different from more typical schools that build and rebuild walls?

> He is all pine and I am apple orchard.
> My apple trees will never get across
> And eat the cones under his pines, I tell him.
> He only says, "Good fences make good neighbors."
> Spring is the mischief in me, and I wonder
> If I could put a notion in his head:
> "Why do they make good neighbors? Isn't it
> Where there are cows? But here there are no cows."

It is my hope that the previous chapters may put the mischief in us— helping us ask new questions, see with different eyes, hear with new ears. I repeat Lisa Delpit's profound insight:

Listening requires not only open eyes and ears, but open hearts and minds. . . . to put our beliefs on hold is to cease to exist as ourselves for a moment—and that is not easy. It is painful as well, because it means turning yourself inside out, giving up your own sense of who you are, and being willing to see yourself in the unflattering light of another's gaze. (1990, 297)

Asking that educators give up their sense of who they are and see themselves in an unflattering light is certainly mischief. It is also, partly, carnival. It stems from a deep belief that we can, through a combination of honesty and playfulness, find new and better models for public education in diverse communities. Frost's farmer states:

> Before I built a wall I'd ask to know
> What I was walling in or walling out,
> And to whom I was like to give offense.
> Something there is that doesn't love a wall,
> That wants it down. . . .

These are important statements. Just because we want the walls to come down, there is no sense in which "everything goes," in which all beliefs, values, and behaviors should be deemed appropriate for a school community. A community of difference is not a relativistic concept, but a deeply moral one in which all members together determine its boundaries. Neither those who traditionally hold power nor those whose culture has traditionally been marginalized make decisions on their own.

> He moves in darkness as it seems to me,
> Not of woods only and the shade of trees.
> He will not go behind his father's saying,
> And he likes having thought of it so well
> He says again, "Good fences make good neighbors."

We do not want to rebuild fences and walls in darkness, but carefully consider where the boundaries of community should be protected and where there do not need to be fences built at all. We want to tear down walls that divide us unnecessarily, carefully building in their place relationships of forgiveness and understanding.

In chapter 9 we consider some additional aspects of what a community of difference might be like; in chapter 10 we reflect on how to make it happen. I will present a contour map—some big picture ideas that each administrator will need to make her own, that each leader can work toward, taking into account the realities of his context, setting, and organization. What does a leader who wants to be *transformative* need to know or do? Here I will offer neither a prescription nor a detailed plan but will focus on data and dialogue as tools of the transformative leader.

In chapter 11 I take a different approach. It has been my observation that even after reading about the educators and schools I describe in this book, after spending time reflecting on how to be a transformative leader, or considering the qualities of a community of difference, many educators become bogged down in traditional, technical approaches to change. Our habitus of education is so strong that we almost automatically fall back on strategies we have used in the past. Hence, in chapter 11, I present a case study of Sherwood Junior Secondary School, a fictionalized case based on many schools I have visited. I ask you to put yourself in the place of Lynn Saver, the school's newly appointed principal, and reflect on how you might approach educational change. Then I enlist the help of Sheila, a vice principal I have taught in graduate classes, and ask her to engage in dialogue with me about the challenges the case presents.

PATTERNS, NOT WALLS

Margaret Wheatley, in her influential 1993 book *Leadership and the New Science* suggests that one of the problems of educational leaders has been a propensity for prediction and control. We want to know, in advance, and with a considerable degree of certainty, what will happen if we engage in a specific course of action, if we introduce a new program, or try a new textbook series. In fact, this desire for certainty undergirds most of the traditional, rational, and functionalist organizational and leadership thinking of the last century.

In contrast, Wheatley suggests that educators should take their lead from science, recognizing that nature consists largely of patterns of relationships. While one cannot predict specific individual changes, it is possible to identify patterns that will vary over time. Understanding the pressure points will help us learn how to change the patterns.

For example, introducing a beaver into an area served by a particular waterway is likely to change the water level and flow. We cannot determine precisely where the dam will be built, nor which branches the beaver will use; we can anticipate whether the dam will have the desired effect and take steps to accommodate to the new pattern of water flow. In similar fashion, Wheatley states that leaders need to pay much more attention to patterns and relationships. By finishing the thought as my friend advocates, we understand that learning where and how to exert pressure to bring about change is more important and, in the long run, more effective than trying to control the behavior of individuals and organizations.

Wheatley reflects:

> I look now for patterns of movement over time and focus on qualities like rhythm, flow, direction, and shape. Second, I know I am wasting time whenever I draw straight arrows between two variables in a cause and effect diagram, or position things as polarities, or create elaborate plans and time lines . . . the time I formerly spent on detailed planning and analysis I now use to look at structures that might facilitate relationships. (1993, 43)

The three chapters in this third section are offered in the spirit of helping us understand patterns that will permit us to engage in behaviors and develop the attitudes and dispositions most likely to effect change. They are not intended to offer ways to predict or control, but simply to deepen our understandings and facilitate new relationships, to help us create fresh images of schools as just, caring, empathetic, and optimistic communities to which to entrust our children and the future of our society.

CHAPTER 9

A New Community

After reading the compelling stories filling the pages of previous chapters and reflecting on the educators' commitments to create inclusive, respectful schools in which all students have better opportunities to achieve, you may be feeling overwhelmed. Or you may be invigorated and ready to move forward, but wondering what to do next.

Creating a community of difference cannot be accomplished if educators fear the task or have false expectations about what can or cannot be accomplished and in what time frame. The previous chapters have focused on a number of concepts that I believe to be key for changing the ways we think about community in diverse school settings. I have provided some ideas and illustrations from educators I have known to show how they have worked toward this idea. I have also provided some examples of attitudes and behaviors that are detrimental.

In this chapter, I want to develop a scaffolding that will help caring and knowledgeable transformative educators in their own contexts to discover their own ways to build this type of school community. I want to help you to create what Senge (1990) might call "mental models" of a community of difference. What does a community of difference look like? In what ways does it differ from a typical school community? As an educational leader, what does it mean to you to implement the ideals of justice, democracy, empathy, and optimism that have been referred to throughout this book?

I will proceed in two ways. Sometimes I present what I consider to be negative, but unfortunately common, examples of ways in which some school communities operate. Many educators will find in these illustrations reflections of their own schools. But you have been thinking about issues of social justice and excellence. You have been developing, as you read the previous chapters, the transformative leadership dispositions of critique, justice, and caring. The negative illustrations will raise red flags for you, reminding you of similar situations in your own workplace that may need to be re-examined.

I also provide more optimistic images of schooling. They will help you reflect on your own situation and give you confidence and hope that with dedication and hard work you can make a difference.

LEADING A COMMUNITY OF DIFFERENCE

Chapter 10 will focus on the topic of *how* transformative leaders might begin to create a community of difference. In this chapter I start with some general concepts. As Schwartz and Ogilvy (1979) found, leadership must be shared. It is heterarchic. No one person can create a new community alone; rather, it takes the vision, commitment, and hard work of many members of a school population. Moreover, I am convinced that most educators have the desire, commitment, and dedication to improve public education. Thus, with effective leadership, I believe that schools not only *must* change but *can* change.

I know of no educator who leaves for work each morning thinking "I am going to do a terrible job today; that's what I'll do." As professionals, we are committed to working together to create the best teaching and learning environments possible for all children. As Alicia stated, describing her staff, "The teachers here want to do well. They want to do what's right, they are devoted, they are not just hanging out here; they really want to do it. Somehow or other we have to get our enthusiasm back because they have become a little resigned and they have just kind of given up a bit."

It is my hope that this chapter will provide an image of schooling that will help those who have become discouraged to find places to begin to get their enthusiasm back.

REVISITING THE CRITERIA

In chapter 3, I suggested that transformative educational leaders might use the criteria of justice, democracy, empathy, and optimism to assess and guide their school communities. I now want to revisit these criteria in light of the stories we have seen and heard, as well as the theories identified in part 2. Here I apply them more broadly to various school situations. Thinking about them again will help you reflect on your context and identify areas in your own school community where you would like to introduce some changes.

Just Schools

Earlier in this volume I associated justice with issues of equity—advantage or disadvantage. Schools that are just are inclusive; policies, structures, attitudes, or practices do not inherently privilege one group of students over another. Schools in which differential achievement or participation are treated as the norm are not *just* by this definition. For example, I visited a number of secondary schools in New Zealand, observed classes, and asked questions. Frequently the conversation went something like this:

> Question: I understand from talking to other people that even though 36 percent [or 55 percent or 70 percent] of your school population is Maori, you might have 5 percent in the senior academic courses. Is that correct?
>
> Response: That would be right. There are issues and this is a real bomb because something really needs to be done.
>
> or
>
> Response: The higher up you go, the fewer Maori students there are in the academic classes, but that's to be expected.
>
> or
>
> Response: Our systems have always been geared to encouraging a 50 percent pass rate in school certificate . . . almost exclusively geared to get the 10 to 20 percent of young people to university. Fifty percent is deemed to be okay. When in actual fact it is rubbish, isn't it, when you think about it?

The expectation that certain groups of children, based on ethnicity or any other group factor, will automatically be disadvantaged, will typically be less inclined to choose academic courses that lead to university, or will drop out of school is obviously not part of a socially just or equitable school. Rejection of commonly accepted beliefs, as indicated by the last comment, that an expectation of a graduation rate of 50 percent is rubbish, comes closer to the attitude one would expect in a school determined to be equitable.

In a just school, every decision, whether it is related to new curriculum or textbook series, staffing, alternative programming, or leasing a new photocopier, will be guided by questions about who is advantaged and who is marginalized, who is included and who excluded by the decision. There are no simple answers to these questions and certainly no answers that are appropriate for all schools in all situations.

In one urban school, for example, allocating funds for the continuation of a football program may be perceived as *unjust* in that the funds may be more needed to provide a school lunch or breakfast program[1] for needy students. One year Alicia of Canyon Collegiate was faced with a decision about whether to permit the football program, which involved only thirteen boys, to proceed. She decided that although it was costly, it was just. It provided opportunities for these young men to engage in an activity not otherwise available in their community, to travel to other schools, and to interact with non-Navajo students—all of which she believed would enrich their educational experience. (The participation has since risen and remains relatively stable at around twenty players.)

In a community of difference, decisions will not only be just; they will be seen to be just. Budget information will be shared and people with legitimate interests will be encouraged to argue persuasively for their positions. No program will be seen as second-class, having a less legitimate call on available funds than any other. In a fiscal climate of restraint and limited resources, not every legitimate program or activity will be funded. But each will be considered. Thus the art teacher, the band teacher, and the athletic adviser should all be at the table when decisions about program funding are made. Traditional funding patterns may ultimately be questioned, sometimes disrupted, but everyone will have a chance to be involved in the discussions.

School policies need to be carefully examined to determine whether their effect is equal or differential with regard to certain groups of students. Does the discipline policy, for example, result in a disproportionate number of suspensions? Many more boys than girls? More students from African American backgrounds than students from Caucasian or Asian families? Are more children from single-parent or low socioeconomic families being expelled? A common response to queries about school discipline is to indicate that the policy is just, if it is applied equally to any student whose actions infringe a school regulation, and all students have been made aware of the policies at the beginning of the year, when they registered and received a school handbook. But this is not enough. Policies are just if they offer equal opportunities for access and for participation to all students. Just making information available does not ensure that all students have equal access to it.

One vice principal, when asked whether she tries to ensure that all groups of students are proportionately represented in various academic programs, explained:

> No, it's not always possible to do that. But what we do try to ensure is that they are equitable in the sense that all students have access. So we ensure, for example, in our senior course booklet, that all of the prerequisites for the courses are absolutely accurate. Then students can't come away and say, "So and so refused to accept me into his or her course." If the student meets the prerequisite, the student has to be accepted. So that's a quality management thing.

And that may well be true. Quality management would necessitate that all students know what the prerequisites for a desired course are. But it must go much farther. Students need advice and guidance to ensure that they develop appropriate educational plans to enable them to achieve whatever career goals they have established for themselves. Listing requirements in a handbook (although necessary) does not guarantee equitable access for all students. Some may need extra support and encouragement to attempt courses in which their group has traditionally not been well represented or successful.

Farrell (1999) suggests that equality relates to questions of access, sustainability, outputs, and outcomes. We need to ask whether all students have equal opportunities to comply with the prerequisites or other school regulations. Do students who have to act as surrogate parents for younger siblings at home have equal opportunities to be on time and in attendance at every class? Do those who suffer the barbs of racist taunts from their classmates have opportunities to share their hurt without being stigmatized as tattletales? Have we been willing to name racism where it exists rather than argue that certain comments are simply the norm for teenagers dealing with hormones? Have we instituted conversation with students and teachers alike to reduce prejudice and enhance students' sense of belonging? Have we permitted the creation of clubs for gay and lesbian students to provide them with an outlet (other than fighting) for feelings of alienation often exacerbated in the close proximity of school relationships from which they may feel excluded?

We may need to look again. Are there elements of the school program that promote a sense of belonging and inclusion for some students while keeping others on the margins of school life? How does suspending a student who has little or no supervision at home do anything other than provide a few days of relief for a teacher and classmates from behavior deemed to be inappropriate? A more just approach, described by Alicia (in words reminiscent of Esther), would be to

> realize that you have to take each kid and each case separately. Not all kids have to be treated the same to make their situations equitable. Listen to the kids, because in almost every situation there are reasons behind why they do what they do. Don't make excuses for them, but listen to them. Find out what resources are available, the support resources in the community, whatever mental health resources, or social services, or whatever. Access as many of those as possible. Again realize that kids are more similar than different, they want the same thing.

And of course, one of the things they want is just and equitable treatment in policy and in practice. However, there are numerous other areas in which justice needs to be ensured for a community of difference to develop. Justice needs to extend to issues of governance and resource allocation, culture and curriculum, and interpersonal and social interactions, as well as the academic aspects of schooling.

Justice as a Curricular Issue

We have seen how schools like Canyon Collegiate and Regal High School have made the cultures of their schools visible and incorporated them in meaningful ways into the curriculum. This is where the emphasis needs to be—on the meaningful incorporation of the cultures of the students.

I reiterate. I do not reject the concept of multicultural activities or the need for newsletters to be translated into home languages. But when cultural recognition and incorporation stop there, they are little more than superficial nods to the diversity within a school.

One school in New Zealand with a diverse and multicultural population enlarged the concept of a *marae* to make it more appropriate for the whole school population. In exterior design, the building looked like a traditional *marae*, but in the details of its decor, it was not. The principal described it:

> In effect it was set up in a way which defines it as being multicultural . . . so the figure on the top is the biblical Noah because Noah is the father of us all , . . in a biblical sense . . . and biblical Noah was chosen as simply being a recognition that we have all come here, Maori included, because there were very few Maori who lived in this area, That means that you could have an Egyptian welcomed and it would be quite okay for the Egyptian to speak in Egyptian.

Developing inclusive symbols for a school is important, but they must not become superficial representations that ultimately marginalize rather than exclude. As school and community demographics change, the symbols may need to be revisited. Situations change, and traditions may need to be modified over time. Here, the intention of inclusion was excellent, but I still wonder how students of non-Judeo-Christian backgrounds could find themselves included in a concept based on the fatherhood of Noah.

In a desire to be inclusive, teachers in Princess Grace School instituted a practice to help elementary students explore their identity. Each student's birthday was recognized with a week in which that student's lived experience was highlighted in class. Each child made a poster, shared photographs of himself or herself as an infant and of his or her siblings, talked about family traditions and experiences, and shared valued objects. In this case, the child was permitted to share over several days; other students asked questions and talked about similar experiences, and class discussion occurred in meaningful ways about the ideas introduced by the child. Thus it was not a single artifact of culture that each child was expected to share, but aspects of his or her daily reality. I recall Anish's discussion of the African curio widely available in tourist shops, which he presented as an artifact of his culture; and I remember how deeply ashamed and hypocritical he felt. I hope this approach would have seemed more authentic.

Permitting each child to share something of his or her own lived experience, without pathologizing it, is a starting point for a teacher wanting to develop a sense of a community of difference within his or her classroom. When the initiative takes on a school-wide character (as Jane, in chapter 8, insists is necessary), then each year's activities build on the ones before it, and learning about others and their cultures becomes an ongoing and intrinsic part of the community. If, however, children are asked to do the same activity every year, the activity soon pales and becomes a superficial exercise devoid of meaning. Hence, one task of educational leaders is to help teachers find multiple ways to open up the curriculum so that the historical realities of the students contribute to the learning and discussion.

Ronald Takaki (2001) intrigued a large audience at the annual conference of the American Educational Research Association in Seattle with a "fifteen-minute history lesson" within a larger address demonstrating how one might open the curriculum. He began by asking why most Irish immigrants came to America and received his expected answer, "because of a potato famine." Moving on from there, he examined not only their reasons for emigrating but also some outcomes. He explained that 52 percent of Irish immigrants were women who found work in the textile industry. The growth of the cotton and textile industry encouraged more family immigration and provided even more employment for Irish women. The resultant demands for better ways to transport the fabric prompted the building of railways and encouraged Chinese immigration. Yet these workers were prohibited from bringing their wives and children, and only 5 percent of Chinese immigrants were women. Takaki talked about the different patterns of development and challenges for the two immigrant communities. Beginning with a common perception (or misperception), he demonstrated how a curriculum concept may be opened to broader discussion that includes other groups and perspectives. Starting from the potato famine idea, his analysis permitted various perspectives to be presented, provided a clearer understanding of some of the ways in which racism has developed in and divided U.S. society, raised issues of access to education for different ethnic groups, and discussed some of the deeper political aspects related to the expansion of America.

Although there are numerous opportunities for teachers to introduce multiple perspectives into classroom discussion, we rarely take full advantage of them, paying lip service to a new idea and quickly retreating to the comfort level of the prescribed core curriculum or lesson plan. "We have a visitor from Canada in class today," teachers often said to their classes when I visited New Zealand. "Do you know where Canada is?" After ascertaining that they recognized it was above the United States in North America, the real teaching began; in other words, most teachers returned to their planned activity for the day.

Two experiences stood out. In one class, a child asked me if there was any difference between Canada and the United States. I responded with a question: "I wonder. What do you think? Is there any difference between Australia and New Zealand?" The response was immediate, "Oh, yes, miss—a big difference!" I then acknowledged that we believed there were similar differences between the United States and Canada; the conversation stopped as the teacher returned to the prepared lesson rather than encourage a discussion of the similarities and differences. In another class, where neither a globe nor a map was available, I sketched a rough map of the world and on it located my home, Vancouver, Canada. As the children interacted with me, I heard one child say quietly to her teacher, "She's drawn it wrong!" Although the teacher looked somewhat embarrassed and shushed her quickly, I publicly acknowledged the comment and redrew the map as a New Zealand pupil would do—with North and South America on the right-hand side, Asia on the left, and New Zealand and Australia in the middle.

I left that school thinking that both teachers had missed wonderful opportunities to talk about national identity, power relationships, and the constructed nature of knowledge, including geographic understanding. The point is not to criticize these two classroom teachers but to demonstrate how deeply ingrained one way of thinking and instruction is; educators must carefully consider how to make their instruction more equitable and more inclusive of new ideas.

Sometimes educators indicate that it is easy to introduce various perspectives if one is teaching history, social studies, or English. From my perspective as a former English teacher, this is true. However, teachers from other subject areas acknowledge that they also find many ways to ensure their instruction is inclusive. Sometimes working in interdisciplinary ways offers excellent opportunities not only for the responsive and interactive pedagogy advocated by Cummins (1989) but for combining math or science with cultural awareness. Practicing graphing by using textbook examples may be supplemented (or replaced) by graphing various elements of school or community life—how many children come from which continents or countries; patterns of immigration, employment, education; or career aspirations of students. (Numerous government and school district websites contain data that might be used.) Calculations of percentages might focus on poverty lines, relative poverty, ways to divide various salary levels to cover basic necessities and luxuries, and it might be accompanied by discussion of social issues or, in more senior grades, of regressive or progressive income tax structures. Learning in science classes may be confined to memorizing the periodic table or focusing on chemicals and formulas. But it may also extend to discussions of how industrial practices (for example, using raw materials from developing countries) may relate to the profit margin of multinational corporations or to explorations of the environmental impacts of various activities.

In one school with a predominantly Navajo population, students in a third-grade class conducted surveys with their peers and other classes in the school and then graphed the results. One girl, who asked about students' favorite musical instruments, learned that many students favored the drum. She showed remarkable insight and presented her teacher with an incredible opportunity to connect the math to deeper cultural understanding when she asked, "I wonder whether they mean drum sets or traditional Navajo drums."

I am not suggesting that teachers should take moral positions—such as "globalization and multinationals are evil" or "the wealthy are unfairly advantaged by current income tax laws"—but I am suggesting that it is difficult to find curriculum that is not infused with issues of culture, gender, ethnicity, class, politics, or economics. Too often we isolate and sanitize curriculum in ways that perpetuate current structures without raising any of the concomitant equity issues that affect the daily lives of many of our students. A more just and equitable environment for teaching and learning will incorporate, rather than eliminate, these issues into ongoing classroom discussion. Justice, conceptualized in this way, is of course at the heart of a school that is also deeply democratic.

A Democratic School

A just school does not guarantee a democratic school and vice versa. Justice implies equal access, equity of opportunity, and fair treatment. Democracy requires that processes related to all of the above be opened up to enable all members of the school community to participate fully in the activities and decisions related to school life.

Educators promoting social justice strive to ensure that all parts of the school's wider community are seen as a resource, not just those parents who have university degrees, professional jobs, or time to act as chauffeurs or chaperones. In a just and democratic school, there will not be talk about the "right" and "wrong" side of the tracks or the town or the river. Rather, conversation will focus on how various elements of the community are supporting, and can support, the ongoing learning of all students.

As a high-school teacher from a privileged white middle-class background, I had not seriously contemplated this issue, until I had a "modified" ninth-grade class in which racial tensions surfaced on a regular basis. At the center of the tension were Sally, a very shy aboriginal girl, and Marilyn, a vocal, angry white girl who regularly taunted Sally with comments like "All Indians are lazy. They are all on welfare. They are all drunks and prostitutes." None of the literature I asked them to read seemed to make a difference. None of my efforts to silence the taunting or appeal to the school's discipline code produced significant changes in Marilyn's attitude, and Sally often retreated to the corner of the class in tears.

In desperation, I spoke to the principal, telling him I needed to try a different approach. I asked for his support while I taught a unit on urban native issues and invited into my class men and women who frequented a Native Friendship Center, the very people Marilyn despised. For a few days, the tension was heightened; on one occasion, a fistfight broke out as class ended. Increasingly anxious, I stayed in close contact with the principal, who continued to support me. Gradually, as the lived realities of the urban native population and their historical situation were presented to my class, taunting was replaced by understanding; animosity was replaced by tolerance and respect. Imagine my surprise at the end of the year when Marilyn announced that she had attended a dance at the Indian Friendship Center and was going on a canoe trip with some of her new aboriginal friends!

I learned that developing a curriculum which enhanced social justice was hard work. It involved risks—for me as well as my students. And it involved bringing into my classroom partners—people I had never met, people who are not traditionally welcomed into the life of a school. As a classroom teacher, I could not have accomplished this alone. It required both the help and support of my colleagues and the participation of people from the community not normally included in schools.

Once I visited a secondary school with a diverse student population. I asked, as I usually do, a lot of questions about how the school accommodated and made decisions about students with various needs. How do you provide for ESL students? For the refugee students who arrive with no prior schooling? How do you relate to the Somali community? What if you need a translator? And the response was always the same: "Ask Wanda. Wanda can tell you about that."

I asked Wanda, a teacher who worked with various children with specific needs—children who were newly arrived, students whose English proficiency was limited, and many with other kinds of challenges. She consistently responded with comments like "What we do have which is quite lucky is that we do have contacts with the Somalian and Cambodian communities. We can get hold of tutors pretty quickly. And it's important that we can do that." I noted that she used "we" but that everyone else had referred me to her.

I asked what would happen if she left the school, and Wanda replied modestly, "If I went they would be a little stuck." (There was no doubt in my mind that the contacts she described were hers, not the school's.) She acknowledged that being the resident expert had its benefits. "People turn up to the [office] window and they will often call me. That's why I've moved from a broom cupboard to the door right next to the office. I've got a bit of power see and . . ." With Wanda's power comes the significant danger of the school losing all of the momentum for which she has worked because the multicultural work has not been democratically shared with her colleagues.

I asked, "What are the basic challenges you deal with in this school?" Her response was not a catalog of various needs, student codes, or a litany of issues related to time and resources or parental support. Instead, she identified teacher attitudes as critical:

> Getting mainstream staff to accept the fact that these students have a right to be in their classrooms. It's better with ESL students. With special education students we're getting there. But I read a really good article a while ago about mainstream teachers being afraid of special ed students and they are. They really, really are. And they say things to me like, "I'm never going to get him up to speed on this." And I'm saying to them, "No one is expecting you to."

Although Wanda has the power that comes with being the sole possessor of specific and necessary knowledge, the lack of interest and understanding on the part of others, as well as her enjoyment of the benefits that accompany her power, are indications that this school is less than democratic. Wanda's autonomy for making decisions about incoming students means that other educators in the school are neither involved in nor aware of decisions regarding student placement and instruction. Too many decisions are left to Wanda. Too few people are working with minority children and their families. Too little knowledge is shared.

In a democratic school, many people will be involved in identifying students with special needs and making decisions about appropriate placement and instruction. In most cases, the planning process should involve an administrator, a group of teachers, some specialists, students, and their parents.

In a democratic school, teachers, parents, and community members should be invited to participate, but differently and often *in their own ways*. Parents, regardless of their background, will be treated with respect; educators will acknowledge that they contribute in multiple and complex ways to support their children's learning. As we saw in Emily Carr Elementary School, students will be respected and accepted as rightful participants in the decision-making structures of their school. As we noted in Stephen Lewis Junior High School, professionalism will be enhanced when teachers are treated as the experts they are and given appropriate responsibility and accountability.

In a school that is both *just* and *democratic,* educators recognize that one size does not fit all, that alternatives need to be provided and choices made from a base of equal but different opportunities. Thus we may offer some heterogeneous, some homogeneous, and some multi-age groups; we may offer some opportunities for children to speak their home languages, some bilingual programs, and some sheltered English-immersion classes; we may provide some classes where students with special needs are fully included and others where they are provided with safe and supportive environments apart from the mainstream class. There will be no dead-end programs but, as one principal put it, there will be "big connecting paths" between and among multiple student options. Teachers and administrators will take responsibility for helping all students become involved in appropriate ways.

In many schools, teachers stated that although all extracurricular activities were open to all students, some people chose not to participate. For example, one teacher from the Academy said, "I think it's up to the kids in this school to join. It's always a question of whether to intervene or not to intervene" (Shields et al. 1998, 112). Engagement is seen as primarily the responsibility of the students, and most teachers believe that if students choose not to participate, it is not their role to interfere.

How does the assumption that students have equal opportunities and abilities to access programs demonstrate justice or empathy? How does it assist students who do not already have a positive peer group or have never joined in because they are concerned that their English proficiency is not adequate? How might targeting and inviting specific students make a difference?

A colleague of mine tells how, when he was a young teenager, his self-confidence was changed forever because teachers reached out to him. He was one of the quiet kids with few close friends, heavily involved in church and Scouting activities but at school a loner on the periphery of school life. Imagine his surprise when one summer he received an official letter from his school, telling him that his teachers had nominated him as a candidate for Boys' State—an activity sponsored by the American Legion to provide students seen to have leadership ability with firsthand experiences of representative democracy.

Swen states that the nomination by his teachers and the opportunity to participate contributed in significant ways to how he thought of himself and to how others related to him. He recalls how, on the first day of school the next fall, when he proudly wore his Boys' State T-shirt, many schoolmates approached him with comments like "What? You went to State?" Had his teachers assumed that school activities were available to Swen only if he chose to get involved, he might never have realized that others saw his potential for meaningful participation in school activities and his leadership ability. Most importantly, he says, the experience taught him that instead of seeing him as an outcast and misfit, "maybe others did not think of me the way I thought they saw me" (personal communication).

Members of a democratic school community take responsibility for helping others participate. They do not wait for people who have traditionally been the least involved to step forward themselves, as that is unlikely to happen,

If I could turn back the clock, the skills, abilities, and interests of my elder son, now a successful welder, would have been valued and encouraged in his schools (and by me) just as much as the more academic orientation of his younger brother (now a graduate of a prestigious political science and history program). His teachers could have discussed the value of trades and the abilities needed to be successful. They could have shown him, and others like him, that there are numerous career opportunities in vocational areas. Moreover, teachers could have provided information about apprenticeship programs and types of qualifications, and perhaps even invited representatives from different occupations to demonstrate their skills and talk to their classes. Although the schools my son attended had elective classes in such areas as automotive repair or wood shop, the only career alternatives presented to students were options that required university education.

On the other hand, if a school legitimately does not have a program to meet the needs of a given group of students, it might implement a just and democratic approach like the option offered by Cosmopolitan High School in New Zealand. Because it no longer has enough students who want a Maori-immersion program and because the number of staff members proficient in Maori has declined, the school provides a bus to take students wanting an immersion program to Regal High School, approximately thirty miles away. Offering choice to meet student needs instead of forcing students to fit into the existing programs is evidence of a just and democratic approach.

Operating on democratic principles for Emily Carr School required the full participation of the community—and the institution of what came to be called the "curriculum of life." Life, including the socio-economic condition of the students and their lived realities—from shoplifting sunglasses to working with the local art gallery to showcase the work of local artists—became the basis for a critical and ongoing conversation that was the curriculum. Into these conversations and realities, the core objectives for the province were infused—not dominating but not omitted either. A just and democratic curriculum may change its starting point; it may change its focus and emphasis; but it does not disadvantage the students by neglecting to teach concepts that students in other schools are taught.

A Democratic Understanding of Multiculturalism

Educators in a school that is becoming democratic understand the basic concepts of the five types of multiculturalism described by Kincheloe and Steinberg (1997). They work toward helping every member of the school community to realize that attempting to eliminate difference is not acceptable. Educators must also take care not to essentialize students from various cultural groups. Maxine Greene identifies a need for the

avoidance of fixities, of stereotypes, even stereotypes linked to "multiculturalism" for, to view a person as in some sense "representative" of

[a] culture, is to presume an objective reality called "culture," a homogeneous and fixed presence that can be adequately represented by existing subjects. (1993, 16)

In one school, as the student population began to change, people needed to confront their assumptions about difference. A teacher explained,

> some Somali people started coming four or five years ago. We also started to get South Africans and that was a significant change because they were the first groups of black people. . . . There were some issues because many people had seen movies and had ideas about Black American people. And Somali people are quite unlike Black American people. So there was a fair bit of getting to know each other.

The key is in the concept of getting to know each other. There was no expectation that the Somali or South African population would make all the adaptations; there was no condemnation of erroneous impressions formed from watching American movies. Rather, in that school, each person was expected to take responsibility for getting to know the others.

Democratic educators also reject both the pluralist and the liberal notions of multiculturalism—concepts that focus on difference in order to minimize or emphasize it, but without dealing with related issues of justice, equity, and inequality. It is important not to promote or validate a superficial recognition of difference in our societies.

We saw in the case of Regal High School that attending to difference in ways that permitted all groups to participate required some personal sacrifice by the principal. She was forced to deal with the conflicts between her own feminist values and those of the Maori traditions in which she was not permitted to speak on the *marae*. Creating democratic schools does not always mean that all members will be able to do as they please or even that each person will always be able to exercise her individual "rights." Instead, it may sometimes mean subjugating one set of traditions and entitlements to another to ensure that people whose voices and cultures have been marginalized will be moved closer to the center of the organization.

This may be threatening to those who currently hold power, who will see they have the most to lose. They may be anxious about changing the status quo because at the outset the outcome is unpredictable. Yet unless others, like Brenda, are willing to act courageously, to give up some "rights" for the greater good of the community, then hegemonic practices will continue and some individuals and cultures will remain on the periphery of the school community.

An Empathetic School

Recognition that justice and democracy sometimes require sacrifices on the part of individuals and groups that have normally been seen to hold power and authority moves us toward the third criterion: empathy. Although Kincheloe and Steinberg (1995) chose to use the word *empathetic,* we have seen that the meaning resembles the notion of caring as explicated by Noddings (1988, 1999) and others. Empathy requires deep understanding of another's position, almost the sense of walking in someone else's shoes. It identifies with the pain and joy of others as they are marginalized or included in our school communities. It is a sense of anguish at hearing tales like the one told by Anish in which he suffered shame and rejection at the hands of classmates and teachers. It is also the experience of celebration when a student who has struggled with racism and prejudice, like Marilyn, ultimately finds a better way to relate to those around her.

Empathy is the quality that makes schools not simply inclusive and just, but pleasant, exciting, and respectful places. Without empathy, we may exercise justice, ensuring that equal access is available to all participants. We may encourage full participation, providing opportunities for various legitimate stakeholder groups to voice their opinions about a given situation. But it will be difficult to convince people that we respect their opinions and need their participation unless we show that we value them as individuals.

Noddings talks about caring as a "moral perspective," not a superficial concern for others (1988, 215). It permeates the fabric of schooling, curriculum, relationships—everything we do in school communities. She says,

> If we were to explore seriously the ideas suggested by an ethic of caring for education, we might suggest changes in almost every aspect of schooling: the current hierarchical structure of management, the right mode of allocating time, the kind of relationships encouraged, the size of

schools and classes, the goals of instruction, modes of evaluation, patterns of interaction, selection of content. (p. 221)

Caring thus conceptualized focuses on student growth as well as student progress toward an ethical life that is "relationally constructed" (p. 222). Caring emphasizes making connections between individuals and powerful ideas, as well as developing relationships among individuals and groups in order for them to grow and learn together.

Mayeroff talks about how such caring necessitates trust—in both oneself and the other: "Only the man who trusts himself to grow, who is not trying to force himself to be something he thinks he is supposed to be, will be able to trust another person to grow" (1971, 22). Mayeroff believes that one lives the meaning of one's own life "through caring and being cared for" (p. 2). For the teacher, this requires trusting in her ability to provide a climate conducive to learning and permitting her students space to find their own way.

Likewise, the transformative leader will not set himself apart. By being firmly rooted in the daily realities in which teachers and students engage together, the leader will demonstrate trust in both teachers and students and will develop positive relationships with them.

It is important to note that neither the deep form of caring advocated by Noddings and Mayeroff nor the form of empathy I am proposing is primarily emotional in nature. At its core it is deeply cognitive. It is easy to demonstrate care when we like someone. It is more difficult to practice care and respect if we tend not to like the other person; yet it is our commitment to care, grounded in a force of the mind and the will, that makes empathic education possible in schools.

Sometimes in order to express caring, school leaders need to take what may appear to be harsh steps. The practice of overt racism or discrimination, or other destructive practices, cannot be permitted. Those who persist in deficit thinking with respect to children whose lived experiences differ from the norm must not go unchallenged. Hence it is critical to build a staff that shares the vision of a community of difference. Alicia from Canyon Collegiate reflected on this aspect of her leadership:

The first year I was principal I made a couple of serious mistakes in hiring. I didn't do enough investigation into who they were and what their educational philosophies were and where they come from and successes and failures in past jobs. So I took them on face value. They seemed like nice people and I hired them and it was a disaster in both cases. . . . And so I have been much more careful since then in who I hire, making sure that they are the kind of people that will basically fit into our educational philosophy, that their reasons for coming here are not because they just need a job but that they want to be here.

Creating an empathetic school starts with building a staff of people who want to be there—who are in the right place with the right kids, as Jane from Martin Popper and Esther from John Howard School would say. Esther went further, identifying strategies she used to help teachers move to another school if they did not seem able to buy in to an empowerment philosophy of education. Esther says that when she goes into a new school as principal, she communicates up front that she values every teacher equally and that she is not going to have any exclusive cliques on her staff. Moreover, she tells teachers that everyone needs to teach in a place where they are happy. That may mean, she recognizes, that she will have to help some of them find a "happier" place somewhere else, a place where there is a better fit between their approaches and the school philosophy.

There is no doubt that in many districts, school principals experience constraints due to contract provisions in terms of how they may hire or transfer teachers. However, if the principal has a clear vision of the kind of teacher who works most effectively with his specific student body and wider community context and if he is explicit about the goals, he can develop a bag of tricks to help build a coherent staff team. Slanting a job description in a particular way, changing the organization of grade-level teams, emphasizing a particular curricular approach—these are only a few ways in which an administrator may discourage some teachers from applying for a particular position or remaining at a given school.

Having a caring staff does not mean hiring any available teacher but choosing carefully to ensure that a shared vision can be developed—in this case, a vision for a just, democratic, empathetic, and optimistic school. However, as Esther and Alicia and many others recognize, hiring the right people is simply a starting point.

Moving everyone along together, ensuring that opportunities for professional development address the needs of all teachers and of the school is the next step. Transformative educational leaders carefully balance opportunities for individual professional growth with the needs of the whole school to acquire understanding and expertise in a particular area. Sometimes a leader may provide incentives and encouragement for new teachers to visit students' homes and learn firsthand about their living conditions. At other times, she may provide appropriate training for the whole staff in interdisciplinary curriculum or in opening up the curriculum to ensure that multiple cultural perspectives are included.

In chapter 5, I described how people use language like *color-blind* or *class-blind* in a well-intentioned attempt to be caring—to develop relationships based on "common humanity," to not focus on difference. Pretending to ignore difference is generally more cruel than kind and tends to make the other feel self-conscious and insecure. Using difference to define someone is, of course, the opposite and equally undesirable extreme.

I once had a friend who was blind. When I first got to know him, in an attempt to be kind, I consciously avoided using words that related to seeing. I soon learned that this artificial constraint was both inappropriate and unnecessary, as Harry often talked about movies or television shows he had "seen." As we became better acquainted, I learned how my failure to acknowledge his blindness placed many more restraints and constraints on him than acknowledging and working with it. I eventually learned, for example, that with a little help and accommodation, Harry enjoyed waterskiing, repairing electronic equipment, and many other activities I had simply assumed were beyond his capabilities. Accepting and acknowledging his blindness as a normal part of our relationship permitted us to share activities I had previously believed impossible. I had mentally used the label *blind* to define him, thereby circumscribing my expectations and constraining the full development of our relationship. Intending to show empathy without taking time to understand Harry's situation had been counterproductive.

To be empathetic, educators need to attend constructively to both personal stories and narratives of history, remember historical injustices, and bring them to the center of the conversation. Bellah and colleagues described this as being a "community of memory," a community that

> does not forget its past. In order not to forget that past, a community is involved in retelling its story, its constitutive narrative, and in so doing, it offers examples of the men and women who have embodied and exemplified the meaning of community. (Bellah et al. 1985, 158)

In Canyon Collegiate, the story of the community and its history is closely tied to narratives and memories of the Long Walk, of what the Navajo call the Fearing Time (Locke 1992, 303), of treaties and relocation. This cannot be retold apart from the creation of a safe and trusting environment in which it is appropriate for all members to identify differences, rather than ignore them, and to speak honestly to one another.

In British Columbia, Canada, many communities with large percentages of Sikh students still ignore such events as the 1914 refusal to permit immigrants on the Kama Gata Maru to land after a difficult fifty-one-day voyage from India via Hong Kong. The official reason was a convoluted policy that prevented immigrants from landing if they had not come *directly* from their home country (in this case India). Because the ship had stopped in Hong Kong, the travelers were not permitted to land. Telling this story of rejection may help all students develop more empathic dispositions toward South Asian immigrants.

In many areas of North America, the history of development and settlement is closely tied to the completion of a transcontinent railway—and the often unjust treatment of thousands of Chinese workers. We know, through historical records and personal narratives, that the Chinese workers were paid very low wages (approximately $28 a month) and many of them perished. In Pendleton, Oregon, Chinese workers were charged a $1 poll tax and a curfew was forced on them. Because the Chinese often were not safe above ground, an underground city grew up. Visitors can now tour the underground city and attend the annual event in which the Pendleton Underground Tours presents its Comes to Life celebration. Williams describes it in the following words.

> Real-life cowboys, saloon girls, gunfighters, Chinese laundry workers, meat market butchers, ice cream parlor patrons, speakeasy gamblers,

bordello madams and working girls trade one-liners with the tourists while keeping in character and acting out vignettes of life in the "good old days." (Williams 2000)

Bringing the past to life by perpetuating stereotypes of immigrants and assuming the hegemonic dominant perspective of the "good old days" is hardly consistent with a caring or empathetic society; yet these are the messages we too often continue to perpetuate in our classroom conversations and curriculum materials.

We must find ways to tell these stories and acknowledge the harm done to the recipients of these unequal policies and practices. But we have to ensure that we do so in ways that are empathic and sensitive. We should remember, as Barman states,

> Every today has a yesterday. The issues that engage us—and enrage us— each have a context. Their shape lies not just in today's priorities but in past desires. Today got to be the way it is, at least in part, because of how we have chosen to interpret the events of yesterday. For the most part we take the past for granted. . . . What we overlook in doing so is that the educational past is just as contested and constructed as is the present day. (personal communication 2001)

Being empathetic includes re-examining our taken-for-granted assumptions about the past and bringing the recognition of hegemonic practices in resolving past tensions to the surface where they can be addressed.

In order for members to begin to take the risk of telling their individual stories, as well as those of their families and communities, a climate of openness and respect will have to replace hostile attitudes that still exist in some schools. As I spoke to one teacher, I noticed a large elk head mounted on the wall of her classroom; she followed my gaze and told me that it frightened many parents and students. Instead of taking it down, she permitted it to constitute a barrier to communication and understanding, dismissing their concern with a single, scornful word, "Superstition!"

Creating schools that are just, democratic, and empathetic requires educators to accept people where they are, offering support, encouragement, and respect regardless of their circumstances, histories, or even superstitions. This does not mean that everything and everyone must be accepted into a given community. Ensuring that a community is empathetic may require making some tough decisions to exclude those who do not share the norms of inclusion and respect, those who want to perpetuate the status quo without regard for those who have been marginalized or excluded by common practices, or those who reject the need for openness, trust, and dialogue. Empathy requires caring deeply about the quality of life and relationships that develop within an organization.

An Optimistic School

Educators who develop attitudes and implement policies and practices that promote justice, democracy, and empathy make considerable progress toward inclusive and respectful school communities in which all students can participate in their own learning. Ensuring that the learning is optimistic is a final step in the development of a school as a community of difference. A school falls short if its educators work to achieve equity of access, full participation, and a caring environment but fail to design the central activities of the school—its teaching and learning core—to provide the basis for success beyond its walls.

Optimism is not to be confused with blind anticipation of a rosy future or an empty belief that if we repeat common platitudes like "all children can learn" often enough, then everything will be all right. Optimism is most closely related to the spiritual notion of *sure hope*—hope that is deeply grounded in the knowledge that good intentions have been replaced by sound practices which help every child develop a positive academic self-concept, achieve to his or her potential, and leave school prepared to succeed in his or her chosen path.

I spoke to two teachers about their positions as visible minority teachers on a predominantly white staff in a diverse school. They recognized it was "partly [their] responsibility to keep pushing justice, to speak about colonization." One added, "However, I think because you're a minority, as a staff member, you feel very ground down a lot of the times."

Feeling ground down is not optimistic. Moreover, as I spoke with the teachers about issues of marginalization and discrimination, they stated that I was "probably touching [their] conscience." They felt defeated and withdrew, tired of the pressures, the critiques, and the sense of exclusion that came with speaking up (and speaking out). An optimistic school would be one in which all teachers feel they can raise issues of concern without fear of reprisal, in which they will not find it necessary to repress critiques of unjust positions and undemocratic attitudes.

In an optimistic school, everyone is united by a sense of common purpose, not an assumed unity but one that has been developed over time with a great deal of hard work and dialogue among individuals and groups both inside and outside the school. In one school, I was told that equity was the responsibility of a committee. An administrator stated,

> I think we still buy into the lip service stuff. We need to start at the staff level. Probably we should be focusing on what we do in our staff development time and we haven't. There have been modest attempts, but I do think we have to address our issues. Raising the achievement level of all students is the responsibility of the equity committee, have you visited them?

In this school, central issues of equity and student achievement were relegated to a small committee, leaving the majority of the teachers unconcerned and unaffected. How can we ensure that equity becomes a priority of the whole staff, rather than the responsibility of only a few members of the community?

Often one hears talk about reducing the achievement gap between advantaged and disadvantaged students. Yet reducing, rather than eliminating, the gap still reflects a deficit model. At one point in Red Rock School District, the explicit goal was a gap reduction of 25 percent. In other words, the district policy makers seemed to believe that reducing the gap between Anglo and Navajo achievement, instead of eliminating it, was good enough. I believe that educators in an optimistic school would question this standard, which still buys into a deficit model. Indeed, in an optimistic school, everyone would take responsibility for equity and student achievement.

Eliminating gaps does not happen all at once but is a process that occurs over time. Nevertheless, ensuring high standards for all students is fundamental to providing hope. I once worked with a school staff, at the principal's request (but in his absence), discussing school programs and resources and setting goals for the coming year. Teachers told me they had acquired training in instructional strategies that they believed would help all students achieve success in reading and math. As a result, they agreed that reading and math would be priorities; they would ask the principal to assign appropriate resources and support to the targeted areas. Their goal would be for all students to be working at grade level by the end of the forthcoming school year. When Don, the principal, arrived from a district meeting, the staff shared their new sense of purpose with him. Their professionalism was quickly shattered as he commented, "Of course, that is the ideal. But as a goal, you are setting yourselves up for failure." He was willing to have teachers implement new programs and learn new instructional strategies, but he was unwilling to commit to the achievement of all students or to believe deeply that all students in his high-risk school really could learn to high standards.

Not only would Jane in Martin Popper School disagree with this principal but she has proven his stance to be wrong. Having successfully moved her school from a D to an A school in Florida's high-stakes environment, she reflects:

> I was thinking even today when I was driving to school. . . . I have one teacher in particular where it's a challenge for me to have her keep her expectations high. I was thinking that we always have to know that if we don't expose the children to certain things they're never going to do better. It is like when I play tennis with someone better than me, if I keep in my comfort zone, I'm not going to get any better. . . . For the student, the light bulb might come on. You don't know when, it may just take that little guy a little bit longer; but he's had the opportunity. You haven't closed your mind to it.

It is critical that transformative leaders provide an environment of constant hope and encourage teachers never to give up on any student. Accepting teachers where they are and working with them to achieve shared goals is one thing. Accepting an inequitable situation and being unwilling or unable to see a way out is neither optimistic nor acceptable.

While Jane's approach—raising the standards, fighting for an A rating—helped increase the self-esteem and academic self-confidence of her school community, Don's does the opposite. Although he states publicly that all children can learn, his reaction to his staff's plans to achieve the explicit goal clearly demonstrates that he is still guided by deficit thinking.

Deficit thinking and an optimistic learning environment are antithetical. It is not possible to enhance the academic self-esteem of children if the implicit message is that they cannot succeed. All the staff-development opportunities and program innovations imaginable will have little positive effect if they are implemented in an atmosphere of resignation.

For a school to be optimistic, people need to feel ownership. There must be a sense that school goals and home goals are congruent. In one school, teachers expressed frustration that students "were not making the grade." Prior to a staff meeting planned to discuss the situation, the principal elaborated, "Our worry is that parents don't feel much ownership of the grand dreams that we have. This meeting is essentially for the school staff, but the next step after that will be to involve community members, to actually see what they think." The intentions are good, but for optimism to replace frustration, parents need to be brought into the process much earlier.

Optimism requires the development of a learning environment that is rich and varied—one that will engage students in their own learning processes. It requires constant examination and re-examination of how students are progressing and identification of new ways to help them learn. One principal stated, "Until we get a handle on this reading deficiency in this school, our kids are not going to be able to do really well in their other academic classes without a great deal of assistance. There is also a real need for teachers to make school more interesting and fun for the kids." Getting a handle on deficiencies, never giving up, not writing kids off—these are the attitudes of optimistic educators. As a friend once said to me, "A transformative leader has chronic optimism."

Sometimes in today's environment of high stakes testing educators and the public are convinced that student results on standardized achievement tests are truly indicative of a school's performance or of students' abilities. In Canyon Collegiate, teachers are often frustrated by extremely low results on standardized tests. However, consistent with Cummins's (1989) approach, they try to overcome the tendency to use this kind of assessment to legitimate deficit thinking or perpetuate myths about lack of student achievement. One way to accomplish this is to ensure that alternative forms of assessment are used and the results disseminated. Alicia states that despite the lack of progress on norm-referenced tests, students have made progress on the sixth-grade writing assessment conducted by the district and on the criterion-referenced tests developed and administered by the state. She says, "Last year we did well on the core math tests." When asked what she meant by well, she replied, "At or above district average in every area." This news must be shared with the community.[2]

Hope is found in individual stories as well as in statistics and test results. The principal of a junior high school told the following story about a young man who was not succeeding in the traditional classroom.

> His mother pulled him out and is home schooling him. He is a fifth grader. We have allowed him as part of the home schooling, to come in and take science with the seventh graders and do some things here in the school. He came into the school with a tested reading level of fourth grade; in less than two months he was up to seventh grade reading level. It's not because of anything that we did, but there was a motivation there I think on his part to try to perform as well as the seventh graders. And so he did.

The principal was wrong; the change was because of something she did. Through flexibility, attention to individual needs, provision of alternatives, and expectation of success, this student was able to find the intrinsic motivation to succeed. The story illustrates clearly the importance of working in creative and positive ways with parents and students. This is a characteristic of optimism.

Educators need to acknowledge what parents know only too well: that there is a difference between an unmotivated student and schooling that is unmotivating. Without my constant prodding, my eleventh-grade son seemed to find it difficult to get up in time for school; yet he had no problem getting ready to leave with his friends at 5 A.M. for a weekend ski trip. Unmotivated? Hardly. But he definitely found traditional schooling to be irrelevant and uninteresting. Differentiating between the two is critical because it helps educators make connections to the lived experiences, backgrounds, cultures, and interests of students in order to tap into their curiosity and motivation for learning. Expecting all students to be actively engaged in learning simply because a topic is specified in a curriculum guide is unrealistic. Expecting all students to succeed and finding ways to achieve that goal is our job.

Optimistic educators go beyond the requirements of their contract. They do not work to a clock, nor do they remain aloof from their students. We have seen, in earlier chapters, that students want to connect with their teachers as real people. We have read about teachers who engage students in simple experiences, like going to the post office, that have been missing from their lived experiences. Examples of successful adults, like Esther, principal of John Howard School, or Ruth Simmons, president of Brown University, have demonstrated clearly that educators can make a difference when they believe in children and identify the support they need to be successful.

Alicia describes how efforts on the part of teachers to identify ways to provide assistance and support for students from Canyon Collegiate have made a difference:

> Those who graduate from high school are being more successful in college, partly because we are being better at helping them choose colleges that will help them succeed. There are some colleges that really have strong support programs for Native American kids and we take them to those schools before they graduate. They make the connections with the college counselors before they graduate, so the kids know who to go to and where to go . . . rather than just dumping them into a whole new culture. And we try to work with the two-year colleges as stepping-stones before they go to the four-year universities. And they are being more successful academically.

Optimistic schooling provides the opportunity for students to make healthy and hopeful choices in their day-to-day lives. It offers hope for the future—for individuals as well as for society.

CONCLUSION: A COMMUNITY OF DIFFERENCE

A community of difference is a community that is inclusive, respectful, and hopeful. In a school that is a community of difference, teachers, parents, students, and administrators work and learn together. Over time, as they share their histories and their daily lived experiences, including their culture, ethnicity, gender, and class background, they develop and demonstrate trust. Increasingly, they communicate their hopes and their hurts. They bring their cultures, traditions, and dreams. They are neither fearful nor ashamed. Because they have learned to trust each other, they are able to participate honestly, engage in debate, disagree, and find resolution in a spirit of openness. When all members of the community know that the principles of justice, democracy, empathy, and optimism are foundational to both daily life and broader policy and decision making at the school, a climate of justice and hope is established. They are free to be and to share themselves.

In this chapter I have tried to provide a glimpse of what a school as a community of difference might be like. There are no prescriptions, but some key concepts that committed educators will take to heart and work out in their own contexts and settings. In the next chapter I examine some strategies and approaches that educators, as transformative cross-cultural leaders, might use to begin to make this vision a reality.

NOTES

1. American readers especially need to be aware that while federal funds provide meal programs in many U.S. schools, this is not a universal practice; in many countries, schools in need of meal programs must find local funds and volunteers to move ahead.

2. Texas House Bill 588, known as the Top 10 Percent Law is consistent with a more holistic emphasis. Because there is evidence that the top 10 percent of students earn grade point averages that exceed averages of other students even though the latter may be admitted with higher SAT scores, high-school class ranking is considered both an excellent predictor of student success and a way of ensuring a broader base of admissions of students from all populations.

Making It Happen

At the beginning of the twenty-first century, an important question for many educators is no longer how to maintain the social order, but how to move beyond previous static conceptions of community to find ways of embracing and including difference in democratic communities. Sidorkin believes that "the greatest failing of this civilization is its inability to deal with difference" (1999, 144). Ultimately, he says, "we humans must confront our differences together. . . . The world of irreducible differences, among other things, requires us to adjust ourselves to it" (p. 144).

Because previous conceptions of community were frequently narrow and oppressive, in this book I have tried to develop a way of adjusting ourselves in educational settings, to understand and embrace difference. This search for a concept of community that recognizes diversity and difference has not been grounded in a romantic or nostalgic quest for a past reality that never was (sometimes exemplified by Tönnies's (1957) notion of gemeinschaft). Instead, I have based my approach on the concept of a deeply moral community, one that is inclusive, liberating, and socially just, one that I call a community of difference. This new community shares some elements of what others have called authentic as opposed to *counterfeit* community (Rousseau 1991). It also contains elements of what Peck (1987) calls real community as opposed to *pseudocommunity*.

A community of difference contains inherent paradoxes. It is tolerant and democratic, accepting of otherness or difference but not perpetuating a relativistic "anything goes." It must be inclusive but intolerant of injustice. It must value difference and otherness, while at the same time finding a sense of purpose or meaning that will bring people together. It must address the challenge described by Henderson and Hawthorne as "cultivating unity *within* diversity" (1995, 135; emphasis added). The preposition *within* is extremely important here. Neither they nor I have suggested that the goal is unity *from* diversity. Instead, in order for an authentic community of difference to occur within a school, members must find areas around which unity may be fostered without expecting to eliminate diversity.

In part 2, I provided some glimpses into the thinking and actions of educators who are working toward the creation of communities of difference. In chapter 9, I tried to create a composite picture of what a community of difference might be like. In this chapter, I focus on data and dialogue as ways to help educators who want to be transformative, who are committed to making changes in their school contexts, to move closer to the normative concept of community I outline in this book. However, I do not provide prescriptions or a how-to list, since none are possible. I rely on the ability of educational leaders to reflect carefully on the ideas presented here and determine how, in each individual setting, they can best bring theory and practice together to create schools that are both academically excellent and socially just. (For as I said earlier, I do not believe one is possible without the other.) McLaren says,

> The key is to make the theories real—to ground them in the contextual specificity of real life and human suffering as well as happiness—to anchor them effectively in people's dreams and agonies, visions and mundane routines. We need to take theories out of . . . academic life . . . in order to get democracy off the ground in the streets and in the classrooms. (as cited in Borg, Mayo, and Sultana 1998, 371)

In this chapter, I begin by offering suggestions about why change sometimes seems so difficult. I hope these ideas will prompt dialogue about the status quo and ways to move beyond it. Next, I present some ways to engage in data collection and demonstrate how data may provide an image of what is as an important starting point for developing a sense of what can be. I suggest two approaches to data collection: a school profile and a conceptual matrix.

Finding ways to move a community from what is to what can be requires a commitment to dialogue, a topic I take up in the next part of the chapter. What is dialogue? How can we facilitate it? How can we sustain it?

Once we gather data, identify needed change, begin to understand and critique it through the use of dialogue, and introduce changes consistent with the goals and criteria we have established, the task is to ensure that the new community can be sustained—not carved in stone but maintaining a dynamic tension. I conclude the chapter with some reflections about how transformative leadership may make it happen.

BARRIERS TO CHANGE

Sometimes we approach the task of introducing educational change with considerable cynicism, not believing that it can be done and resigning ourselves to the idea put forward by Cuban (1990) that despite our best efforts educational change occurs in predictable patterns, like the swing of a pendulum. Sometimes we are tempted to resist calls for reform or appeals for change, convinced that if we just close our eyes, shut our doors, and hang on for a while, the new wave, like many in the past, will wash over us and leave us virtually unscathed. At times, we take stock, recognize the need for change, resolve to take the moral high road, and introduce sweeping reforms to make our schools more just, democratic, empathetic, and optimistic—only to realize that we don't know where or how to begin. Even when we muster our courage, put in hours of work, and expend considerable energy at the expense of sleep or personal relationships, we are sometimes confronted at the end with the question How do we know whether or not we have made a difference for children? Meaningful change is so difficult that often the mere thought of it leaves us mired in confusion.

Fullan attributes the difficulty of achieving educational change to the intrinsic conservatism of today's schools:

> On the one hand we have the constant and expanding presence of educational innovation and reform. It is no exaggeration to say that dealing with change is endemic to post-modern society. On the other hand, however, we

have an educational system that is fundamentally conservative. The way that teachers are trained, the way that schools are organized, the way that the educational hierarchy operates, and the way that education is treated by political decision-makers results in a system that is more likely to retain the status quo than to change. When change is attempted under such circumstances, it results in defensiveness, superficiality or at best short-lived pockets of success. (1993, 3)

There is some truth in Fullan's analysis. Our education system is inherently conservative and often those who are hired, especially to administrative positions, may seem to have the most to lose if the status quo is changed. Most principals are hired *because* they have been successful in the system as it is, not because they have been involved in efforts to overthrow or change it.

Bourdieu (1990, 1993), a French sociologist, provided a different explanation. He believed that culture is composed of a variety of fields (such as education, the state, religion, and political parties) all occupying positions due to their possession of various forms of economic, social, and symbolic capital. Each field is a relatively autonomous social microcosm, with its own separate sphere built up over many years through an accumulation of traditions, rules, and common practices.

Bourdieu advanced the concept of habitus, "a system of dispositions common to all products of the same conditionings" (1990, 59) to explain why members of the same institutions tend to share cultural and social experiences that shape them and constrain their understandings and ability to change. While the concept of agency is intrinsic to his ideas, agency is not unlimited but restricted by these durable dispositions of habitus. Choice is therefore bounded by what we know:

> Habitus tends to generate all the "reasonable" and "commonsense" behaviours (and only those) which are possible within the limits of these regularities, and which are likely to be positively sanctioned because they are objectively adjusted to the logic characteristic of the field, whose objective future they anticipate. At the same time . . . it tends to exclude all "extravagances" ("not for the likes of us"), that is, all the behaviours that would be negatively sanctioned because they are incompatible with the objective conditions. (pp. 55–56)

This position helps us understand why the creation of a community of difference seems so difficult. Circumstances have changed, but our awareness of the range of possibilities for change has not kept pace. Finding unity in diversity seems to lie outside our general range of possibilities. We may suspect that attempting to change the status quo, even to be more socially just, would be negatively sanctioned.

Sometimes societal and demographic pressures are ignored as those in control maintain links to traditional ways of operating without taking into consideration changed circumstances. Bourdieu called this the "short circuit effect" (as cited in Swingewood 1998, 89). Others (Tichy and Devanna 1986; Senge 1990) have called it the "boiled frog syndrome."[1] Regardless of the name, it frequently appears that the worldview of the most powerful groups—administrators, parents, or community members—is not conducive to a change in the status quo. This is not surprising, since those with the most power have come to expect and enjoy the benefits that accrue to them from the status quo, which therefore becomes the habitus of education.

Bourdieu's theories of fields and habitus are helpful in understanding why educational change is so difficult. His primary point is that social and cultural boundaries are established by a complex interplay of past and present experience, and are quite resistant to transformation. However, despite the difficulties, change is possible. With effort, we may expand our repertoire of responses to enable us to react to changing external conditions.

Change theorists suggest that the way forward is not to wait for beliefs to change nor to attempt to persuade all members of a group, through argumentation, that a certain change should occur. Rather, they suggest that both vision and belief follow action. Too often in educational life, we engage in futile and endless talk, trying to convince colleagues to adopt a new rule or curriculum or program.

I once worked in a school in which offering enriched classes in some subjects was the subject of much controversy. Some people argued on ideological grounds that these classes were elitist; others took a more practical position that there was no need for enriched classes as all students were challenged through the availability of elective subjects. As debate coach, I was helping two ninth-grade students (who happened to be in the enriched program) prepare for a regional competition about a famous historical figure, Louis Riel. I approached the twelfth-grade history teacher and asked if the girls could practice their speeches in his class and whether his students, who had been studying Riel and his era, could ply my debaters with questions. He reluctantly agreed.

Following the class, my colleague effusively complimented my debaters everywhere he went. These freshman students, he had learned, were thinking, probing, analyzing, and arguing at a higher level than his seniors. Although lengthy discussion had not persuaded Geoff that some students benefit from more challenging approaches and peer groups who share their interests, he became an advocate and signed up to teach classes in the enriched program the following year.

Fullan believes that while vision is essential for successful change, it "emerges from, more than it precedes, action" (1993, 28). He suggests that change is so complex and the stakes are so high that educators who want to be change agents must develop a deep and coherent understanding of how to effect change. In his 1999 discussion of change forces, Fullan emphasizes that change must be inspired by moral purpose. Educators wanting to effect change need to clarify their pedagogical assumptions, accept the reality and validity of conflict, diversity, anxiety, and chaos, and recognize that "there can never be a silver bullet of change" (Fullan 1999, 28). Fullan concludes that

> leaders at all levels from the classroom to the state house need to conceptualize and continue to construct ever more sophisticated practical theories of action. These theories of action will enable them: to understand the critical importance of incorporating all three forces—the intellectual, the political, and the spiritual in their thinking and action. (1999, 83)

I have been suggesting that a morally grounded theory of education will foster both thinking and action that are socially just. I have talked about how transformative educational leaders recognize the imperatives for change that are required if we are to provide more just and equitable educational experiences for all students. In the next section, I suggest that if we are serious about effecting meaningful reform, we will recognize the importance of data as an impetus for change.

UNDERSTANDING WHAT IS

Few educators would consciously decide to implement or perpetuate an inequitable or unjust system—not when we are there, as we often say, for the good of the kids. Yet, as we have seen, numerous inequitable practices do exist and are perpetuated by caring, well-intentioned individuals in the present system. Knowing how to identify and address inequities in practices and attitudes can be a daunting task. One way to begin is collecting data to provide a snapshot of what is. Developing a school profile is one useful way to approach data collection.

Developing a School Profile

A school profile is a collection of information, including anecdotes and statistics, that provides a snapshot of a school at a given time. We recall Gardner's (1990) assertion that to effect change, we need to understand the context, the organization, and the setting. Because these vary widely, there are no set rules or components for a school profile, but we might begin by examining the teaching staff of a school. What is the range of age and experience, the gender balance, the ethnicity representation? Which teachers are in formal positions of authority? What programs does the school offer? Who are the students? How many students have been identified as having special education needs or requiring an educational aide or assistant? What is the ethnic breakdown of the student body? What do we know about the socioeconomic status of students or their home situations? What students are in which programs or classes or extracurricular activities?

Once these basic items have been determined, you may want to extend the data collection. In an elementary school, one might ask how much time each student spends in a pullout program rather than with his or her classroom teacher. Do the support systems work together to help create a sense of community or to fragment? How are children with special needs integrated into full classroom participation? What is the makeup of the parent advisory council?

Scrutinize records of disciplinary actions, suspensions, attendance. Identify the students who have been selected to represent the

school at various functions. Are some groups of students disproportionately represented in select activities? Or on the other hand, are
members of other groups of students noticeably absent from certain
school activities?

Additional questions may be posed in a secondary school. Who is on
the honor roll? Which students are in college preparatory or advanced
academic classes? Is there inequitable representation in any of these
groups? What about student academic performance? Are there groups
of students who are consistently below average or excluded from certain honors or classes? What about the rest of the school's programs—
including clubs, athletic activities, leadership responsibilities?

The creation of a school profile is a time-consuming activity that
raises numerous questions about things we often take for granted. On
the one hand, it requires that we maintain careful records of various aspects of school life, records that for some schools in some districts are
not readily available. On the other hand, it raises questions we are frequently not prepared to answer. Who, for example, should be counted
as an aboriginal student—one who has a tax number or treaty status?
Who counts as an Asian teacher? One who is a third-generation citizen
whose first language is English but who looks Asian?

Creating the profile requires opening dialogue about some difficult
issues of identity and identification. It is therefore a powerful tool for
beginning to understand what is in a given setting. By way of illustration, I present some data collected by Holly, a teacher in a diverse urban secondary school, who developed a profile as part of a graduate
course assignment.[2] In this case, after providing an extensive overview
of the school population, Holly zeroed in on a program of special interest to her (a program for teen moms) and conducted an extensive
analysis that included interviews with the students themselves. I share
only a small portion of the information provided in her profile, but it is
evocative of what is possible.

Holly describes her school, which encompasses grades 8–12, as an
"inner-city school." She writes,

> It serves an ethnically diverse population and enrolment as of September
> 2000 was 1378 students. Approximately one third of the students come
> from homes in which a language other than English is spoken; it is esti-

mated that 43 different languages are spoken in the homes of our students. In all, 225 students are receiving English as a Second Language Instruction and an additional 18 percent of our population is enrolled in special education or other special programs. Our student body includes a large number of students of aboriginal descent and we have the highest transiency rate of secondary schools in the district. (course assignment, used with permission)

She then illustrates in dramatic fashion some of the key challenges faced by educators in Granite High School. First, in table 10.1, she provides a breakdown of the students, reflecting the languages spoken in the homes of students who were being served by the school's ESL program.

Table 10.1. Home Languages in Granite High School

Language	Students	Language	Students	Language	Students
Tagalog	47	Taiwanese	7	Albanian	2
Korean	35	Polish	6	Bangladeshi	2
Arabic	17	Ethiopian	5	French	2
Czech	16	Punjabi	5	Japanese	2
Mandarin	16	Bengali	3	Ghanian	1
Persian	13	Russian	3	Greek	1
Hindi	12	Serbo-Croatian	3	Tamil	1
Vietnamese	10	Urdu	3	Thai	1
Spanish	8	Indonesian	2	Yugoslavian	1

She then shows the ethnic distribution of the teaching staff in figure 10.1. Clearly, although more than 33 percent of the students come from homes where languages other than English are spoken, the teaching staff is predominantly white or Caucasian and native English speaking.

Holly then proceeded to search available databases and census information to better understand the student body of her school. These data helped her identify areas in which her school population differed from the regional norm and hence might need special attention from teachers in her school. Figure 10.2 demonstrates that the school population averages more families with annual incomes less than $30,000 than does the geographic region in which it is located, more single-parent families, and a generally lower level of education.

Teaching Staff-Ethnicity

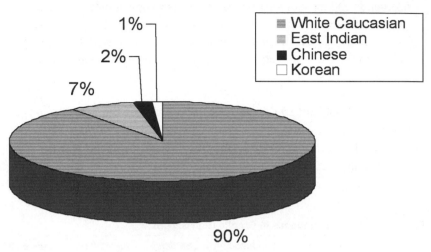

Figure 10.1.   Ethnic Origin of Teachers in Granite High School

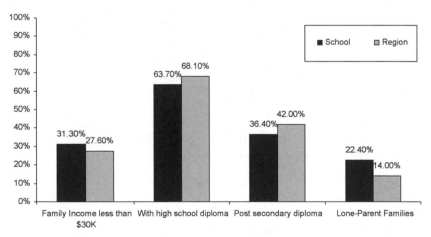

Figure 10.2.   Income and Education Levels of Granite High School's Geographic Area

From these data, she extrapolated that the school will likely need to be creative and persistent if it wants to relate to parents. Many parents will likely be unavailable to come into the school during the day; moreover, the relatively low education level suggests that many adults may not be particularly comfortable approaching the school at all. Thus it will be important to identify ways in which the school may help families, perhaps offering adult GED classes in the evenings or on weekends.

As shown in figure 10.3, Holly goes on to identify some of the specific populations served by the school. One question prompted by these data is how the school can ensure that the large non-English-speaking population is able to find a place and a voice in the school community. For example, the author of this school profile became increasingly concerned that the only languages offered in the school were French and Spanish, with no instruction in Tagalog, the predominant second language of the population.

Holly proceeded to examine the available achievement data. Table 10.2 reports the scores from a standardized criterion-referenced writing skills assessment. They are intended to illustrate not only the data available but how they provide a basis for asking questions about the equity and equality of various programs.

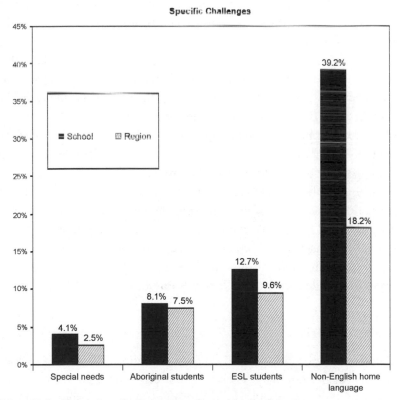

Figure 10.3. Some Specific Populations Served by the School

Table 10.2.   Tenth-Grade Writing Assessment Data

| | 2000–2001 Writing Skills Assessment: Grade 10 | | | | | |
| | Not Yet within Expectations | | Meets Expectations | | Exceeds Expectations | |
	School	District	School	District	School	District
Total (%)	31	14	67	82	2	4
Male (%)	42	20	56	77	2	3
Female (%)	19	7	78	87	3	5
Aboriginal (%)	63	33	38	66	0	1

Even a cursory examination of these data demonstrate that tenth grade students in Granite High School are performing below the district average in writing. Moreover, males and aboriginal students seem to be faring worse than the female students in the school.

Armed with these data, educators in Granite High School may begin to enter into dialogue about what the challenges are and how to address them. They will, of course, need to avoid falling into the trap of deficit thinking and blaming the victim as they discuss the school's demographic data. They will need to ask why the aboriginal students in their school are performing at a lower level than those in other schools, not only examining their own programs, attitudes, and assumptions but spending time finding out what others are doing. They will want to gather more data to help them understand and interpret the profile, for example, whether there are some groups of male students who are performing satisfactorily and others who are not.

A school profile encourages everyone to get involved in collecting information, asking questions, interpreting the findings, determining what the school is doing well and where there may be problems. It does not identify causes, point fingers, or assign blame; hence, it is a useful starting point for educational leaders wanting to ensure that their schools are academically excellent, equitable, and socially just.

Creating a Matrix

Another way of engaging in data collection might be to develop a matrix of ideas from this book or other sources and assign each cell to a triad of faculty members who could investigate the issues raised and identify areas needing discussion. Sometimes creating a matrix leads to a belief that there are no other topics that need to be discussed, or that the matrix is a complete and comprehensive examination of relevant data. Although these are dangers to be avoided, the development of a matrix may serve as a useful tool to prompt reflection and dialogue and provide the basis for further investigation. The matrix presented in table 10.3 is an illustration of one approach to some of the issues raised in this book. One might, for example, use the criteria of just, democratic, empathetic, and optimistic as one axis and invite members of the group to list relevant topics, such as culture, structure, identity, parent and community involvement, carnival, or power, along the other axis. It might be useful to ask small groups at a staff meeting or during a staff-development activity to define what they understand by each term on the matrix and to fill in each cell with some ideas relevant to their particular situation in the school.

For example, after spending time defining identity, and deciding that identity includes how we represent others, how others represent us, and how we see ourselves, a group might decide to focus on empathy as it relates to identity. What are the current problems? How might we help students feel proud of who they are? Likewise, after thinking about the

Table 10.3. A Matrix of Important Issues

	Justice	Democracy	Empathy	Optimism
Culture	How to include all cultures	How do we hear the Tagalog parents when no one speaks their language?	How can we demonstrate caring to students who have and/or who are single parents?	How do we ensure that our children from welfare families have a better future?
Structure				
Identity	Not: color-blind, class-blind, spiritually blind	Open dialogue, not show & tell	Each should feel proud & safe	Opportunity to express all three registers (Taubman)
Parent involvement				
Community partnership				
Carnival				
Power		Who makes decisions about class enrollment and course offerings?		How can we help all students feel capable of success?

justice issues related to identity, they might decide to help everyone understand some of the potential problems of using well-intentioned terms like *color-blind* to discuss visible minority students, or "kids from single-parent families" as a way of labeling children without recognizing other individual characteristics.

In table 10.3 I filled in a few ideas that might relate to Granite High School to illustrate that there are many ways to start the conversation. Although one does not always need to start by examining data, developing a profile or matrix provides a focused and blame-free way of engaging fundamental questions and not being derailed by topics that may seem important to a few people but are peripheral to enhancing the social justice and academic excellence of the whole school.

Providing time for teachers to discuss specific ideas among themselves may help begin the dialogue and raise their consciousness about what constitutes a community of difference. Whether you choose to develop a matrix or a school profile, the important thing is to start somewhere and commit to a process that will permit you to clarify your beliefs, values, and assumptions, understand your practice, and develop some agreed-on criteria that will move you closer to your goals.

DREAMING WHAT CAN BE

Once we have an idea of what is, the next step is to identify what could or should be. Please note that I am not talking about strategic planning or another sequential, linear process. This type of planning is decried by Wheatley, who says:

> We've spent years moving pieces around, building elaborate models, contemplating more variables, creating more advanced forms of analysis . . . . We have reduced and described and separated things into cause and effect, and drawn the world in lines and boxes. (1993, 27–28)

Rather, I am increasingly convinced that if we are to effect change, we need to recognize the power of ideas and the power of relationships. In 1930 astronomer James Jeans said, "The universe begins to look more like a great thought than a great machine" (as cited in Wheatley 1993,

32). A half century later, Temes defined leadership as "the action of ideas to make change through the agency of individuals" (1996, 74). In this book, I have relied on the power of ideas like transformative leadership and a community of difference to excite us and help us effect educational change.

When we acknowledge the power and potency of ideas to move us forward, we come to recognize the second important truth—the importance of relationships. Wheatley asserts that with relationships we "give up predictability for potentials" (1993, 34). The problem is that relationships are often confusing, always complex, and difficult to manage. Nevertheless, we are on a journey of discovery, exploration of powerful ideas, and exciting potential—all defined, at least in part, by our valued relationships.

Buber recognizes this in his emphasis on "I-thou" relationships. Bakhtin puts it slightly differently when he states "Two voices is the minimum for life, the minimum of existence" (as cited in Sidorkin 1999, 33). Alexander Sidorkin goes further. He states, "A person of integrity is deeply committed to truth, and truth is being born between us. This requires a commitment to dialogue, a commitment to ascertain the other (Thou art, therefore I am), to discover the human dimension of this world" (p. 63).

To move forward in new ways, in a new time, for a new outcome, transformative leaders must build relationships based on powerful ideas and exciting opportunities. We must begin to understand, facilitate, and encourage moral dialogue.

MORAL DIALOGUE: A WAY TO GET THERE

Bryck has eloquently identified commitment to discourse as the first moral principle of a democracy:

> In writings as ancient as Aristotle, as contemporary as Gadamer, Habermas, and Arendt, as secular as Dewey, and as religious as Aquinas, we find strong support for the contention that the survival of a pluralistic democracy requires a belief that mutual understanding among diverse parties can be achieved through genuine dialogue and commitment of its citizens to such a discourse. (1988, 259)

Dialogue can move us forward and provide the fabric from which the new community will be woven, from which the new norms of a heterogeneous community of difference will be negotiated. It will be the task of each transformative leader in his or her context to create the norms of continuous dialogue—in the halls, in the staff room, at staff meetings, by disseminating articles, by a judicious comment or a strategically posed question in daily e-mail, by encouraging teachers to attend workshops and classes and engage in peer observation or team teaching. The possibilities are endless. Although many serendipitous understandings may emerge from these interactions, dialogic moments should also be intentional, designed to support the agreed-on norms of the community.

In chapter 2, we examined the five disciplines that Senge believed are important for a learning organization. Returning to these disciplines may provide an excellent starting point for a dialogue about the strengths and weaknesses of the school. Senge reminds us, for example, that team learning "involves mastering the practices of dialogue and discussion" (1990, 237) and distinguishing between them. Dialogue, he tells us, is different from discussion or casual conversation. Discussion shares its etymological roots with the words *concussion* and *percussion* and is often nothing more than a clash of convictions—each participant defending a particular view, striving to persuade the others to his or her obviously correct way of thinking. Dialogue, on the other hand, comes from the Greek *dia* (through) and *logos* (the word or the meaning). Dialogue represents a flowing through of ideas, with each person listening and striving to understand the other's position. Although dialogue and discussion are potentially complementary, few seem to have learned how to deal creatively with the conflicts often produced by discussion. Too often, we try to smooth over differences rather than figure out how to unlock and then redirect the energy in them.

Both discussion and dialogue are necessary for the emergence of a community of difference. Both strategies force us to seriously examine our own positions and perspectives, to identify how we may be inhibiting the development of community. If we listen to different perspectives, attempt to understand them and learn from them, we will grow, learning will occur, and new norms can develop.

Gadamer talks about how dialogue contrasts with rigid statement certainty. Dialogue, he says, uses a "process of question and answer, giving and taking, talking at cross purposes and seeing each other's point" (as cited in Burbules 1993, ix). Burbules emphasizes that engaging in dialogue is something "we learn to do through practice, not by following any sort of recipe or algorithm" (1993, xi). His concept of dialogue is a fundamentally relational "activity directed toward discovery and new understanding" (p. 8). The relationship may be filled with tension, but it must be one in which the participants are firmly committed to what he calls an "ongoing communicative relationship" (p. 19).

Note that difference does not preclude dialogue, but that it is an intrinsic part of it. Dialogue requires a "level of reciprocity that binds partners together in a mutual relation of concern and respect (a relation that is fully cognizant of their differences" (Burbules 1993, 27). Burbules elaborates: in dialogue, one "cannot assume that people will speak the same way, mean the same things, or share the same concerns when they speak (or for that matter will feel safe speaking at all)" (p. 37).

Although there are no recipes for successful dialogue, Burbules does propose three rules: participation, commitment, and reciprocity (1993, 79–83). Although dialogue (especially in a community of difference) requires the participation of all members, people need to participate freely and voluntarily, feeling free to remain silent or even withdraw at times, as necessary. Moreover, they must not participate in a way that excludes others or appear to dismiss alternate positions as unworthy of consideration. Second, all participants must be committed to seeing the interaction through to a point where understanding (although not necessarily consensus) is achieved. The third rule, reciprocity, requires that dialogue be undertaken in a "spirit of mutual respect and concern, and must not take for granted roles of privilege or expertise" (p. 82).

For a student to be able to engage in dialogue with a teacher, to understand a teacher's situation, there will need to be a high level of trust and openness. I recall with amusement the indignation of a colleague whose senior high-school French class was being taught by a teacher intern. During the morning break, she came angrily into the staff room, commenting that a couple of rude girls had just asked her if she was paid her regular salary when an intern was teaching the class. Without the ability to politely ask such questions, how might the students ever understand the role of internships and mentoring in many occupations in society?

Dialogue comes in many forms and serves several purposes. The rules of participation, commitment, and reciprocity are useful in normal conversation, in debate, and in classroom instruction, as well as for engaging in more extensive and purposeful inquiry for the purposes of increased understanding. Dialogue can be either convergent or divergent. It may seek some sort of agreement or it may simply focus on increasing understanding of the different perspectives held by members of the community. Dialogue in a community of difference will at times serve one purpose, at times another; but it will be grounded, as the community itself is grounded, on the norms of inclusion and respect and a desire for excellence and social justice. Regardless of the purpose, dialogue is often hard work and requires concerted attention by educational leaders.

STRATEGIES FOR DIALOGUE: THREE QUESTIONS

There are several tendencies that need to be overcome when we approach dialogue and decision making for a community of difference. We have become so used to jumping to conclusions, to listening only long enough to begin to formulate our response, or to find reasons for *not* doing things rather than ways to facilitate change, that it is useful to become explicit about how we engage in dialogue and interaction with others. Three useful questions that open up dialogue are: Why is that a problem? For what problem is that a solution? and In what ways might we . . . [accomplish whatever]? I take these in order.

Why Is That a Problem?

Learning to ask this question is an important step in changing the thought processes of a group, getting people to think outside the box, and finding new and creative solutions for what sometimes seem to be either routine or intractable problems.

A classic situation described in problem analysis literature (Hills and Gibson 1988; Kahney 1986) goes something like this. A driver is proceeding along a deserted country road when he suddenly realizes he has a flat tire. Opening his trunk, he finds he has no jack. About to walk the ten miles back to town, he stops and asks himself, "Why is that a problem?" and quickly answers, "I need to get the car raised so I can get the tire off" and immediately begins to hunt for a log and stone he might use as a pry. However, the terrain is barren, so he begins again. Why is the need for a pry a problem? He reflects, "I need to create a space between the wheel and the ground to remove the tire! Oh! . . . I have a shovel in the trunk and the ground is soft." Asking Why is that a problem? helps us reframe a problem and begs novel solutions. Using a shovel to assist with changing a tire is not a typical response.

IWWMW *In What Ways might I/we.*

A useful companion question is, In what ways might I (or we) (IWWMW) . . . ? In some ways, asking In what ways might we get the tire changed? could lead to a similar solution, although the detailed thought processes in the foregoing example may not be identified. The second question is, however, useful in many educational situations. We often hear that parents of minority children do not come to school for parent-teacher interviews. Our typical response is to bemoan the fact that they do not seem to care. First asking why it is a problem may lead us to conclude that if they do not attend the meetings, we will not be able to talk with them about how to help their child or inform them about their child's progress. We then might use the second question and ask, In what ways might we provide information about student progress to minority parents? Brainstorming responses to this question may lead to various other solutions, including student-led conferences, special sessions with interpreters for minority parents, meeting with some parents in a setting where they are comfortable (perhaps a community hall, church, or mosque), or even setting up a schedule of home visits.

Another example relates to the common request of teachers to introduce stricter school-discipline policies. Depending on our inclination and particular set of beliefs, we may either agree that it is a good idea and set up a discipline committee or reject the idea, saying that if teachers would only enforce the existing policy, everything would be fine. Asking Why is that a problem? might lead to an understanding that a particular group of students was smoking where they were not permitted to gather. Turning to the follow-up question, In what ways might we address the student smoking problem? may lead to seminars on the dangers of smoking, working with neighboring stores (if underage children are buying cigarettes), setting aside a smoking area, giving students longer breaks to leave the school grounds, and so on. The solution is not the issue; rather, the dialogue that ensues when such questions are asked is a way to explore beliefs and alternatives without allocating blame.

For What Problem Is That a Solution?

It is amazing how frequently in education someone makes a proposal in the absence of meaningful dialogue about the underlying issues. A few years ago, many North American newspapers reported that a southern district had instituted a policy requiring that students use formal terms of address, "sir" and "ma'am," when speaking to teachers. This is an excellent example of a situation in which the third question, For what problem is that a solution? might have been useful. Another example is the decision often made by a school or district to introduce school uniforms. On such occasions, it is useful to ask, For what problem is that a solution? If formal terms of address are intended to resolve undue familiarity between students and teachers, the solution may be appropriate; if, on the other hand, they are intended to improve student discipline or enhance the academic climate of a school, one might well revert to the IWWMW to encourage a fuller discussion of the underlying issues. Likewise, if school uniforms are to lend a sense of decorum or encourage a sense of belonging, they may be appropriate, although asking why there is a problem and exploring other ways of creating a sense of belonging to a community are still warranted.

Dialogue offers a way for everyone's voice to be heard; for people to avoid jumping to conclusions; and to find new and creative ways of addressing issues that may have been festering for some time. Dialogue offers a way for everyone to express an opinion, explore issues, and find where resolution may occur, but this cannot happen in an atmosphere of blame. One clear ground rule for responding to all of the above questions is to deal with issues and avoid assigning blame to any individual. One of the advantages of framing an issue in terms of "we,"

IWWMW, instead of identifying individual responsibility, is that it points to collective solutions to community problems rather than singling out individuals.

BLOCKS TO DIALOGUE

Earlier in this chapter, I suggested a question that might be useful for encouraging dialogue in an organization: Why is that a problem? I used the commonly used term problem. Yet many people suggest that most issues facing educators are better thought of as dilemmas (which may only be balanced on a temporary basis) than as problems (for which a solution may be found). Others suggest that it is wise to distinguish between tame problems (like fixing a photocopier) and wild problems (like calming an angry bus driver). One of the most difficult lessons for educational leaders to learn may be that not all problems can be solved and that the best approach may well be to "satisfice," to use a word coined by A. H. Simon (1957). By that he meant that we do what we can, choose an approach that is the best available at the time, but recognize that most solutions are temporary. We need to acknowledge that any new solution enters an already crowded policy space. Although it may offer a way to balance immediate concerns, it may also raise new concerns that ultimately will need to be brought into balance as well. Believing that we can and must find a resolution to all conflicts instead of finding ways to balance them may actually block dialogue.

Sometimes framing situations in blame-free ways is deemed impossible. I have heard educators insist that the cause of a particular problem is Mr. C. or Miss G. Yet the old adage that you can lead a horse to water but not make him drink seems to apply here. You may believe you are absolutely correct and tell the computer technician that she is to blame for the number of machines not working in the school computer lab. But that does not necessarily lead to her taking responsibility or to a positive resolution. Asking some of the foregoing questions may lead to a re-examination of the role of the lab as well as the responsibilities for its upkeep. One group I know expressed considerable frustration and anger about their computer technician. After spending time working through the problems, they decided to downsize the lab, decentralize many of the computers, and change their expectations of the designated technician, who could not teach all the required computer classes and keep up with the maintenance as she had been trying to do. Blaming seems to be a common initial reaction, but it is one that must be overcome if trust is to be established and dialogue permitted to occur.

Another tendency that organizations need to overcome is the "yes, but . . ." response so often heard in schools when common problems emerge. Establishing the practice of approaching issues through the question method sets boundaries of hope and encouragement. We will explore the issues, talk about underlying values and beliefs (Why is that a problem?) and attempt to find new ways of handling them. There is no room, when using the previous three strategies for encouraging dialogue, either for blaming or for the negatives: "yes, but we've tried that before," "yes, but they won't let us," or "yes, but we don't have the money."

Sometimes an educational leader wanting to introduce dialogue in an organization feels frustrated at what appears to be the slow pace of progress. Another block to dialogue is forgetting that people are at different stages in their personal and professional lives, some more ready than others to make the required commitments. Rather than give up or denounce the process as unworkable, educators need to recognize that dialogue occurs on many levels. Two individuals may engage in dialogue; small subgroups may work through issues that pertain to them. Dialogue is a process that needs to permeate an organization, to occur on many levels simultaneously and concurrently, in order for progress toward understanding to be made. While whole-group dialogue is desirable, and sometimes necessary, transformative leaders will encourage and foster dialogic relationships wherever they occur instead of becoming discouraged that dialogue does not happen all at once.

There are numerous blocks to dialogue, including behaviors that send implicit messages of inclusion or exclusion, superiority or inferiority; however, there is one further paradoxical block to dialogue that I wish to mention here. Praise may be a block to dialogue. There is an oft cited "teacher rule" that a teacher should find three items to praise before offering criticism of a student's work or performance. Although it is common, many educators and students recognize the hollowness of seeking three positives for every error, offering glib or empty praise, or complimenting an inferior performance. Although well-intentioned, the rule leads as often to mistrust as it does to the development of a positive relationship or the enhancement of self-esteem. Moreover, praise of one person may unintentionally overlook or neglect another, leading to a sense of privilege that is counterproductive. That does not mean that a sincere comment about a job well done should be withheld; but it is important to realize that the one who is seen as having a legitimate right to praise may also be feared as having a legitimate right to criticize. Sincere, just, and empathetic comments are more conducive to dialogue than empty praise.

Many other blocks exist, of course. Where dialogue falters and trust seems elusive, it is advisable for educational leaders to spend time reflecting on the impediments within their contexts and find ways to overcome them.

The Content of Dialogue

Once we have an understanding of the nature and importance of dialogue, as well as ways to move ahead positively and openly, we must examine its substantive content. Purposeful dialogue focuses on what we believe to be the desired ends of education, the kind of society we hope to create for ourselves and our children, the kind of life we believe to be meaningful and rewarding, and what we mean by terms like *success, justice,* or *democracy.* Although there are innumerable topics that can move us forward, a leader needs to start somewhere.

Having read this book, an educational leader might create a list of topics and ideas from each chapter that caught her imagination, examine the data from her school profile, and notice that one area jumped out as the logical starting point or as the area in need of critical attention. A school principal who examined her school's standardized test data and learned that no aboriginal students had passed the eleventh-grade algebra exam, might invite a group of interested teachers to interpret and explain the finding. Likewise, if an examination of course-enrollment patterns showed that none of the 30 percent Asian population was enrolled in any of the school's fine-arts courses, one might ask whether there were systemic barriers that prevented some students from acquiring a balanced, broad-based educational experience.

In chapter 3, I suggested several questions that are useful for examining decisions to ensure they respond to the agreed-on criteria. (Recall that the four I propose—just, democratic, empathetic, and optimistic—are not the only possible criteria, simply four I find to be useful and reasonably comprehensive.) The questions included items like: Who is advantaged and who disadvantaged by this decision? Who is privileged or marginalized? Who might be excluded or included? These questions may be used once a tentative decision has been reached to assess its congruence with your goals and values.

Suppose you have some very persuasive teachers who claim that as numbers of ESL students in the school increase, many graduate without being willing or able to speak in public, a skill they judge to be important for contributing fully in a democratic society. The teachers are convinced that instituting a compulsory public-speaking requirement would ensure that all students, including those for whom English is a second language, acquired the necessary skills. The justice grounds seem covered—all students will participate; democracy may be well served by providing practice and skills to all students. But when one asks who might be disadvantaged by the decision, one teacher raises the issue of several students in the school known to have speech impediments. They will find the new criteria particularly difficult to meet.

Does that mean the idea has no merit? It might, but there may also be other considerations. Asking Why is that a problem? may lead to the idea that it is a problem because these students may be uncomfortable and embarrassed, especially if their peers laugh at them. The next step may be to focus on empathic solutions. What if we established small, supportive peer groups and helped these students practice until they felt comfortable with speaking in public? What if we also spent some time ensuring that other students understand how respect, one of the foundational values of the school community, involves encouraging and accepting differences. In other words, applying criteria does not necessarily mean we will reject an idea but that we might find better ways to make it work—empathetically and optimistically for all students. Wisdom, data, and dialogue complement good intentions and help ensure that they will be effective.

NEGOTIATING CULTURE(S) THROUGH DIALOGUE

In chapter 7, we examined Bakhtin's notion of carnival and how it might help us change existing norms, particularly those of hegemonic power, and find new ways of being together in our organizations. Bakhtin also addresses the role of language, particularly that of dialogue, in moving us forward. He is not just thinking of common everyday speech and interaction but, like Burbules, advocates a particular understanding and practice of dialogue that may help us overcome the paralysis of tradition (what Bourdieu identified as bounded fields and habitus) and move us to a position from which change may be possible.

For Bakhtin, cultures are dynamic and constantly renegotiated through the relationship between the self and other by means of language, dialogue, communication, development, and change. Bakhtin "sees culture as an unfolding, incomplete process which lives on borders consisting of differences which find their unity through dialogue" (Swingewood 1998, 116). Differences find their unity though the process of dialogue that gives words meaning:

> In order for dialogue to occur, one must recognize that meaning belongs to a word in its positions between speakers . . . realised only in the process of active, responsive understanding. Meaning does not reside in the word . . . [but] in the effect of interaction between speaker and listener. (Bakhtin and Volosinov 1973, 95)

Where educational change initiatives are successful, they appear to be the result of this type of dialogic interaction. For example, telling people that the school teaches the dominant culture and hence does not serve every child equally well assumes the meaning is in the word. It does not attend to the emotional impact of the listener's traditions and culture. The listener's personal experience of schooling may be so tied up in the present school organization that he or she cannot conceive of it being outmoded or inappropriate. Giving people an opportunity to express their opinions, emotional responses, fears, and concerns is a necessary part of the dialogical process that creates active, responsive understanding. It is a prerequisite for understanding one's personal borders with respect to educational change. Moreover, without this enhanced understanding, change will not likely occur.

Bakhtin distinguishes between dialogism and monologism. The latter "conceives the other as finished, complete, an object of consciousness" (Swingewood 1998, 115). Monologism, represented by a turning inward and by an enclosing of self, is typical of too many attempts at educational reform in which borders are not negotiated, language is not interactive, and participants develop entrenched positions and argue for them without engaging in active or responsive listening. Rather than define ourselves by the rigidity of our positions and our ability to argue for them, we need to find alternative ways of interacting. Sidorkin calls this "dialogical integrity," which represents a different type of organizing—one in which "the self integrates around the need to remain open and unfinished, and around the purpose of dialogue with others" (1999, 65).

Bakhtin calls this type of organizing dialogism. In contrast to the typical forms of educational discourse, dialogism helps us remain open. It creates the "means whereby different social groups represent ideological values, and affirm their cultural, political, and social aspirations in relation to others" (Swingewood 1998, 123). If we apply this notion to schools we find that, in order to discover what a particular community wants from its educational institutions, what it might define as the good life for its members, we must create opportunities for dialogue. Sidorkin (1999) puts it this way:

> Utterly simplified, my claim is this: there must be a multitude of distinctive voices, these voices must hear each other, and there must be some moments when these voices become "purely human" (or lose their social attachments). (p. 112)

When we temporarily lose our social attachments and become purely human, we have transcended our differences through the dialogic relationship. We have not silenced the differences but learned from them, in order to move forward together in just, democratic, empathetic, and optimistic processes.

Dialogue is not simply a vehicle for individual discourse but a way for borders to be broken down and renegotiated in an arena of struggle represented by opposing groups and diverse cultural voices and ideas. To effect educational change, therefore, individuals and groups need to be willing to speak and listen, look both inward and outward, and recognize that boundaries can be, are, and eventually always will be changed.

The transformative leader will infuse the organization with dialogue, grounded in moral principles, about the meaning of a community of difference. Building on some substantive criteria for assessing both new ideas and current practice, he or she can help the group move forward. I agree with Sidorkin, who argues persuasively that "the formation or transformation of a school requires nothing less than a personal transformation of its leader" (1999, 117).

TRANSFORMATIVE LEADERSHIP: KEY TO DYNAMIC COMMUNITIES OF DIFFERENCE

Community does not emerge, as did Athena, full-blown from the forehead of Zeus. Neither is community an entity that can be created piece by piece as a puzzle or LEGO construction. It is much more holographic. The norms and values on which it is founded must pervade each part of the community, as people learn together, through respect and dialogue, to understand each other's similarities and differences and negotiate a new center for their organization.

Community is created incrementally and sometimes painfully. Taking small steps may lead to the possibility of taking larger steps. Developing small commitments may lead to the creation of greater commitments. Learning to trust in small things may lead to deeper levels of trust in more important matters. Engaging in dialogue leads to better understanding that in turn leads to a clearer sense of community that facilitates greater dialogue, and so on. The process is a continuous spiral, one that turns back on itself at many stages yet constantly changes, is refined, and is perfected through the efforts of the members of the community.

Establishing and maintaining a tenuous balance is an important leadership task, one that is more difficult to accomplish than attempting to solve every problem that comes along. Balancing the needs of individuals with the good of subgroups and the community as a whole, deciding how to be respectful and inclusive without adopting a relativistic "anything goes" philosophy, recognizing and valuing difference while neither essentializing or pathologizing it—are critical challenges and constant dynamic tensions facing the transformative educational leader.

Scott Peck describes four steps he believes to be necessary in the creation of a deeply meaningful community. He calls the normal state of working together pseudocommunity, a stage in which we pretend to respect each other and share some common goals but rarely take time to even acknowledge, let alone understand, differences among us. The second stage he calls chaos, a time of fighting and struggle in which various value perspectives and power bases become explicit. This is followed by emptiness, a time during which the bridges between chaos and community have yet to be built. Only after a time of struggle and emptiness, Peck suggests, can we achieve anything resembling community. He asserts that in "genuine community there are no sides," that people have learned how to "give up cliques and factions. They have learned to listen to each other and how not to reject each other" (1987, 71).

As we saw in chapter 2, a community of difference is not based on existing norms, but on newly agreed-on shared norms based on a comprehensive and inclusive dialogue among all of its members. Tierney asserts that

> democratic community revolves around contradictions. We search for commonalities while encouraging difference. We seek community through conflict. We act as leaders by following. We develop voice by listening. We learn about ourselves by trying to understand others. (1993, 143)

The transformative cross-cultural leader will need to have patience, sensitivity, persistence, and above all a deep moral conviction of the rightness of the chosen path. It is a slow, sometimes difficult, always challenging, but often highly rewarding educative process.

In the final chapter, I put those challenges to the test, reflecting on how we, as transformative leaders, might begin to achieve social justice and academic excellence in Sherwood Junior Secondary School.

NOTES

1. See the introduction to part 2.

2. It may be of interest to know that I use the creation of a school profile as one assignment for a course I teach about the administration of the instructional program. It is followed by a requirement that students interview one of the school administrators about the data they have uncovered. The final assignment is a paper, based on the theoretical readings and class discussions, about what they would change if they were in the leadership position in the school.

CHAPTER 11

New Lenses, Sharper Focus

As you read through the previous chapters, I anticipate that you were developing the transformative leadership dispositions of critique, justice, and caring and that you have been considering your own workplace in light of the ideas discussed. You have likely been wondering if you are, or can become, a transformative leader—one who can help introduce meaningful change in your community. The concept of a community of difference may resonate with you, and you may have found yourself reflecting on how to make your school more just, democratic, empathetic, and optimistic. Some of the data you have examined in your own community may have caused concern, even raised some red flags, but you may want confirmation about your insights.

In this chapter I present a fictionalized case called "Saving Sherwood Junior Secondary School." I outline some of the challenges faced by a newly appointed principal, Lynn Saver, as she tries to figure out how to change an ineffective school into one that is successful. I invite you to study the case and reflect on what you would do and how you would start. Following the case, I share some typical responses the case evokes from educators. Then I engage in a dialogue with Sheila, an educational leader familiar with the concepts in this book. We explore how the idea of transformative leadership might provide a lens for creating a community of difference. The chapter concludes with some reflections about removing the walls and fences in educational institutions.

CASE STUDY: SAVING SHERWOOD
JUNIOR SECONDARY SCHOOL

Part 1

December 27, 2000

Lynn Saver has just been appointed principal of Sherwood Junior Secondary School—effective immediately. Throughout her career, Lynn has been known to search out and access opportunities for personal and professional growth. As a classroom teacher, she served on curriculum committees in her school system, took full advantage of staff development opportunities, served as recording secretary for a networking group of literacy educators, and coordinated a professional reading group that met after school. She has recently completed a graduate program in educational administration as well as leadership training offered by her school district.

Before she went through the selection process for the principalship, she refined her views on the purpose of education and began to develop some priorities for reform. She was honest about these views in her interviews and in informal discussions with school committees, parents, and teachers. She recognized that in a time of cutbacks, declining resources, and rapidly changing demographics, the climate was not particularly conducive to educational change. And yet she was convinced she was ready for the challenge and looked forward eagerly to her first assignment—until she received notification of her placement.

Sherwood Junior Secondary School was built in 1995 in a heterogeneous, rapidly growing urban area. When it opened, it was heralded as the finest public school in its district, destined to be a lighthouse school for years to come. As a facility, Sherwood is unsurpassed. It boasts a modern science lab, an auditorium with a stage and theatrical lighting for public presentations, a centrally located library, and a technology center with media-production capabilities and computer applications necessary to perform any task students might require or think of. Each teacher's classroom is wired to the school's local area network, and students can search the World Wide Web for projects and communicate with peers around the world through e-mail.

The school itself is midsize and houses approximately eight hundred students with forty teachers and a variety of other personnel to staff the seventh- through tenth-grade program. The student body is mixed, with students from families with a wide range of careers, ethnic backgrounds, and socioeconomic status ranging from very wealthy to single-parent families, with a few families receiving some form of government assistance. About 5 percent of the student body come from a nearby aboriginal community; another 40 percent of the students represent visible minority groups who have recently moved into the community, many of whom do not speak English at home.

To serve the student body, the newly hired staff decided to offer a full range of academic programs as well as extracurricular activities and an adult-education program. Sports are emphasized because staff believe they foster a sense of achievement and well-being that will help students get ahead in the "real world." Teachers also hope that sports and other extracurricular activities will help bring the students together to overcome some of the tensions that are apparent in the halls and classrooms. Although many do not, every student is encouraged to participate in at least one activity.

The staff is experienced and predominantly white and middle-class. Only four (including the two ESL teachers) are from a visible minority group. Ten of the teachers are female, with all of the department heads and the assistant principal being male.

Mr. Smart had been hired by the Brilliant School District in 1994 to be the first principal of the new school. Thus he had input into planning the school, ordering equipment, hiring the first faculty, and deciding on the programs that would be implemented. Mr. Smart took great pride in keeping tight control over everything that was going on at the school. Although there were numerous committees, each with a parent and student representative on it, Mr. Smart was careful to attend all meetings and approve both preliminary agenda items and ultimate decisions. Not surprisingly, perhaps, it had become increasingly difficult to find people willing to serve on school committees.

Lynn's conversation with the assistant superintendent had left her somewhat uneasy about how she might help the school achieve the glory that had originally been envisaged. She had recently read a newspaper article reporting that the technology was not being used and that student performance as assessed by standardized tests and district assessment instruments had declined annually since the school opened.

fact, the school ranked in the bottom 25 percent of the region's schools. The assistant superintendent informed her that the previous year an unprecedented 25 percent of the staff had requested a transfer to another school.

Mr. Smart suffered a serious heart attack shortly before Christmas and was advised to take early retirement. Lynn was to take over beginning in January. Immediately following her appointment, she began to hear rumors that Kelly Climber, the vice principal hired by Mr. Smart, was very unhappy because he expected to be appointed principal. Although no one would ever admit it, it had almost become policy in the district to promote vice principals through the old boys' network.

Part 2

March 25, 2001

Lynn has been reflecting on what she has learned about the school. Many students are failing—30 percent of the school's students failed at least one class during the January exam period and 20 percent are failing more than half of their classes. The school has a serious attendance problem, particularly among Caucasian students of lower socioeconomic status, aboriginal students, and visible minority students. Over two thousand days had been missed between September and November, and another two hundred student "lates" had been recorded. Teachers were demanding implementation of a strict attendance and discipline policy, supported by the school administration.

Last year, a committee had been established to find ways to address the identified needs of the school. Many teachers had worked in small groups to adapt the core curriculum so that even the students who had learning and language deficits would be able to succeed. Many of these activities permitted students to work independently and at their own pace on the key concepts, using packaged modules or computer programs. In addition, many teachers tried hard to become caring and sympathetic friends of the students, offering support for family problems and allowing considerable leeway if they arrived late or without their assignments completed.

Teachers have also established a special program for students with attendance problems. A select group of students has been assigned for the whole day to two teachers tasked with managing an instructional program whereby students can come and go and feel safe and accepted. The other feature of this program is an attempt to find work-study partnerships with the local business community so students can be more directly prepared to enter the world of work.

Other teachers have attempted to increase the amount of teacher-led instructional time and provide many small group activities in which students have ample opportunity to drill and practice their basic skills. In addition, to ensure that all students develop English-language proficiency, the staff has adopted a policy of English-only at school.

In her first three months, Lynn identified a number of other special programs. In addition to the Plato lab, used for remedial help during the day, the school sponsors a Bright Futures program, a computer-assisted learning program for returning adults, offered in the evening. There is also a well equipped portable in which the special education program is located. Students in this program are encouraged to play games, use the computer, and raise funds for field trips to visit community businesses or go on overnight camping trips.

In addition to the academic programs, Lynn has learned, the staff has tried to be responsive to the cultural needs of the students by implementing quarterly cultural days—activities to which parents and community members are invited. However, few community members attend. Students nevertheless seem to enjoy holding the assemblies, at which classmates perform ethnic dances and songs, and they especially like the opportunity to try different ethnic foods in the cafeteria on those special days. One of the cultural workers has written a memo complaining that during the last multicultural presentation, there was too much emphasis on Chinese traditions and presentations to the exclusion of students from South Asia, whom she feels are always ignored.

When Lynn inquired about the parent advisory council, she learned that although it exists on paper, there are few meetings. The PAC executive seems to have a difficult time getting people to participate, perhaps because the PAC has little power or influence, except that it plans the annual spring dance. Lynn has already heard from one group of vocal and influential parents who are not in favor of having a spring school dance take place during the school day because it detracts fro valuable instructional time. Another group, predominantly from a local church, believes that schools should not hold dances at all because of their potential to encourage inappropriate sexual behavior. Still others fear that the small group of gay or lesbian students in the school would experience discrimination and thus also argue that a dance should not be supported at all. Some parents want a dance held in the evening, with others claiming it disadvantages children who live farther away from the school and South Asian girls whose families will only permit their participation in "school" activities.

As Lynn reviews the list of staff, she is amazed at the number of nonenrolling teachers and noncertified staff. It seems there are people to deal with any conceivable student problem: ESL teachers, two learning assistance teachers, an area counselor, a part-time speech pathologist, a neighborhood worker, an aboriginal worker, a Vietnamese worker, two short-term urgent-intervention workers, and a variety of volunteer tutors. How could she ever sort out the roles and programs and determine what is needed to help improve the school?

She had barely unlocked her office door when the phone began to ring. The first call was from a newly elected school-board member demanding a meeting that very afternoon in order to talk about how she was going to improve student academic performance and how she planned to deal with the new curriculum policies. Next came a call from a parent, angry that the school had not informed her of her son's absence on Friday afternoon, which she had found out about from the mother of her son's friend. Lynn was writing a note to herself to discuss school-home communications, when the union rep, Tim Idate, began to pound on the door.

The phone rang one more time. The superintendent told her that the press was going to do a story about Sherwood School; he demanded that she show up at his office in three days with a plan for turning things around. Otherwise, it was clear, her three-month tenure as principal might be the shortest in the district's history.

A TYPICAL DISCUSSION

As an educator I have often used a case such as this in a university course for experienced teachers and aspiring administrators. Invariably

I tend to leave frustrated because my students seem to have missed the boat. They often turn to familiar strategies and explanations and to focus on what I perceive to be at best partial, simplistic, and technical solutions.

Sometimes educators suggest that Lynn has a staff morale problem. They then proceed to explain that the previous principal had not empowered teachers or developed a collaborative approach. Teachers are affected by the unhappiness of the vice principal and by the lack of attendance, achievement, and participation of the students. Lynn should, they suggest, implement social events, have potluck suppers for staff, try fun activities for students, and figure out how to get more parents involved in the PAC.

Other educators indicate that the basic problem is communication. This is evident because students do not seem to follow the rules, parents are not always advised when their children are absent, multicultural events are poorly attended, and the PAC cannot seem to achieve consensus about the spring dance. Teachers claim that there are so many adults in the school for one reason or another that they rarely see the students in their own classes. It is hard to keep up with schedules and to know when students are expected to attend learning assistance, ESL, computer, or remedial speech classes. Translating newsletters into various home languages, instituting a computerized phone system to notify parents when their children are absent, making better use of e-mail for internal communications are common suggestions to address the problem.

Still others claim the school has a "standards problem." They argue that if students would comply with the English-only rule and take advantage of the opportunities provided through the after-school tutoring and the Plato lab, and if more teachers would use the self-paced modules that had been prepared, the achievement scores would go up. Lynn would still need to address the lax attitude of the "special attendance classes" but generally everything is in place, and it is just a matter of finding ways to make teachers conform.

I do not dispute that all of these problems are in evidence in the case of Sherwood Junior Secondary School, but it is my students' failure to pull back and consider the case in the context of the big ideas about leadership, community, academic excellence, and social justice that we have spent weeks discussing that most troubles me. Sometimes I have heard educators make comments like, "This is just like our school. It's just too big a task. It's impossible to make significant changes or turn it around." And I suspect that many people, faced with the complexity of leading a school that has some obvious difficulties and challenges, may feel inundated.

Perhaps it is the sense of being overwhelmed that prevents people, even those who have read and discussed the ideas in this book or those who have taken a class about communities of difference and transformative leadership, from moving beyond their good intentions and seeking new approaches. Perhaps as Bourdieu (1993) believes, our *habitus* of education is so deeply ingrained that it is difficult to step out of previously attempted strategies and modes of thinking to move toward a more dialogic and less technical approach. Yet I am convinced, based on my eighteen years as a school-based educator and what I have learned from others, that a different process, one consistent with the ideas I have presented in this book, may offer a productive way forward.

TURNING TO DIALOGUE

In this section I present an alternative approach, one not based solely on good intentions, intuition, or traditional practices, but one designed to demonstrate how to refocus and move away from the typical technical analysis to a more thoughtful one. Here I present a dialogue with Sheila, an assistant principal in a secondary school, who was a student in one of my classes.

Like many of you, Sheila is both a thoughtful scholar and a passionate educator who is concerned with how to improve schools. She and I sat down to explore how an administrator might use dialogue as a starting point for effecting change at Sherwood Junior Secondary School. I retain my current role as a faculty member, teacher, and author of this book and Sheila takes on the hypothetical role of Lynn Saver, an educational leader wanting to facilitate educational change. In many ways, the dialogue in which we engage is also one that Lynn might want to begin with a few trusted and interested members of her staff and ultimately with the whole staff.

CS   Sheila, I wonder what you mean when you say you want the school to be more successful. Are you talking about staff morale, communications, or achievement?

SS   I don't think I am really talking about any of those, at least not directly. It seems to me that a successful school, particularly in this diverse, urban context might really be what you have called a community of difference. I understand the concept to be a holistic one that includes attention to the various purposes of schooling, including students' sense of belonging, academic achievement, and collective purposes.

CS   I certainly intend for a community of difference to be broad enough to embrace multiple purposes and diverse aspects of schooling. It is not just creating a sense of feeling good within a school or developing better communication with the wider school community, but something much deeper.

SS   I agree. Sometimes we use words in a pretty vacuous way. We talk about meaningful change or high standards or democratic schools as if the words in and of themselves have any meaning.

CS   Of course, that's why I introduced the notion of criteria. Educators often assume that everyone else in a school shares their perceptions and is trying to achieve the same thing. In our own department of the university, we have recently held discussions about our purpose. Many of my colleagues claim that we are united by a goal of social justice and seem to believe that any disagreement is like being against motherhood. How could anyone not agree with "social justice" as a unifying concept? But other colleagues think that it is too narrow a focus, and that it is important to acknowledge distributive justice, economic justice, and so on.

SS   These discussions about purpose are not easy. They really do require commitment to see it through. I remember that Burbules says commitment is a prerequisite for meaningful dialogue.

CS   He also talks about the rules of participation and reciprocity. I wonder how, as a leader, you can ensure that people really do participate.

SS   I am a strong believer in narrative. If we tell stories, stories about ourselves and our experiences, then I think others may begin to feel there is space for their stories as well. This seems to be a nonthreatening way to invite participation because people can select what they share and what they choose to protect. We need to create time and inviting spaces for people to participate on their own terms.

CS   Are you talking about developing trust as a foundation for dialogue?

SS   I certainly think so. Without trust, people are reluctant to say what they really believe or to raise issues that may seem controversial.

CS   Yet without honesty and even some degree of risk taking, we are unlikely to move ahead. It is so easy to rely on what Irving Janis called groupthink and let ourselves be swayed by loud or popular opinions.

SS   I wonder what would happen if I asked my staff to explain what they think we are trying to accomplish and then identify some criteria to use as benchmarks for our discussions. I'd like to ask them in what ways the school is presently just, democratic, empathic, or optimistic.

CS   It might be useful to take the criteria in turn and explore evidence of both justice and injustice, empathy and lack of caring, and so on.

SS   That might help them avoid focusing too narrowly or jumping to a solution for a superficial aspect of the situation.

CS   If you could achieve some consensus, you might also use the criteria on a regular basis to guide decision making and actions as well as assess the progress you are making.

SS   One of the challenges with Sherwood Junior Secondary School is that everyone has a different idea of what the problem is and how to solve it. We have not taken the time to sit down and figure out what happened. The school opened with such promise and now it seems to have become quite a disaster.

CS   Yes, it certainly does. And yet, I think there are some germs of good ideas, some promising initiatives and programs, and definitely some committed staff. Sometimes we put too much emphasis on new buildings, resources, and technology, and fail to understand that it is the fundamental moral principles on which an institution is founded that make it excellent, mediocre, or even worse. In this case, I think there was too much glitz and too little thought given to guiding principles.

SS   True, but it was not just hype; there are also some really misguided and ill-informed practices. Take for instance the English-only policy. You teach us that the research shows it is not the way to go. I'm also concerned about the emphasis on direct instruction and on individualized and self-paced packets for student learning, not to mention the special attendance classes and the fragmentation that seems to occur as a result of our many pullout programs.

CS   You have certainly put your finger on several of the troubling elements I also identified. As you well know, the literature suggests that English-only programs do not facilitate students' ability to conceptualize or to achieve proficiency in a second language. They certainly do not help students achieve a level of comfort that empowers and emboldens them to keep trying. They are often frustrating for students who want to explore ideas but lack the conceptual vocabulary to enable them to participate.

SS   You are so right. I have heard a colleague say that if she permits the Mandarin-speaking students in her class to speak their home language, the three-English speaking students will be disadvantaged. What nonsense! How could we ever disadvantage children who are advantaged at every turn in our educational system by curriculum that has been developed from a Eurocentric perspective, by policy makers who come from the elite governing groups in our society. Yet I know we can't ignore the needs of these three students.

CS   I heard a nice story from a principal the other day. She told me that she visited an ESL class and found a student totally engrossed in a book. When she approached, however, he seemed embarrassed and tried to hide it. As she conversed with him, she found that he had been reading *To Kill a Mockingbird*—in Korean. She shared how she had praised the teacher and encouraged the student. This was a significant departure for her. In fact, she said it had been an "ah ha" moment when the discussion from her master's class came to life in practice.

SS   I am really concerned when teachers place too much emphasis on self-paced, individual learning packets. They do not seem either just or optimistic. Although they are intended to permit students to learn at their own pace, they tend to promote lower-level learning and prevent students from speaking their own languages.

CS   My concern is that they keep students from talking at all. We know that knowledge is socially constructed; for those children who do not have proficiency in English, enforcing silent, individualistic activities helps them neither to better understand the content nor become integrated into the social structure of the class.

SS   I think we are letting our "moral outrage" show.

CS   Maybe that is a good thing. It is definitely an element of effective transformative leadership.

SS   I'd like to get back, though, to a discussion of the criteria and how I could use them to help the teachers in my school think differently about what we are doing and how we are going about it.

CS   Okay. What do you have in mind?

SS   I am often amazed that we ignore available data and the kind of information we can gather through the development of a school profile. I think it is a useful starting point in that it provides an opportunity to come together, in a blame-free environment, to begin to assess where we are and what we need to do.

CS   So, if you have data, for example, about student enrollment patterns and achievement, you can then examine whether there are inequities that prevent justice and optimism from occurring.

SS   Yes. If, for example, we find that there are no aboriginal students in our advanced placement classes, we can begin to ask about access and determine whether it is teacher attitudes, identification instruments, or other institutional barriers that inhibit these students' success.

CS   I know what you mean. When we find that there is a significantly higher dropout rate among South Asian or Hispanic male students, we need to ask questions about the optimism of our programs. How do we ensure that their life chances and choices are opened rather than restricted by our schooling practices?

SS   An examination of student involvement in extracurricular activities could prompt a discussion of whether our practices are really democratic and inclusive.

CS   In Sherwood School, starting with a school profile might provide ways for the teachers to come together to identify clusters of issues that relate to the justice criteria. That might help them focus on attitudes and assumptions and determine what the research says, for example, about student engagement, instead of zeroing in on superficial and quick fixes.

SS   You mean, for example, they might come to understand that having a wide variety of activities available does not necessarily mean that all students will be equally able to participate in them.

CS   Absolutely right. Some South Asian girls, for example, may not be permitted to return to school for evening activities; other students have responsibilities after school for younger siblings. Some sports require out-of-town travel, which may disadvantage those who have jobs or whose families are poor.

SS   It goes deeper than that, though. Some students just hang back. They think they are not skilled enough or popular enough to participate.

CS   And of course, these are the very students we need to find ways to encourage if we are to become more democratic and empathetic.

SS   If we started with some really comprehensive questions about what we are trying to accomplish and how best to achieve it, then we might find that a dialogue about the inclusivity and openness of a community of difference would be useful. I am always uncomfortable about going straight to a discussion of the "communication problem" without figuring out who needs to communicate with whom and for what purposes.

CS   I agree. Often I hear educators saying that the school has tried to communicate with parents and has even translated newsletters in an attempt to ensure that parents know the expectations and rules of the school. I wonder what might happen if educators turned it around and tried to learn about parents' expectations of the school: how they think the school could help support them in their efforts to educate their children and what they would like to see in terms of procedures and rules, as well.

SS If that really happened, I think educators might realize that even parents who do not come to the school often are fundamentally concerned about the education of their children. I know that some of the Southeast Asian families in my school send their children to North America to get a good education. The father often stays in Asia, earning enough money to support them and sustain their quality of life, while the mother lives, almost as a hermit, isolated in a large house in a foreign country, waiting for the children to come home from school. They feel they are doing their utmost to support their children's education.

CS I know that is true in other cultures as well. Sometimes parents are intimidated when they have little or no formal education; some truly do believe that it is the job of the school to educate their children and they don't want to interfere.

SS That is an example of Delpit's conviction that we need to make the rules explicit, especially for people who are not part of the decision-making or power groups. We likely need to spend much more time helping parents understand how important a partnership can be.

CS And helping educators understand that a partnership truly is mutual. We need to learn from parents about what they can do and about what they need, just as they can learn from us.

SS It is the relational aspect of education that we so often ignore. We have been talking about ethics and moral leadership and even dialogue. We must make explicit our understanding that all of this is fundamentally relational. Without relationship there can be no dialogue and no partnership. Yet the reality of dialogue is that it often creates relationships that develop and are strengthened through the dialogic process.

CS I think people are often very confused. They think it is necessary to like someone, to be friends, in order for there to be meaningful relationships. I have come to believe that ethical educational relationships must be founded on respect and deeply democratic principles — not on what we usually think of as caring.

SS We use Noddings's word *caring* glibly but fail to use it as she meant it — as a foundation for everything we do in schools, including curriculum and policy.

CS   When we like someone, we often say we are caring, but that falls far short of having an empathic school grounded in moral principles. I have a few colleagues that I find really difficult to deal with. Sometimes, when I see their ID on my answering machine, I even ignore the call. And yet I am committed to caring about them, to helping them achieve their potential within the community of the department. I cannot just avoid working with them because it is difficult and tiring.

SS   So, what are you suggesting—that we don't need to think about the emotional aspects of caring? I think you are wrong. We definitely need to pay attention to the emotional environment in schools in order for children to feel safe and respected.

CS   I need to clarify. Too often we rely on feelings, but my sense is that feelings are fleeting and hence are not a good basis on which to build a community of difference. I might like you today because we are in agreement and seem to be working well together, but if our ideas come in conflict, or if you do something with which I disagree, I might feel less kindly disposed toward you. If this is the only basis for caring, then the good feelings might dissipate, as well as the foundation for our relationship. If, on the other hand, my caring is based on a fundamental respect for you and for your right to disagree with me, then the emotions become part of the background and not the foreground. I am not suggesting that we can or should ignore emotions. Healthy individuals need to be in touch with their emotions; and the affect is critically important. I just think caring is more than emotional connections.

SS   So, when Ms. S. comes running in to my office saying that she can't stand Mr. L. and that she is really tired of being the "race police" for the school, I don't need to worry about her feelings?

CS   On one level, you need to address the feelings first. Then you can help her identify the reasons for her frustration. You can help her understand that she can (and likely must) address the issues of injustice that she is concerned about in a respectful way, but that it is quite all right if she does not really like Mr. L.

SS   Last week, we had a really disturbing incident at my school. I wonder how I might deal with it. A number of teachers decided to go out and meet some of the parents from the school community who rarely come to the school. So they arranged a meeting in one of the homes. When the teachers arrived, many people were smoking. The teachers asked if they would refrain but were told that this was a normal part of community social get-togethers. At that point, the teachers left in a huff, saying that if the parents could not be respectful, they would not stay and talk. Now what do I do?

CS   I expect that there has been a considerable worsening of relations over that incident and that you will need a great deal of patience to try to reopen the door. What do you intend to do?

SS   I think first I should ask the teachers what they expect of guests in their houses. They need to understand that they were the guests and that it was not their role to make demands. But I'm not even sure they want to talk. They are so convinced they are right.

CS   But, at one point, the teachers were concerned enough to want to go out to the community. What prompted that? How can we get them to articulate their goal? That might defuse the emotional aspect and their unwavering principles about smoking and let them think about the consequences of their demands.

SS   You mean, make use of Hodgkinson's notion of different levels of values. If they are convinced they took a principled stand against smoking and that the community was wrong, there is little room for change. If I can get them to examine the desired goal and the consequences of their stand, then perhaps we can consider alternative ways they could have acted.

CS   If won't be easy because they are convinced they are right. But being right is not necessarily the goal in a community of difference, especially if it means creating winners and losers. Listening to and understanding the other, identifying a common goal or purpose, and developing new ways of working together toward that end seem more important.

SS   If the teachers articulate their concern for the students and if I could somehow invite the parents to meet with me and to share their concerns, we might find a way to get past the hurt and embarrassment.

CS   If we have stood on principles that excluded or devalued other people, we need to acknowledge that and apologize. I don't think any potential relationship can be restored until the teachers recognize that they were trying to impose their values on the community in ways that were inappropriate. We cannot go into someone else's home and ask that they be like us.

SS   I have a lot of work to do there. It is symptomatic of the whole mess at Sherwood School. We want to improve. We really do. The teachers have put a lot of time and effort into developing new programs, creating units, and volunteering in extracurricular activities. We just seem to keep going about it in the wrong way.

CS   I wonder if it might be possible to use some ideas about identity and carnival as a new starting point. What if we could find a way to give teachers and parents different masks to wear, different roles, and new ways of interacting? I'm not sure what it would look like, but if we could find something that would involve a lot of people, make extensive use of humor, and challenge existing roles and power hierarchies, we might be able to start again.

SS   Well, we won't fall back on another multicultural fair—those have certainly not accomplished our goals. You may recall that the press wants to do a feature on Sherwood School. I wonder if we could use that as a starting point.

CS   You mean, find a way to highlight the hard work of the teachers, the excellent resources of the school, and the assets of the community all at once?

SS   What if we hosted an "urban school conference"? We could call it "Good Intentions Are Not Enough." We could invite speakers from the university and the community. Parents could work with the teachers to help them showcase different parts of the community, its history, recent development, and so on. We could ask students to tell some of their own stories. They could use our high-tech equipment to create a television program or make videos with stories about their families, and include interviews with teachers.

CS   I wonder if the various businesses in the community would like an opportunity to advertise by setting up booths telling about themselves. There are so many new enterprises in the community and I'll bet that some of them might actually welcome the opportunity to become involved in the school.

SS   There are also service clubs and religious organizations. I wonder how many there are?

CS   I can really become excited about the potential of a conference of this nature to bring people together but with enough space for people to make various kinds of contributions in their own ways. Maybe we should pull back for a moment and ask that fundamental question, For what problem is a conference the solution?

SS   I think it is one possible solution to the problem of fragmentation, different goals, and lack of understanding in our school and wider community. If we could get people together for a common purpose, we might be able to discuss the fundamental challenges in our school and find ways to begin to address then.

CS   I wonder if there are other ways to accomplish the same thing. That might be a good question to ask your staff and the parent advisory council. If they think you want a conference, there might be resistance. If they think it is really their idea, it might work.

   SS   Let me sleep on it. I expect we will have many more conversations about this.

A TEMPORARY RESTING PLACE

When Sheila and I began to talk, we had no sense of where the conversation would go. We had known each other in a particular kind of faculty-student relationship but had never had an extended conversation. At the outset, we thought that we would focus on the criteria previously identified for a community of difference. We anticipated that we would focus on how to use a school profile as a starting point for developing common goals in a blame-free manner. When we agreed to engage in this dialogue, we decided that we would talk about transformative cross-cultural leaders using the ethics of critique, justice, and caring. In so doing, we expected to focus on the need for authentic and moral leadership to create a deeply ethical community, one that is inclusive, liberating, and socially just; one that ensures the attainment of appropriately high academic standards by all students.

   We did not start with the idea of a conference or any other specific action. Nor did we discount any ideas out of hand. Indeed, our dialogue took the form of what Burbules (1993) would call a nonteleological dialogue, leading to better understanding rather than a predetermined solution. In many ways, our dialogue was grounded in, and emerged from, our engagement with some of the ideas in this book.

   We were quite astonished that we had actually come to a concrete course of action. We were even more surprised by what happened between us. Although we had begun in a friendly and somewhat casual way, we found that as we explored the ideas and thought about the issues, our understanding of each other increased and our relationship was consolidated. Trust and relationship grew out of the exchange; they were not prerequisites for the dialogue. Through this brief dialogic experience, we came to a better understanding of the interactive, nonlinear structure of the experience. At the outset, for example, Sheila had not planned to share the teachers' failed outreach initiative to the community. I certainly had not anticipated telling her about some of my more difficult colleagues. Trust, commitment, and respect emerged as we explored together, permitting increasing engagement, risk, and exploration to occur.

CONCLUDING COMMENTS

Let me try to summarize where I think we are in this exciting quest for educational leadership that will lead to the creation of more socially just and academically excellent school communities. I have found no recipe for creating community and I have suggested none. But I have learned that we cannot decontextualize the process. Throughout this book, I have suggested that educators need to take seriously the charge to explore a concept of community as a moral endeavor based on dialogical processes. This would help all members of the school community to identify underlying differences as well as commonalities of belief, recognize the moral and ethical nature of their role, and strive to create inclusive and culturally democratic communities. Inclusive, however, does not mean homogeneous. Thus I have presented the notion of unity within, and not from, diversity.

We have acknowledged that community is complex, dynamic, and public—grounded in notions of dialogue and processual strivings. We have recognized that dialogue among individuals who respect each other deeply and wrestle with the meaning of culture, power, empowerment, and community may be as complex as the context itself. The dialogical process may, in fact, increase the levels of cognitive dissonance; but, in turn, the resulting discomfort may promote reexamination and reconstruction of power and decision making within the school.

Despite these challenges, the transformative cross-cultural leader will need to persevere in the complex and deeply moral processes that are essential for the development of community in a heterogeneous context. The community that emerges will not strive for sameness or elimination of difference; rather, it will be a unique combination of the values, beliefs, personalities, and situations of its members. Through the synergy which develops, it is my hope that all participants will develop a deeper sense of self and of each other, a sense of community within which students may learn to overcome the gulf between the past and the future, and between the modern and the postmodern.

Bakhtin's notion of dialogue and dialogism permits us to move forward, open the boundaries, overcome the inertia of a fixed notion of culture or power, and recognize the fluidity and ever changing nature of an educational community. Near the end of his life he wrote,

> There is neither a first nor a last word and there are no limits to the dialogic context (it extends into the boundless past and the boundless future). Even *past* meanings, that is, those born in the dialogue of past centuries, can never be stable (finalised, ended once and for all)—they will always change (be renewed) in the process of subsequent future development of the dialogue. (1986, 170)

Educators will need to continuously renegotiate and reconstruct our understandings of history, leadership, community, democracy, and social justice. Until we understand that change is part of the natural development of organizations as well as of society, we will continue to have an outdated, hegemonic, inequitable, and inefficient educational system. If we learn to negotiate the boundaries of educational change, to become transformative cross-cultural leaders, to combine good intentions with new knowledge, examined assumptions, open attitudes, extensive dialogue, and deep and abiding respect for others, then the way forward may not be as difficult as it sometimes seems.

If the school becomes a place where young people and adults together explore deep understandings of culture, where power differentials are minimized or eliminated, and where unity is found within recognition and celebration of diversity, then we will have a clearer image of what a deeply democratic community of difference is really about. In a successful "community of learners" in a diverse or multicultural setting, students would not have to choose between tradition and success, between family and self, between feeling good and achieving academic excellence.

Frost's farmer describes his neighbor:

> I see him there,
> Bringing a stone grasped firmly by the top
> In each hand, like an old-stone savage armed.
> He moves in darkness as it seems to me,
> Not of woods only and the shade of trees.
> He will not go behind his father's saying,
> And he likes having thought of it so well
> He says again, "Good fences make good neighbors."

Good fences make good neighbors, he says. And one might therefore believe that good fences make good communities. But we have learned that the words are ironic, said with that sardonic twist that implies exactly the opposite. Good fences do not necessarily make good neighbors or good communities. In communities that are just, caring, democratic, and optimistic, communities that help all members move outside their borders to a more optimistic beyond, we do not need walls but permeable boundaries. We must go underneath, behind, and beyond the sayings of our fathers, our culture, our society, and move out of the darkness, away from the armed savagery and say with Frost's neighbor:

> It comes to little more:
> There where it is we do not need the wall.

For Further Reflection

CHAPTER 1: TRANSFORMATIVE CROSS-CULTURAL LEADERSHIP

1. What are the central characteristics of transformative leadership?
2. Why is it essential for educational leadership to be firmly grounded in moral and ethical principles?
3. How does the idea of authenticity help us to sort through the confusing plethora of leadership theories?

CHAPTER 2: SCHOOLS AS COMMUNITIES OF DIFFERENCE

1. How can we reconcile the need to respect, and perhaps value, diversity with the needs of civil society?
2. What does it mean to develop a community of difference within, rather than from, diversity?
3. Whose perspectives would need to be included if your organization were to be a community of difference?

CHAPTER 3: CRITERIA FOR EXCELLENCE AND SOCIAL JUSTICE

1. Choose a recent decision made in your workplace and show how it fulfills (or does not fulfill) the criteria of being just, democratic, empathetic, and optimistic.

2. Use the questions on page 81 to help you explain how the criteria were (or were not) met.
3. Is something missing? To achieve the goals of academic excellence and social justice, are there other criteria that need to be added? If so, what are they?

CHAPTER 4: MAKING CULTURE(S) VISIBLE AND MEANINGFUL

1. What cultures are represented in your school and how could they be made visible?
2. What rules of the dominant culture(s) need to be made explicit in your school?
3. How can the diverse cultures of your school become meaningful in the dialogues, programs, and activities of the school community?

CHAPTER 5: IDENTITY CRISIS

1. How do our present educational practices
   a. pathologize the lived experiences of children?
   b. demonstrate color-blindness?
   c. demonstrate class-blindness?
   d. demonstrate spirituality blindness?
2. What can you learn from Anish, Esther, and Ruth Simmons? What would you like to ask each of them?
3. How do the practices described in this chapter—color-blindness, class blindness, spiritual blindness, and pathologizing the lived experiences of children—contribute to negative self-concept and lack of positive self-identity?
4. How might you build understanding in your school of the effects of these practices?

CHAPTER 6: BREAKING THE BOUNDARIES

1. Which individuals and groups in your school community are not involved in the life of your school?
2. What could you offer them and they, you?

3. What cultural rules in your school must be made explicit in order for those who are not involved to be able to participate more comfortably and more fully?

4. If you began to conceptualize curriculum as a "conversation that makes sense of life," what are some topics you would like to pursue?

CHAPTER 7: CRITIQUE, CARNIVAL, AND CONSCIOUSNESS

1. Identify areas in your school in which power is used in ways that dominate or marginalize some members of the school community.

2. What type(s) of multiculturalism are common in your school?

3. What inequities might a more critical multicultural approach help to address?

4. What elements of carnival can you identify in the current practices of your school?

5. How can the characteristics of carnival be extended to permeate the structures, cultures, and curriculum of the school?

CHAPTER 8: WALLS, FENCES, AND OTHER STRUCTURAL CHANGES

1. What structures (policies, organizational or governance factors, physical constraints) in your school act as barriers to equitable student learning?

2. Who are the children who experience the least success in your school and how might structural changes act as a catalyst for change?

3. How might you introduce a consultative process about structural change to increase community understanding of, and support for, your school?

CHAPTER 9: A NEW COMMUNITY

1. Explain what is meant by each criterion: a community of difference is just, empathetic, democratic, and optimistic.

2. Identify one aspect of your school that meets each criterion and one that does not.

3. What changes would you like to see in your school that would create a deeper sense of community for (a) teachers, (b) parents, and (c) students?

CHAPTER 10: MAKING IT HAPPEN

1. If you were to create a school profile, what are five questions you would like to address?
2. Do your current practices tend to involve more dialogue or more discussion?
3. In what ways might you facilitate more dialogue in your school?
4. How could you build better relationships in your school?
5. What are three powerful ideas you would like to use as a basis for dialogue and relationships in your community?

CHAPTER 11: NEW LENSES, SHARPER FOCUS

1. What are three aspects of your school community you would like to change? Why? Which criteria are not being met?
2. What would be your first step toward achieving your desired goals?
3. What are the patterns of power in your school? What are some pressure points that might change the patterns?
4. As you reflect on your own leadership, how could you become more transformational? authentic? democratic?
5. What are your goals for the next three years
   a. for yourself?
   b. for your school community?

A Multitrack YRS Calendar

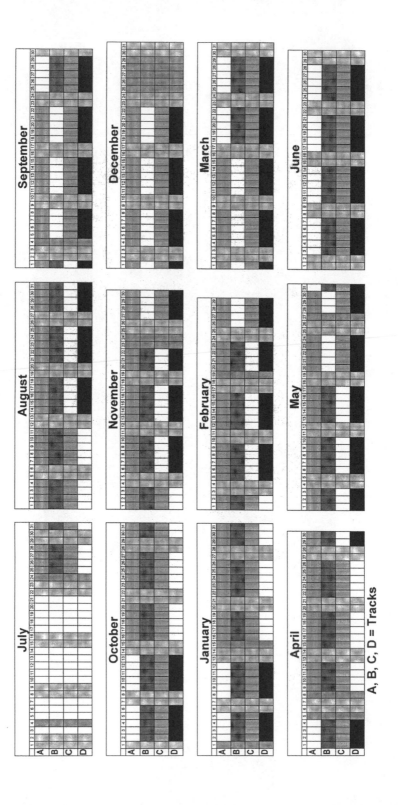

A, B, C, D = Tracks

References

26.4 foreign-born live in USA. 2000, October 3. *USA Today*, n.p.

Adams, L., and Karabenick, S. A. 2000. *Impact of state testing on students and teaching practices: Much pain, no gain?* ERIC ED 443870.

Ah Nee-Benham, M. K. P., and Cooper, J. E. 1998. *Let my spirit soar! Narratives of diverse women in school leadership.* Thousand Oaks, Calif,: SAGE.

Akintude, O., and Cooney, M. H. 1998. *On confronting white privilege and the "color-blind" paradigm in a teacher education program.* Laramie: College of Education, University of Wyoming.

Alexander, K. L., Entwisle, D. R., and Olsen, L. S. 2001. Schools, achievement, and inequality: A seasonal perspective. *Educational Evaluation and Policy Analysis* 23, no. 2: 171–91.

Anderson, G. L. 1990. Toward a critical constructivist approach to school administration. *Educational Administration Quarterly* 26, no. 1: 38–59.

Astin, A. W., and Astin, H. S. 2000. *Leadership reconsidered: Engaging higher education in social change.* Kellogg Foundation, at: www.wkkf.org/documents/youthed/leadershipreconsidered/ (accessed October 10, 2002).

Baber, C. R. 1995. Leaders of color as catalysts for community building in a multicultural society. *Theory and Research in Social Education* 23, no. 4: 342–54.

Bachmann, H. 2000. Not one of us: The people of Emmen decide who is worthy of Swiss citizenship. *Time Europe,* March 27.

Bakhtin, M. 1984. *Rabelais and his world.* Translated by H. Iswolsky. Bloomington: Indiana University Press.

———. 1986. *Speech genres and other late essays.* Edited by C. Emerson and M. Holquist. Translated by V. W. Mcgee. Austin: University of Texas Press.

Bakhtin, M. M., and Volosinov, V. N. 1973. *Marxism and the philosophy of language.* Cambridge Mass.: Harvard University Press.

Banks, J. A. 1991. Multicultural education: For freedom's sake. *Educational Leadership* 49, no. 4: 32–36.

Barth, R. S. 1990. *Improving schools from within*. San Francisco: Jossey-Bass.

Bass, B. M. 1990. *Bass and Stogdill's handbook of leadership: Theory, research, and managerial applications*. New York: Free Press.

Bass, B. M., and Avolio, B. J. 1997. Shatter the glass ceiling: Women may make better managers. In K. Grint, ed., *Leadership*. Oxford: Oxford University Press.

BBC. 1999, November 26. Private firm to run Islington's School. *BBC News*, at news.bbc.co.uk/1/hi/education/536949.stm (accessed October 10, 2002).

Bellah, R. N., Madsen, R. D., Sullivan, W. M., Swindler A., and Tipton, S. M. 1985. *Habits of the heart*. Berkeley: University of California Press.

Bennis, W., and Nannus, B. 1985. *Leaders: The strategies for taking charge*. New York: Harper & Row.

Bishop, R. 2001. Changing power relations in education: Indigenous Maori messages for teacher education. Paper presented at the annual meeting of the Canadian Society for Studies in Education, Quebec.

Bishop, R., and Glynn, T. 1999. *Culture counts: Changing power relations in education*. Palmerston North, New Zealand: Dunmore.

Blackmore, J. 1989. Educational leadership: A feminist critique and reconstruction. In J. Smyth, ed., *Critical perspectives on educational leadership*. London: Falmer.

Borg, C., Mayo, P., and Sultana, R. 1998. Revolution and reality: An interview with Peter McLaren. In W. Pinar, ed., *Curriculum: Toward new identities*. New York: Garland.

Bourdieu, P. 1990. *The logic of practice*. Oxford: Polity.

———. 1993. *The field of cultural production*. Oxford: Polity.

Boyer, E. L. 1995. *The basic school: A community for learning*. Princeton University. ERIC ED 381284.

Brake, N. L. 2000. *Student course-taking delivered through a high school block schedule: The relationship between the academic core and student achievement*. Bowling Green University. ERIC ED 448194.

Brewer, D., Feifs, H., and Kaase, K. 2001. *Accountability policy for North Carolina's alternative schools, year one results*. ERIC ED 453271.

Bryck, A. S. 1988. Musings on the moral life of schools. *American Journal of Education* 96, no. 2: 256–90.

Bullivant, B. M. 1984. *Pluralism: Cultural maintenance and evolution*. New York: Taylor and Francis.

Burbules, N. C. 1993. *Dialogue in teaching*. New York: Teachers College Press.

Burns, J. M. 1978. *Leadership*. New York: Harper & Row.

Burrell, G., and Morgan, G. 1979. *Sociological paradigms and organizational analysis*. Aldershot, U.K.: Gower.

Capper, C. A. 1992. A feminist poststructural analysis of nontraditional approaches in educational administration. *Educational Administration Quarterly* 28, no. 1: 103–24.

Chapman, J. D., Sackney, L. E., and Aspin, D. N. 1999. Internationalization in educational administration: Policy and practice, theory and research. In J. Murphy and K. S. Louis, eds., *Handbook of research on educational administration*. 2d ed. San Francisco: Jossey-Bass.

Chartrand, M. R. J. 2001. *Listening to the voice of marginalized communities within a secondary school structure*. Master's thesis, University of British Columbia.

Christenson, S. L., Hurley, C. M., Sheridan, S. M., and Fenslermacher, K. 1997. Parents' and school psychologists' perspectives on parent involvement activities. *School Psychology Review* 26 no. 1: 111–30.

Clavell, J. 1998. *The art of war by Sun Tsu*. New York: Delta Trade Paperbacks.

Coleman, P., et al. 1996. Learning together: The student/parent/teacher triad. *School Effectiveness and School Improvement* 7, no. 4: 361–82.

Comer, J. P. 1988. Is "parenting" essential to good teaching? *NEA Today* 6, no. 6: 34–40.

Connelly, Owen. Napoleon I. *Encarta*, at encarta.msn.com/oncet/refpages/refarticle.aopx?refid=761566988 (accessed October 10, 2002).

Cooper, H., Nye, B., Charlton, K., Lindsay, J., and Greathouse, S. 1996. The effects of summer vacation on achievement test scores: A narrative and meta-analytic review. *Review of Educational Research* 66, no. 3: 227–68.

Craft, M. 1984. Education for diversity. In M. Craft, ed., *Education and cultural pluralism*. London: Falmer.

Cronon, W. 1992. A place for story: Nature, history, and narrative. *Journal of American History*, March, 1347–1376.

Cuban, L. 1990. Reforming again, again, and again. *Educational Researcher* 19, no. 1: 3–13.

Cummins, J. 1989. Empowering minority students: A framework for intervention. *Harvard Educational Review* 56, no. 1: 18–36.

Dantley, M. E. 2001. "Transforming school leadership through Cornel West's notions of African American prophetic spirituality." Paper presented at the annual meeting of the University Council for Educational Administration, Cincinnati, November.

Davies, S. 1999. Stubborn disparities: Explaining class inequalities in schooling. In R. F. Arnove and C. A. Torres, eds., *Comparative education: The dialectic of the global and the local*, 138–50. Lanham, Md.: Rowman & Littlefield.

Dean, S. 2000. *Hearts and minds: A public school miracle*. Toronto: Penguin.

Delpit, L. D. 1990. The silenced dialogue: Power and pedagogy in educating other people's children. In N. M. Hidalgo, C. L. McDowell, and E. V. Siddle, eds., *Facing racism in education*. Reprint Series no. 2. Cambridge Mass.: Harvard Educational Review.

Dewey, J. 1989. Renascent liberalism. In H. B. McCullogh, ed., *Political ideologies and political philosophies*. Toronto: Thompson Educational Publishing.

———. 2001. Democracy and human nature. In S. J. Goodlad, ed., *The last best hope: A democracy reader*. San Francisco: Jossey-Bass.

Dillard, C. B. 1995. Leading with her life: An African American feminist for an urban high school principal. *Educational Administration Quarterly* 31, no. 4: 539–63.

Dufour, R. 2001. How to launch a community: A new school principal talks openly about the challenges and benefits of creating a professional learning community. *Journal of Staff Development* 22, no. 3: 50–51.

English, F. W. 1992. *Deciding what to teach and test*. Newbury Park, Calif.: Corwin.

Entwisle, D. R., and Alexander, K. L. 1992. Summer set-back: Race, poverty, school composition, and mathematics achievement in the first two years of school. *American Sociological Review* 5, no. 7: 72–84.

Epstein, J. L., Coates, L., Salinas, K. C., Sanders, M. G., and Simon, B. S. 1997. *School, family, and community partnerships*. Thousand Oaks, Calif.: Corwin.

Estrada, K., and P. McLaren. 1993. A dialogue on multiculturalism and democratic culture. *Educational Researcher* 22, no. 3: 27–33.

Evans, R. 1996. *The human side of change*. San Francisco: Jossey-Bass.

Fantini, A. E., Arias-Galicia, F., and Guay, D. 2000. *Understanding the differences*. A working paper series on higher education in Mexico, Canada, and the United States. Consortium for North American Higher Education Collaboration, at conahec.org and elnet.org (accessed December 8, 2001).

Farrell, J. P. 1999. Changing conceptions of equality of education: Forty years of comparative evidence. In R. F. Arnove and C. A. Torres, eds., *Comparative education: The dialectic of the global and the local,* 149–77. Lanham, Md.: Rowman & Littlefield.

Ferguson, K. E. 1994. The bureaucrat as the second sex. In *Educational administration: The UCEA document base*. Primus: McGraw-Hill.

Fine, M. 1993. Parent involvement. *Equity and Choice* 9, no. 3: 4–8.

Fine, M., Weis, L., and Powell, L. C. 1997. Communities of difference: A critical look at desegregated spaces created for and by youth. *Harvard Educational Review* 67, no. 2: 247–84.

Firestone, W. A., and Louis, K. S. 1999. Schools as cultures. In J. Murphy and K. S. Louis, eds., *Handbook of research on educational administration,* 297–322. 2d ed. San Francisco: Jossey-Bass.

Foster, W. 1986. Foundations for critical analysis in administration. In *From paradigms and promises: New approaches to educational administration,* 71–91. Buffalo, N.Y.: Prometheus.

Freire, P. 1970. *Pedagogy of the oppressed.* New York: Continuum.

———. 1994. *Pedagogy of hope: Reliving pedagogy of the oppressed.* New York: Continuum.

Frost, R. 1915. "Mending Wall." In *North of Boston.* New York: Henry Holt.

———. 1999. *Change forces: The sequel.* New York: Falmer.

Fullan, M. 1993. *Change forces.* New York: Falmer.

Furman, G. C. 1996. The promise and paradox of community in schools: A postmodern analysis. Paper presented at the annual meeting of University Council for Educational Administration, Louisville, Kentucky.

———. 1998. Postmodernism and community in schools: Unraveling the paradox. *Educational Administration Quarterly* 34, no. 3: 298–328.

Furman, G. C., and Starratt, R. J. 2001. Leadership for democratic community in schools. Paper presented at the annual meeting of the University Council for Educational Administration, Cincinnati.

Furman-Brown, G. 1999. Editor's foreword to *Educational Administration Quarterly* 35, no. 1: 6–12.

Gardner, J. W. 1990. *On leadership.* New York: Simon & Schuster/Free Press.

Gaventa, J. 1980. *Power and powerlessness: Quiescence and rebellion in an Appalachian valley.* Urbana: University of Illinois Press.

Gemmill, G., and Oakley, J. 1997. Leadership: An alienating social myth? In K. Grint, ed., *Leadership: Classical, contemporary, and critical approaches,* 272–88. New York: Oxford University Press.

Gilligan, C. 1993. *In a different voice.* Cambridge Mass.: Harvard University Press.

Giroux, H. 1997. *Channel surfing: Race talk and the destruction of today's youth.* New York: St. Martin's.

Goeglein, A., and Hall, M. L. W. 2001. *Systems, values, and transformative leadership,* at www.sysval.org/Impact31.html (accessed October 9, 2002).

Gorinski, R., and Davey, B. 2000. Transformative leadership and the development of a community school culture, phase 2. Paper presented at the annual conference of the Australian Council for Educational Administration, at www.cdesign.com.au/acea2000/pages/con08.htm (accessed October 9, 2002).

Gould, S. J. 1996. *The mismeasure of man.* New York: Norton.

Government of British Columbia Ministry of Education. 2002. Special education, at www.bced.gov.bc.ca/specialed/iep (accessed October 11, 2002).

Green, J. M. 1999. *Deep democracy: Diversity, community, and transformation*. Lanham, Md.: Rowman & Littlefield.

Greene, M. 1977. Toward wide-awakeness: An argument for the arts and humanities in education. *Teachers College Record* 79, no. 1: 119–25.

———. 1993. The passions of pluralism: Multiculturalism and the expanding community. *Educational Researcher* 22, no. 1: 13–18.

Grint, K. 1997. Introduction to *Leadership: Classical, contemporary, and critical approaches,* 1–26. London: Oxford University Press.

Grumet, M. R., 1995. The curriculum: What are the basics and are we teaching them? In J. L. Kincheloe and S. R. Steinberg, eds., *Thirteen questions,* 15–21. 2d ed. New York: Peter Lang.

Hallinger, P. 1995. Culture and leadership: Developing an international perspective of educational administration. *UCEA Review* 36, no. 2: 1, 4–5, 10–13.

Hallinger, P., and Leithwood, K. 1996. Culture and educational administration: A case of finding out what you didn't know you don't know. *Journal of Educational Administration* 34, no. 5: 98–116.

Hanushek, E. A. 1998. *The evidence on class size*. Occasional Paper. Rochester, N.Y.: W. Allen Wallis Institute of Political Economy, University of Rochester.

Hargreaves, A., and Fullan, M. 1998. *What's worth fighting for out there?* New York: Teachers College Press.

Heck, R. 1998. Conceptual and methodological issues in investigating principal leadership across cultures. *Peabody Journal of Education* 73, no. 2: 51–80.

Henderson, J. G., and Hawthorne, R. D. 1995. *Transformative curriculum leadership*. Englewood Cliffs, N.J.: Prentice Hall/Merrill.

Hills, J., and Gibson, C. 1988. Problem analysis and reformulation skills for administrators. Unpublished document, Department of Educational Studies, University of British Columbia, Vancouver, B.C.

Hodgkinson, C. 1983. *The philosophy of leadership*. Oxford: Basil Blackwell.

Hoff-Somers, C. 1994. *Who stole feminism? How women have betrayed women*. New York: Simon & Schuster.

Hofstede, G. 1991. *Cultures and organizations: Software of the mind*. New York: McGraw-Hill.

Holcomb-McCoy, C. C. 1999. Understanding "whiteness" in academia: A Black woman's perspective. Paper presented at the annual meeting of the American Educational Research Association, Montreal.

Holquist, M., ed. 2000. *The dialogic imagination: Four essays by M. M. Bakhtin*. Austin: University of Austin Press.

Janis, I. 1982. *Groupthink: Psychological studies of policy decisions and fiascos*. Boston: Houghton-Mifflin.

Johnson, L. 1999. "My eyes have been opened": White teachers coming to racial consciousness. Paper presented at the annual meeting of the American Educational Research Association, Montreal.

Kahney, H. 1986. *Problem solving: A cognitive approach*. Milton Keyes, Pa.: Open University.

Kakabadse, A., Myers, A., McMahon, T., and Spony, G. 1997. Top management styles in Europe: Implications for business and cross-national teams. In K. Grint, ed., *Leadership*. Oxford: Oxford University Press.

Kannapel, P. J., Aagaard, L., Coe, P., and Reeves, C. A. 2000. *Elementary Change: Moving toward Systemic School Reform in Rural Kentucky*. Office of Educational Research and Improvement, Washington, D.C. ERIC ED 449927.

Kets de Vries, M. R. 1997. The leadership mystique. In K. Grint, ed., *Leadership: Classical, contemporary, and critical approaches*, 250–71. London: Oxford University Press.

Kincheloe, J. L., and Steinberg, S. R. 1995 The more questions we ask, the more questions we ask. In J. L. Kincheloe and S. R. Steinberg, eds., *Thirteen questions*. 2d ed. New York: Peter Lang.

——. 1997. *Changing multiculturalism*. Philadelphia: Open University Press.

——. 1998. Reconfiguring white identity in a pedagogy of whiteness. In J. L. Kincheloe, S. R. Steinberg, N. Rodriguez, and R. Chenault, eds., *White reign: Deploying whiteness in America*. New York: St. Martin's.

Knapp, M. S., and Woolverton, S. 1995. In J A. Banks and C. A. McGee Banks, eds., *Handbook of research on multicultural education*, 548–69. New York: Macmillan.

Kneese, C. C. 1996. Review of research on student learning in year-round education. *Journal of Research and Development in Education* 29, no. 2: 61–72.

Knozal, J. L. 1997. A dilemma for secondary school leaders: Developing common understandings about "good" classroom practices among parents and between parents and educators. Paper presented at the annual meeting of the American Educational Research Association, Chicago.

Kozol, J. 1992. *Savage inequalities*. New York: Harper Perennial.

Kumashiro, K. K. 2001. "Posts" perspectives on anti-oppressive education in social studies, English, mathematics, and science classrooms. *Educational Researcher* 30, no. 3: 3–12.

Larson, C. L., and Murtadha, K. 2001. Leadership for social justice. Paper presented at the annual meeting of the University Council for Educational Administration, Cincinnati, November.

Laszlo, K. C. 2001. Learning, design, and action: Creating the conditions for evolutionary learning community. *Systems Research and Behavioral Science* 18, no. 5: 379–92.

Learning, retention, and forgetting. 1978. Technical Report no. 5 for the Board of Regents of the State of New York. Albany: New York State Department of Education/University of the State of New York.

Leithwood, K. 1994. Leadership for school restructuring. *Educational Administration Quarterly* 30, no. 4: 498–518.

Leithwood, K., and Jantzi, D. 1990. Transformational leadership: How principals can help to reform school cultures. *School effectiveness and school improvement* 1, no. 4: 249–80.

Levin, B. 2001. *Reforming education: From origins to outcomes.* New York: Routledge/Falmer.

Lightfoot, S. L. 1983. There are many ways up: Portrait of an urban school. *College Board Review* 129: 4–10.

L'Iniative de la septième génération. 2001, at www.cyberus.ca/choose.sustain/mb-e/7em-g.shtml (accessed October 7, 2002).

Locke, R. F. 1992. *The book of the Navajo.* Los Angeles: Mankind.

Lopez, G. R. 2001. On whose terms? Understanding involvement through the eyes of migrant parents. Paper presented at the annual conference of the American Educational Research Association, Seattle.

Lopez, G. R., Scribner, J. D., and Mahitivanichcha, K. 2001. Redefining parental involvement: Lessons from high-performing migrant-impacted schools. *American Educational Research Journal* 38, no. 2: 253–88.

Louis, K. S. 1996. Putting teachers at the center of reform: Learning schools and professional communities. *NASSP Bulletin* 80, no. 580: 9.

Macedo, D. 1995. Power and education: Who decides the forms schools have taken, and who should decide? In J. L. Kincheloe and S. R. Steinberg, eds., *Thirteen questions.* 2d ed. New York: Peter Lang.

Macridis, R. C. 1992. *Contemporary political ideologies.* New York: Harper Collins.

Martin, J. R. 1995. Cultural citizenship. *Democracy Project,* February–March.

Maxcy, S. J. 1991. *Educational leadership: A pragmatic perspective.* New York: Bergin & Garvey.

May, S. 1994. *Making multicultural education work.* Clevedon, U.K.: Multilingual Matters.

———. 2000. Multiculturalism in the 21st century: Challenges and possibilities. Paper presented at the annual meeting of the American Educational Research Association, New Orleans.

Mayeroff, M. 1971. *On caring.* New York: Harper & Row.

McCarthy, C., and Crichlow, W. 1993. Introduction to C. McCarthy and W. Crichlow, eds., *Race, identity, and representation in education*. New York: Routledge.

McDaniel, P. 1993. Making it happen: How to handle the politics of year-round education. *Year-Rounder,* Fall, 4–9.

McKnight, J. L. 1993. A sampling of ideas for involving schools in community revitalization. *Equity and Choice* 9, no. 2: 30–31.

Merz, C., and Furman, G. C. 1997. *Community and schools: Promise and paradox*. New York: Teachers College Press.

Minnich, E. K. 1995. The drama of diversity and democracy, higher education, and American commitments, 68. Report to the Association of American Colleges and Universities, Washington, D.C.

Mintzberg, H. 1983. *Power in and around organizations*. Englewood Cliffs, N.J.: Prentice-Hall.

Mitchell, C. 1999. Building learning communities in schools: The next generation or the impossible dream? *Interchange* 30, no. 3: 283.

Morgan, G. 1997. *Images of Organization*. Newbury Park, Calif.: SAGE.

Murphy, J. 1992. School effectiveness and school restructuring: Contributions to educational improvement. *School Effectiveness and School Improvement* 3, no. 2: 90–109.

Murtadha-Watts, K. 1999a. Negotiating the primacy of culture, race, and class with city school accountability policy formation. Paper presented at the annual meeting of the University Council of Educational Administration, Minneapolis.

———. 1999b. Spirited sisters: Spirituality and the activism of African American women in educational leadership. In L. Fenwick, ed., *School leadership: Expanding horizons of the mind and the spirit*. Lancaster, Pa.: Technomic.

Neugebauer, B. 2000. Creating community, generating hope, connecting future and past: The role of rituals in our lives. *Child Care Information Exchange* 136: 48–51.

Nichols, J. D. 2000, April. *The impact of block scheduling on various indicators of school success*. Paper presented at the annual meeting of the American Educational Research Association, New Orleans, Louisiana. ERIC ED 451593

Nieto, S. 1992. *Affirming diversity: The sociopolitical context of multicultural education*. New York: Longman.

Noddings, N. 1988. An ethic of caring and its implications for instructional arrangements. *American Journal of Education,* February, 215–30.

———. 1999. Caring and competence. In G. A. Griffin, ed., *The education of teachers: Ninety-eighth yearbook of the National Society for the Study of Education*. Chicago: University of Chicago Press.

Oakes, J. 1985. *Keeping track: How schools structure inequality*. New Haven: Yale University Press.

Ogawa, R. T., and Bossert, S. T. 1995. Leadership as an organizational quality. *Educational Administration Quarterly* 31, no. 2: 224–43.

Ogbu, J. U. 1992. Understanding cultural diversity and learning. *Educational Researcher* 21, no. 8: 5–14.

Ogbu, J. U., and Simons, H. D. 1998. Voluntary and involuntary minorities: A cultural-ecological theory of school performance with some implications for education. *Anthropology and Education Quarterly* 29, no. 2: 155–88.

Omi, M., and Winant, H. 1986. *Racial formation in the United States*. New York: Routledge.

Paris Tourisme. Château de Versailles, at www.paris-tourisme.com/places/Versailles/index.html (accessed October 11, 2002).

Peck, M. S. 1987. *The different drum*. Toronto: Touchstone.

Pillsbury, J., and Shields, C. M. 1999. Shared journeys and border crossings: When "they" becomes "we." *Journal for a Just and Caring Education* 5, no. 4: 410–29.

Pinar, W. 1993. *Understanding curriculum as racial text: Representations of identity and difference in education*. Albany: State University of New York Press.

Pintus, S. That strange clock by Paolo Uccello. *Speciale Duomo*, at www.catpress.com/fanmega/art/tiduomq.htm (accessed October 11, 2002).

Pisapia, J., and Westfall, A. L. 1997. *Alternative high schools: Scheduling, student achievement, and behavior*. Paper presented at the Metropolitan Educational Research Consortium, Richmond, Virginia. ERIC ED 411337.

Plant, A. M. 1998. *The current status of school councils in Canada: Changing structures for parental involvement*. A report of the Manitoba Association of School Trustees, commissioned by the Canadian School Boards Association to develop a national strategy on governance, March, at www.cdnsba.org/govern/status.htm (accessed October 9, 2002).

Powers, S. M., and Barnes, F. M. 2001. Alternative routes for teacher professional development and resources: The MERLOT online community. *NASSP Bulletin* 85, no. 628: 58–63.

Purkey, S. C., and Smith, M. S. 1986. Too soon to cheer? Synthesis of research on effective schools. In R. S. Brandt, ed., *Readings on research from Educational Leadership*. Alexandria, Va.: Association for Supervision and Curriculum development.

Rae, K. 1996. *Ara hou, ara tuku iho:* A new pathway, an ancestral pathway: Alternative models of educational management in the schools of Aotearoa/New Zealand. Paper prepared for the CCEA Regional Conference, Kuala Lumpur.

Raivetz, M. J. 1992. Can school districts survive the politics of state testing initiatives? *NASSP Bulletin* 76, no. 545: 57–65.

Reyes, P., Velez, W., and Peña, R. 1993. School reform: Introducing race, culture, and ethnicity into the discourse. In C. A. Capper, ed., *Educational administration in a pluralistic society,* 66–85. Albany: State University of New York Press.

Riehl, C. J. 2000. The principal's role in creating inclusive schools for diverse students: A review of normative, empirical, and critical literature on the practice of educational administration. *Review of Educational Research* 70, no. 1: 55–81.

Roman, L. G. 1993. White is a color! White defensiveness, postmodernism, and antiracist pedagogy. In C. McCarthy and W. Crichlow, eds., *Race, identity, and representation in education*. New York: Routledge.

Rost, J. C. 1993. *Leadership for the twenty-first century*. New York: Praeger.

Rousseau, M. F. 1991. *Community: The tie that binds*. New York: University Press of America.

Sayani, A. 2001. Identity, power, and narrative in curriculum and educational leadership. Unpublished master's thesis, University of British Columbia, Canada.

Schmuck, P. A. 1993. Invisible and silent along the blue highways. Paper presented at proceedings of the Annual Rural and Small Schools Conference. Manhattan, Kansas, October 25–26, 1993.

Schnarr, G. R., and Moore, R. 2000. *The art of spiritual warfare: A guide to lasting inner peace based on Sun Tzu's The art of war*. Chicago: Quest.

Schwartz, P., and Ogilvy, J. 1979. *The emergent paradigm: Changing patterns of thought and belief*. Analytical Report 7, Values and Lifestyles Program. Menlo Park, Calif.: SRI International.

Senge, P. 1990. *The fifth discipline: The art and practice of the learning organization*. New York: Doubleday/Currency.

Senge, P. M., Smith, B., Lucas, T., Dutton, J., Kleiner, A., and Cambron-McCabe, N. 2000. *Schools that learn: A fifth discipline fieldbook for educators, parents, and everyone who cares about education*. New York: Doubleday/Currency.

Sergiovanni, T. J. 1992. *Moral Leadership: Getting to the heart of schooling*. San Francisco: Jossey-Bass.

———. 1993. Organizations or communities? Changing the metaphor changes the theory. Paper presented at the annual meeting of the American Education Research Association, Atlanta.

———. 1994. *Building community in schools*. San Francisco: Jossey-Bass.

———. 2000. Leadership as stewardship: Who's serving who? In *The Jossey-Bass Reader on Educational Leadership*. San Francisco: Jossey-Bass.

Shakeschaft, C. 1987. *Women in educational administration*. Newbury Park, Calif.: SAGE.

Shields, C. M. 1995. A comparison study of student outcomes in two types of classroom placement. *Roeper Review* 17, no. 4: 234–38.

———. 1996. To group or not to group academically talented or gifted students? *Educational Administration Quarterly* 32, no. 2: 295–323.

———. 2002a. Cross-cultural leadership and communities of difference: Thinking about leading in diverse schools. In K. Leithwood and P. Hallinger, eds., *Second international handbook on educational leadership*.

———. 2002b. Learning from educators: Insights into building communities of difference. In G. Furman, ed., *School as community: From promise to practice,* chap. 7. Buffalo: State University of New York Press.

———. 2002c. Thinking about community from a student perspective. In G. Furman, ed., *School as community: From promise to practice,* chap. 10. Buffalo: State University of New York Press.

Shields, C. M., and Oberg, S. L. 1999. What can we learn from the data? A study of the effects of different school calendars on student outcomes. *Urban Education* 34, no. 2: 125–54.

———. 2000. *Year-round schooling: Promises and pitfalls*. Lanham, Md.: Scarecrow/Technomics.

Shields, C. M., and Seltzer, P. A. 1997. Complexities and paradoxes of community: Toward a more useful conceptualization of community. *Educational Administration Quarterly* 33, no. 4: 413–39.

Shields, C. M., LaRocque, L. J., Hoar, M., and Nicol, J. 1998. British Columbia: BC2. In W. J. Smith, H. Donahue, and A. B. Vibert, eds., *Student engagement in learning and school life: Case reports from project schools*, 1:87–116. Montreal: Office of Research on Educational Policy, McGill University.

Sibicky, M. E. 1996. Understanding destructive obedience: The Milgram experiments. In P. S. Temes, ed., *Teaching leadership: Essays in theory and practice*. New York: Peter Lang.

Sidorkin, A. M. 1999. *Beyond discourse: Education, the self, and dialogue*. Albany: State University of New York Press.

Simmons, R. 2001. Interview by M. Safer. *60 Minutes*. CBS, March 4, 2001.

Simon, H. A. 1957. *Administrative behavior*. New York: John Wiley & Sons.

Skrla, L., and Scheurich, J. J. 2001. Displacing deficit thinking in school district leadership. *Education and Urban Society* 33, no. 3: 235–59.

Sleeter, C. 2000. Critical multiculturalism and curriculum analysis. Paper presented at the annual meeting of the American Educational Research Association, New Orleans.

Smith, A. 1995. Eliminating tracking in the middle schools: Derailing the pursuit of excellence? *American Secondary Education* 23, no. 3: 9.

Smith, M. K. 2001. Martin Buber on education. *Informal education,* at www. infed.org/thinkers/et-buber.htm (accessed October 9, 2002).

Starratt, R. J. 1991. Building an ethical school: A theory for practice in educational leadership. *Educational Administration Quarterly* 27, no. 2: 155–202.

——. 1995. *Leaders with vision: The quest for school renewal.* Thousand Oaks, Calif.: Corwin.

——. 2002. La spiritualité, thème émergent en éducation. In Lyse Langlois et Claire Lapointe, eds., *Le leadership en éducation: Plusieurs regards, une même passion.* Montreal: Chenelière-McGraw/Hill.

Strike, K. A. 1999. Can schools be communities? The tensions between shared values and inclusion. *Educational Administration Quarterly* 35, no. 1: 46–70.

Strodl, P., and Johnson, R. 1994. Multicultural leadership for restructured constituencies. *Reports.* ERIC ED 375190.

Sun Tsu. 1997. The art of war. In K. Grint, ed., *Leadership.* Oxford: Oxford University Press.

Swingewood, A. 1998. *Cultural theory and the problem of modernity.* New York: St. Martin's.

Takaki, R. 2001. Multiculturalism: The disuniting or the reuniting of America? Presentation to the American Educational Research Association, Seattle.

Taubman, P. 1993. Separate identities, separate lives: Diversity in the curriculum. In Castenall, L., and Pinar, W., eds., *Understanding curriculum as a racial text: Representing identities and difference in education,* 289–307. New York: State University of New York Press.

Taylor, G. G. 1999. Mentoring of female African American adolescents. Paper presented at the annual meeting of the American Educational Research Association Montreal, Quebec, April.

Temes, P. S. 1996. Teaching leadership/teaching ethics: Martin Luther King's "Letter from Birmingham Jail." In P. S. Temes, ed., *Teaching leadership: Essays in theory and practice.* New York: Peter Lang.

Terry, R. W. 1993. *Authentic leadership: Courage in action.* San Francisco: Jossey-Bass.

Tichy, N., and Devanna, M. A. 1986. *The transformational leader.* Toronto: John Wiley.

Tierney, W. 1993. *Building communities of difference: Higher education in the twenty-first century.* Toronto: OISE.

Tönnies, F. 1957. Of sociology: Pure, applied, and empirical. In W. Cahnman and R. Heberle, eds., Chicago: University of Chicago Press.

Torres, C. A. 1998. *Education, power, and personal biography: Dialogues with critical educators.* New York: Rutledge.

Trompenaars, F. 1993. *Riding the waves of culture.* Bath, U.K.: Avon.

Tyack, D. B. 1974. *The one best system: A history of American urban educa- tion.* Cambridge Mass.: Harvard University Press.

Utah State Board of Education. 2002. Vision statement, at www.usoe.k12.ut. us/board/DOCS/Brd%20Mission%20Stmny.pdf (accessed October 11, 2002).

Vadasy, P., and Maddox, M. 1992. Building bridges: *The Yakima equity study. The conditions of success for migrant, Hispanic, and Native American Stu- dents in the Yakima Valley.* ERIC ED 359009.

Vendler, H. 2001. Value: Ups and downs with Harvard during a lifetime of in- volvement, a senior scholar comes to discern a university community of af- fection, justice, and reciprocity. *Harvard Magazine* 104, no. 2: 48–50.

Vergon, C. B. 2000. A legal and empirical analysis of the disparate impact of school exclusions on students of color: A wrong without remedy? Paper pre- sented at the annual meeting of the University Council for Educational Ad- ministration, Albuquerque.

Vibert, A. B., Portelli, J. P., and Leighteizer, V. 1998. Nova Scotia: NS1. In W. J. Smith, H. Donohue, and A. B. Vibert, eds., *Student engagement in learn- ing and school life: Case reports from project schools* 1:119–60. Montreal: Office of Research on Educational Policy, McGill University.

Wagstaff, L., and Fusarelli, L. 1995. The racial minority paradox: New leadership for learning in communities of diversity. Paper presented at the annual meet- ing of the University Council for Educational Administration, Salt Lake City.

Walker, J. W. St. G. 1989. "Race" policy in Canada: A retrospective. In O. P. Dwivedi, R. D'Costa, C. L. Stanford, and E. Tepper, eds., *Canada2000: Race relations and public policy.* Proceedings of the conference held at Carlton University, Ottawa, October 30–November 1, 1987. Guelph, Canada: Department of Political Studies, University of Guelph.

Weissberg, R. 1998. *Political tolerance: Balancing community and diversity.* Thousand Oaks, Calif.: SAGE.

Wheatley, M. 1993. *Leadership and the new science.* San Francisco: Berrett- Koehler.

Williams, R. 2000. Volunteers bring Pendleton Underground tours to life. *East Oregonian,* May 30, at www.eonow.com/news/stories (accessed October 9, 2002).

Wing, R. L., and Sunzi 1988. *The art of strategy: A new translation of Sun Tsu's classic, The art of war.* New York: Anchor.

Young, B. 1994. Another perspective on the knowledge base in Canadian ed- ucational administration. *Canadian Journal of Education* 19, no. 4: 351–67.

Young, I. M. 1990. *Justice and the politics of difference.* Princeton: Princeton University Press.

Index

About the Author

Carolyn M. Shields has been an educator since 1970, when she started teaching school in a remote village in Labrador, accessible only by cable car. Drawing from her training in English, French, and special education, she taught for eighteen years in the public K 12 system in three Canadian provinces before acquiring her Ph.D. in educational administration from the University of Saskatchewan.

She then took a faculty position at the University of Utah, where she began what has turned out to be an ongoing relationship with educators and schools on the Navajo reservation. Since her return to Canada, where she currently serves as head of the department of educational studies at the University of British Columbia, she has pursued her passionate interest in issues related to social justice and academic excellence.

She has traveled widely and conducted extensive research into cross-cultural leadership, schools as communities of difference, and how changing educational structures (particularly school calendars) affects the academic outcomes of all children, particularly those from the least advantaged homes. Her ten-year study of the perceptions of stakeholders and the impact of year-round schooling in numerous states and districts in the United States and Canada is summarized in *Year-Round Schooling: Promises and Pitfalls* (ScarecrowEducation, 2000), co-authored with Steven Oberg. She has published over seventy other articles and reports related to educational leadership.

Dr. Shields has held a variety of leadership positions including coordinator of the Educational Administration and Leadership Program (EADM) at UBC, president of the Canadian Association for Studies in

Educational Administration, member of the British Columbia Advisory Council on Multiculturalism, and board member of the Commonwealth Council for Educational Administration and Management. She also sits on the UBC senate and an advisory committee to the British Columbia Ministry of Education.

Shields's ongoing concern is helping school leaders to understand that social justice and academic excellence are not contradictory goals, but are integrally related. Moreover, she believes that they can help to provide a moral purpose and focus for the work of educational leaders.

Shields's says that her two sons, two young grandchildren, and her friends and graduate students are her source of support; they also energize her, and challenge her to take risks, to experience new activities, and to strive for new insights.

pathologize = abnormal

marginalize. - relegate or
confine to
a lower —
as of social
standing

Essentializing - equates certain
characteristics of all members
of a group or minority culture

— Transformative leaders
create schools that are just
empathetic, democratic, and
optimistic.

p239 Social Justice Criteria
justice, empathy,
democracy, optimism

p242
data + dialogue as tools of the
transformative leader

p244 Transformative dispositions of
critique, justice, and caring